W9-CJX-234

DISCARDED

DATE			
MAY 25 '81			
APR 5 '83			

© THE BAKER & TAYLOR CO.

Anti-Movements
in America

McCARTHYISM

THE FIGHT FOR AMERICA

Joseph McCarthy

ARNO PRESS

A New York Times Company

New York / 1977

Reprint Edition 1977 by Arno Press Inc.

Reprinted from a copy in
  The University of Illinois Library

ANTI-MOVEMENTS IN AMERICA
ISBN for complete set: 0-405-09937-1
See last pages of this volume for titles.

Manufactured in the United States of America

Library of Congress Cataloging in Publication Data

McCarthy, Joseph Raymond, 1908-1957.
  McCarthyism.

  (Anti-movements in America)
  Reprint of the ed. published by Devin-Adair,
New York.
  1. Communism--United States--1917-
2. Allegiance--United States. 3. United States--
Foreign relations--1945-1953. I. Title.
II. Series.
[HX89.M27 1977]   335.4'0973   76-46087
ISBN 0-405-09960-6

McCARTHYISM

THE FIGHT FOR AMERICA

Documented answers to questions asked

by friend and foe

by

SENATOR JOE McCARTHY

THE DEVIN-ADAIR COMPANY : PUBLISHERS

NEW YORK : 1952

PRINTED IN THE UNITED STATES OF AMERICA

DEDICATED
TO MY OFFICE STAFF

CONTENTS

FOREWORD

It should be evident to everyone that the United States of America is facing a major crisis, on the outcome of which depends the integrity and security of the American people. In 1945 most Americans were living in a fool's paradise. America had just emerged as the victor in a great world war. Germany, Italy, and Japan, all formidable enemies, had been crushed. It seemed incredible to most people that America would again be imperilled for at least a century. Yet in 1952 it is obvious that America's position in world affairs is seriously weakened, and that in the absence of capable leadership the American people may be headed toward disaster.

During the period 1945-1952 the Communists were permitted to consolidate their position in Eastern Europe with the result that all of Western Europe is threatened with sudden and complete collapse and America has felt it necessary to make desperate efforts to maintain independent and friendly governments in that area. In the Far East the amazing failure of our foreign policy is even more evident. For over fifty years one of the major items in our foreign policy has been to maintain the Open Door policy in China. By the Open Door policy is meant that the United States demands with respect to China, equal opportunity for all, special privilege for none, and the political, military, and economic independence of the Chinese government. It was because the United States was insistent upon maintaining the Open Door policy in China that she became involved in the war with Japan.

During the war with Japan, America spent many billions of dollars and suffered hundreds of thousands of casualties. But this enormous sacrifice seemed to be worth while, in 1945, when Japan was crushed and it appeared that the Open Door policy was completely restored. In the following few years, however, it became evident that the sacrifice was made in vain. Today the Open Door policy is far closer to being nullified than in 1941. Today the whole principle of equal opportunity has vanished into thin air. Today there is special privilege for power only, an unfriendly power, and to talk of the political, military, or economic independence of China is a farce.

In Korea we have met with disaster after disaster. Despite expert diplomatic and military advice, we withdrew our troops from South Korea in 1949, and made no plans to defend this area in case of attack. In 1950, when the Communist attack was launched, we suddenly threw in ill trained and ill equipped troops to check the invading hordes with the result that we came very close to complete defeat in that area. In the end, the courage and vigor of our fighting forces stemmed the tide and we were able to hold the enemy at bay even when they were reinforced by the Chinese army. But political and diplomatic blunders have prevented our achieving a real military victory. We have reached a hopeless impasse, while the enemy has been slowly but surely building up defensive and offensive potential.

It is clear that our government has been guilty of colossal and abysmal failures in the field of international relations since 1945. Some of these failures were due to the fact our responsible leaders grossly miscalculated the intentions and the capabilities of the Communist powers. In spite of the fact that the Communist leaders have frequently and definitely declared that they were actively working for the communization of the whole world, our leaders refused to believe them, and were startled when Communist efforts to seize power in country after country became apparent. Our leaders refused to believe that the Communists were capable of carrying out their expansionist schemes, even when these schemes became obvious to every casual observer.

The inability of our leaders to understand the intentions and capabilities of the Communists in the Far East is especially noteworthy. For several years the dominant clique in the Far Eastern section of our State Department refused to admit that the Chinese Communists were really Communists. The public was given to understand that the so-called Chinese Communists were merely agrarian reformers, or forward looking liberals, who were anxious to cooperate with the democratic powers. Yet all during this period it was clear to serious and dispassionate observers that the Chinese Communists were clearly and admittedly wholehearted Communists, closely tied up with the Kremlin crowd, and aimed at the total communization of the whole of the Far East. Our leaders were equally incompetent when it came to estimating the capabilities of the Chinese Communists. Even in 1947 our Department of State declared that there was no danger of China falling into Communist hands for another twenty years.

It is clear that much of our failure in international affairs was due to incompetence, the inability of our leaders to understand or to cope with the major problems which confronted us. But it also becomes increasingly clear that our failures were aggravated by the fact that disloyal elements had infiltrated into several of our government agencies. The number of actively disloyal persons was comparatively small, but they were able to do an enormous amount of damage. In 1945 much of our power and prestige was due to the fact that we alone were possessors of the secret of the atomic bomb. It has now been clearly proved that several American citizens, working in connection with various atomic energy projects, gave or sold extremely important items of information to the Soviet authorities. This is undoubtedly one of the reasons why the USSR has made such rapid strides in developing its own atomic bomb. It has also been clearly proved that several persons occupying high and responsible positions in the government were, at one time or another, active members of Communist cells, and that such persons perjured themselves when they denied this fact.

Of even greater importance and significance was a group of "fellow travellers," persons who never joined the Communist party, persons who are horrified when accused of treason or disloyalty, but who joyfully followed the Communist party line in their advocacy or rejection of causes and policies. A person may agree with the Communist position on one or two points, even on three or four, without necessarily coming under suspicion. But when a person, during the course of several years, always speaks and writes in favor of ideas which closely parallel the policies advanced by the Communist hierarchy, it would appear obvious that either his intelligence or his integrity as an American citizen is open to doubt. Such persons are unworthy of being considered "experts," as they often claim to be, or else are guilty of hoodwinking the American public as to what is going on in national and international affairs. I do not believe that such persons should be persecuted, but I do believe that such persons should be eliminated from positions where they are able to influence national policy.

During the period 1945-1950 there were a number of clear-sighted people who realized that we were being led along a disastrous path in the conduct of our affairs with foreign nations. These men raised their voices in protest, but in nearly all cases these protests were either suppressed or ignored. General Hurley, U. S. Ambassador to China, Stanley Hornbeck and Joseph Grew in the State Department pointed out the dangers which were likely to arise from the Chinese Communists, and they were quickly removed from their posts. General Wedemeyer, one of the most brilliant of our strategists, with an intimate knowledge of the Far East, wrote his famous report on China, pointing out the seriousness of the situation. His report was suppressed, and before long Wedemeyer himself was driven to retire from active service. "Bill" Bullitt, former Ambassador to Russia, Senators Brewster, Bridges, Mundt, and Knowland and Congressmen Judd and Busbey all pointed out the futility of our foreign policy. They were all politely or impolitely ignored. In the academic field Prof. Colegrove and I tried to indicate that our foreign policy was based upon ignorance and incompetence in high quarters. There were hundreds of others who embarked upon a similar task, but the public refused to be aroused.

Then there arose a new and forceful figure, with a new and vigorous voice, the junior Senator from Wis-

consin named Joe McCarthy. Senator McCarthy soon proved that he had the faculty of commanding public attention. He has a dynamic personality and an ability to speak directly and to the point. As the result of McCarthy's speeches, the man on the street, the average American citizen, became alerted to the perilous situation with which we are faced. I have not always agreed with Senator McCarthy on matters of detail, but I greatly admire his courage and his sincerity, and I am profoundly grateful that he has been able to awaken the American public out of its complacent slumber and make it realize that there was something radically wrong with the caliber of our leadership in international affairs.

It is not at all surprising that McCarthy's success in exposing the weakness of our leadership has aroused a great deal of resentment and animosity. Attempts were made to suppress or smother his charges, or to kill them by ridicule. When these attempts proved unsuccessful, McCarthy was made the object of a barrage of venomous attacks. His ideas and his charges have been grossly twisted and misrepresented, and every conceivable effort has been made to smear his private life. Time after time I have heard people launch into a violent attack on McCarthy, and when I questioned them, I found that they had only the haziest and most inaccurate notions of what the Senator had really said and really done. I am, therefore, delighted that McCarthy has taken this opportunity to clarify his position and to clear up numerous misrepresentations. His most vicious enemies will not be silenced— such enemies never are and never can be. But I am sure that a great number of persons of independent thought, who are willing to investigate and learn the truth, will find this book interesting and valuable. I am sure that many such persons will be convinced that Senator McCarthy has rendered valuable service to the American public in exposing the messy situation which has long existed among the group of men who are chiefly responsible for guiding America's national policy during a period of great peril.

William M. McGovern

(Professor of Political Science,
Northwestern University)

CHAPTER I

Hearing Room—March 8, 1950

"To sin by silence when they should protest, makes cowards of men."
Abraham Lincoln

WHEN the inter-office buzzer across the room on my desk sounded, it seemed as though only ten minutes had passed since I had stretched out on the leather couch in my office after a night's work.

Actually, an hour had passed since I had asked my office manager to wake me at 10:15.

It was now 10:15 a.m.

This was March 8, 1950.

In fifteen minutes I was due in the Senate Caucus room to begin testifying before the Tydings Committee.

My office manager walked into the room and placed a pot of coffee on the desk. "Everything you dictated last night is typed," he said. "Still a few more pages to put in order, but by the time you're ready to go, we'll be set."

I quickly shaved and checked through my briefcase to see that the documents, photostats, and other exhibits were all there.

On my way to the corridor I detoured through the outer office. To my surprise I found even those members of the staff who had been alternately typing and taking dictation practically the entire night, still on duty—sleepy-eyed but going strong. I shall never cease to be amazed at the pace which the office set in those early days in 1950—a pace which they have maintained ever since. Without the day and night work of my loyal and efficient office staff, my task would have been impossible.

As I walked down the long marble corridors to the Senate Caucus room, I wondered if I would be able to accomplish what I had set out to do.

The Senate had authorized the Tydings Committee to investigate Communist infiltration of government. The Senate had given that committee power, investigators, and money to run down every lead on Communists in government which I gave them. Today, March 8, 1950, my task was to give the committee the leads which would be a basis for their investigation.

In the back of my mind there was faintly echoing the chairman's statement, "Let me have McCarthy for three days in public hearings and he will never show his face in the Senate again."

Over two weeks had elapsed since my Senate speech which had forced the creation of the Tydings Committee. Already it had become very apparent that this was to be no ordinary investigation. It was to be a contest between a lone Senator and all the vast power of the federal bureaucracy pin-pointed in and backing up the Tydings Committee.

The picture of treason which I carried in my briefcase to that Caucus room was to shock the nation and occupy the headlines until Truman declared war in Korea. But there was nothing new about this picture. The general pattern was known to every legislator in Washington, except those who deliberately blinded their eyes and closed their ears to the unpleasant truth.

As I walked toward the hearing room, many things crossed my mind. For example, in a few seconds I relived the first trip which I had taken in the rear seat of an SBD to divebomb Japanese anti-aircraft on the then southern anchor of the chain of Japanese Pacific defenses at Kahili on the southern tip of Bougainville. Apparently I had complained too much about the lack of photo coverage for our dive and torpedo bombing strikes for I suddenly found myself the Pacific's most reluctant "volunteer" cameraman in the rear seat of a dive bomber. As we flew over the Japanese airfield on Ballale island that morning, a few minutes before our break-off for the dive through Kahili's anti-aircraft fire, there crossed my mind the thought: "McCarthy, why are you here? Why isn't it someone else? Why did you have to be the one who objected so much to the bad photo coverage?" But then I remembered the next thought which I had as my pilot—I believe it was little Johnny Morton—cracked his flaps and I saw the red undercover as the dive bombing brakes opened up. My thought was: "Hell, someone had to do the job. It might as well be me."

In a split second my thoughts shifted from the Pacific to the Arizona hills and I found myself riding a long-legged black mule rounding up cattle in the hills and canyons of the rim-rock country beyond Young, Arizona. It was on the ranch of Kelly Moeur, father of one of the less retiring and modest Marines of my acquaintance, who in his more generous moments admits that the Army and Navy also helped him win the war.

Ten saddle-sore days which I spent on that desolate but friendly cattle ranch, played a most important part in my anti-Communist fight. It was a link in a chain of events leading up to that morning of March 8, 1950. Six years before, after having spent thirteen months as combat intelligence officer for Marine Dive Bombing Squadron 235, I was ordered to the Intelligence Staff of COMAIR-SOLS (Commander of Army, Navy, Marine, and New Zealand aircraft in the Solomon Islands area). My major task was to study the de-coded messages from and concerning the activities of all of our search planes in the entire Pacific. That was my task under General Mitchell of the Marine Corps, General Harmon of the Army, and General Field Harris of the Marine Corps. Morning after morning I briefed some 30 of the top officers of Army,

Navy, and Marine Corps on what our search planes had found throughout the entire Pacific area during the previous 24 hours.

In performing that task I came to know the Pacific and the coast of Asia almost as well as I knew Dad's farm when I was a boy. And for the first time I began to fully appreciate the great wisdom of America's long-time foreign policy on Asia—the policy of maintaining a free, independent, friendly China in order to keep the Pacific *actually* pacific in fact as well as in name.

Upon my return to the United States I discovered that our wise long-time foreign policy was being scuttled—scuttled without the approval of either of America's two great political parties. At that time, I frankly had no idea that traitors were responsible. In my campaign for the United States Senate in 1946, I referred to the State Department planners as "starry-eyed planners, drifting from crisis to crisis, like a group of blind men leading blind men through a labyrinth of their own creation." I then thought that we were losing to international Communism merely because of abysmal incompetence. At that time I had not even heard the names of many of those whom I was to later expose and force out of policy-making jobs.

Many of them I heard discussed for the first time by a man who was later to be hounded to his death by the Communists. I arrived in Washington in December, 1946, about two weeks before being sworn in as a senator. Three days later my administrative assistant and I received an invitation to have lunch with Jim Forrestal.

I have often wondered how the extremely busy Secretary of the Navy discovered that a freshman Senator had arrived in town and why he took so much time out to discuss the problems which were so deeply disturbing him. More than an equal number of times I have thanked God that he did.

Before meeting Jim Forrestal I thought we were losing to international Communism because of incompetence and stupidity on the part of our planners. I mentioned that to Forrestal. I shall forever remember his answer. He said, "McCarthy, consistency has never been a mark of stupidity. If they were merely stupid they would occasionally make a mistake in our favor." This phrase struck me so forcefully that I have often used it since.

When I took on my duties as a Senator, I discovered that certain outstanding Senators and Congressmen for years had been intelligently trying to alert the American people. They belonged to both parties. Unfortunately, when they clearly and intelligently presented a picture of incompetence or treason which should have commanded banner headlines in every newspaper, the story was found, if at all, hidden in want-ad space and type. I witnessed the frustration of those honest, intelligent, loyal Americans who were attempting to expose our suicidal foreign policy. Day after day I came into contact with convincing evidence of treason. Obviously, unless the public was aroused, the downward course upon which we were embarked would continue and at an accelerated pace. But how to arouse the public to the danger before it was too late?

The tempo of events and the pressure in Washington make difficult the careful laying of plans and drafting of blueprints for an effective fight against the inconceivably powerful Communist conspiracy.

The best place to lay the plans for this fight, I decided, was in the lonely relatively uninhabited rim-rock country of Arizona, which had been so thoroughly pictured to me by J. K. Moeur while I was in the Marine Corps. It was there in the lonely Arizona hills that I carefully laid the plans for the one great fight which, as a Senator, I had to make. There I became convinced that the American people could not be awakened by merely a discussion of traitorous policies *generally*. The men who made those policies—the specific traitors or the dupes, well-meaning as they might be—had to be exposed. Foreign policy, after all, does not just happen. It is carefully planned by men with faces and names. Those faces and names had to be exposed. As J. Edgar Hoover has said, "Victory will be assured once Communists are identified and exposed, because the public will take the first step of quarantining them so they can do no harm."[1]

I decided that it did but little good to argue about changing our suicidal foreign policy so long as the men in charge of forming that policy were in the camp of the enemy. The change which had to be made—if this country was to live—was a change of the "experts"—the "experts" who had so expertly sold out China and Poland without the American people realizing what was happening.

The planning was made infinitely easier by my contact with real Americans without any synthetic sheen—real Americans who are part of the Arizona hills—real Americans like J. K.'s mother and his father, Kelly Moeur, like Rillabelle, old Jim Sands, and Old Jack with the hounds, whose last name I cannot recall.

All of those things crossed my mind as I headed toward the Senate Caucus room. And thoughts of those real people who are the heart and soul and soil of America; thoughts of the young people in my office, toiling night and day, some of them not even fully understanding the fight, but knowing that this fight was their fight; thoughts of the many young men, friends of mine, who went to their death in the Pacific for what they thought was a better world—those thoughts convinced me that this fight I had to win.

So it was that I walked into the huge, red-carpeted Caucus room on that Wednesday morning more than two years ago.

Chairman Tydings and the other four committee members were seated behind a long mahogany table at one end of the room. The committee staff moved around in the background placing papers, notes, and questions in front of the Democrat Senators. The Republican members of the committee had not been given a counsel. A court reporter was setting up his stenotype machine.

The chair in which I was to sit faced a table directly in front of the committee. Several microphones were on the table. On either side and in back of me were press tables. All of them were filled. Over to my right I could

[1] J. Edgar Hoover, House Committee on Un-American Activities. Hearings on H.R. 1884, H.R. 2122, Pt. 2, March 26, 1947, p. 44.

see the tape recording machines of the radio men, and on my left the newsreel cameramen's huge, bright kleig lights were focused on my chair.

I glanced down the press table to my right. Elmer Davis, easy to identify by his heavy black-rimmed glasses, was seated at one end of the table. I remembered that Davis had headed the Office of War Information. Many of the cases I was about to present had once been employees in the OWI under Davis and then had moved into the State Department.

As I glanced at Davis I recalled that Stanislaw Mikolajczyk, one of the anti-Communist leaders of Poland, had warned the State Department, while Davis was head of OWI, that OWI broadcasts were "following the Communist line consistently," and that the broadcasts "might well have emanated from Moscow itself."[2]

There could be no doubt about how Davis would cover the story.

As I began to take files and documents out of my briefcase, a photographer braced his face against his camera for a shot. Another crouched down for an angle shot. Others stood on chairs.

At one of the other press tables I noticed one of Drew Pearson's men. I could not help but remember that Pearson had employed a member of the Communist party, Andrew Older, to write Pearson's stories on the House Committee on Un-American Activities and that another one of Pearson's limited staff was David Karr, who had previously worked for the Communist Party's official publication, the *Daily Worker*.[3]

No doubt about how Pearson would cover the story.

I saw Marquis Childs stop Senator McMahon on his way into the Committee room to chat with him. As I saw Childs with his hand on McMahon's shoulder, I remembered that Childs had defended both Remington and Hiss and had bitterly attacked General MacArthur's headquarters for exposing Communist Agent Agnes Smedley who later was to will her estate to Chu Teh, one of the Chinese Communist leaders.

The wire services were there—Associated Press, United Press, and International News Service. In their presence I felt some sense of security. Traditionally, their job was to present the facts without any editorializing or distortion. In my opinion, they thus differed from men employed by papers such as the St. Louis *Post-Dispatch*, New York *Post*, Milwaukee *Journal*, and the Washington *Post*. I was later to learn, however, that the cards were stacked even there. The wire service men assigned to the Hill are almost to a man honest, fair, capable reporters. But after several experiences there was impressed upon me the painful truth that the stories written by the competent, honest AP, UP, or INS men assigned to cover the Senate or the House, might not even be recognized by them when those stories went on the news ticker to the thousands of newspapers throughout the country. Before being sent out to America's newspapers the stories pass across what is known as a rewrite desk. There certain facts can be played up, others eliminated. For example, so often we found that in the stories about McCarthy, a word like "evidence" was changed to "unfounded charges," "McCarthy

stated" would become "McCarthy shouted," "digging up evidence" became "dredging up evidence." In one case I recall the story as written on the Hill was "McCarthy picked up his briefcase full of documents and left." When the story left the rewrite desk it was "McCarthy grabbed his briefcase and stormed from the room."

Dave McConnell, one of the intelligently honest young men who covered the hearings that morning in 1950 was later to describe the press coverage as follows:

"To a reporter comparatively new to the Washington scene, the intensity, frequently highly emotional, with which many have approached the McCarthy story has come as a surprise. It has come, too, as a surprise to many veterans who cling to the old mandate that personal bias or personal opinions belong on the editorial page and not in the news columns.

"It is not unusual for reporters to quip to one another during the course of a Congressional hearing, but it is highly unusual when members of the Washington press corps maintain a running commentary while a witness is testifying. Such was the case when Senator McCarthy was called early in March before the Foreign Relations Subcommittee to make his initial charges to that group.

"The uproar in the press section during Senator McCarthy's testimony at one point made it difficult even to hear what the Wisconsin Republican was telling the subcommittee."[4]

The news coverage of the first day's testimony of Louis Budenz illustrates the extent to which the picture was to be distorted as the hearings progressed. It is an excellent example of what the American people were told about the hearings as compared to what actually happened.

Budenz for years had been the editor of the official newspaper of the Communist Party, the *Daily Worker*. He had also been a member of the national board of the Communist Party. Since he has renounced Communism, he has been used by the government as one of its principal witnesses in practically every criminal action or deportation proceeding against Communists.

I had told the Senate that Budenz could testify that Lattimore was a member of the Communist Party and could give the committee part of the story of the important tasks assigned to Lattimore by the Communist Party. This had been widely covered by the press. Interest had been built up. If Budenz did not so testify, McCarthy would be discredited.

Budenz' testimony was a story of a deadly conspiracy against America. He testified as to the part which Lattimore played in that conspiracy. He gave the detailed story about this man who was a respected university professor and enjoyed the distinction of being considered America's top expert on the Far East. He testified that this man, who had been employed by the government, consulted for years by State Department officials on Far Eastern policy, and looked to by newspapermen and magazine editors for news on Far Eastern trends, had been a member of the Communist Party.

Budenz testified that as editor of the *Daily Worker* he

[2] Stanislaw Mikolajczyk, The Rape of Poland (Whittlesey House, 1948), pp. 25, 58.
[3] Congressional Record (Unbound), Dec. 19, 1950, pp. 16805, 16912, 16914, 16915; House Committee on Un-American Activities, July 11, 1951, pp. 744, 745.
[4] New York Herald Tribune, Dave McConnell, "Reporting the McCarthy Story," May 16, 1950

had been ordered to treat Lattimore in the official Communist newspaper as a concealed Communist. Lattimore, according to Budenz, had been a member of a Communist cell in the Institute of Pacific Relations, a Communist-front propaganda organization. He further testified that when an important party line change was sent from Moscow to the American Communist Party, it was delivered via Lattimore and Communist Frederick Vanderbilt Field. Budenz testified that this party line change was confirmed by Moscow sources.[5]

After Budenz repeatedly and positively testified that Lattimore was a member of the Communist Party, Tydings' counsel, Ed Morgan, attempted to break down Budenz' testimony by showing that Budenz had not called Lattimore a Communist in an article which he had written in 1949 for *Collier's* Magazine.

Morgan's question was: "Did you refer in this article to Mr. Lattimore as a Communist or someone carrying out this program?" Budenz replied: "Oh, no, no, no." He then went on to explain that *Collier's* did not want him to use Lattimore's name in connection with the story let alone name him as a Communist. Budenz stated: "As a matter of fact, Mr. Lattimore is directly, so far as I could, referred to there by mentioning all the Communist writers who wrote for the *Pacific Affairs*."[6]

Even after the repeated positive testimony that Lattimore had been a Communist, one of the major wire services *misreported* Budenz' testimony as follows:

"... Budenz a onetime Communist who renounced the party in 1945 ... said he was not saying that Lattimore is a Communist."

Papers like the Milwaukee *Journal* used this story. The *Journal* headlined it thus:

"Budenz Says Lattimore 'Aids Reds' But Refuses to Call Him Communist."

The subhead read:

" 'No, no.' His Answer at Senate Hearing to Flat Question About Party Membership."[7]

The Milwaukee *Journal*, of course, was completely dishonest in running this wire service story because their own Washington correspondent was present at the hearings and heard Budenz repeatedly testify that Lattimore was not only a member of the Communist Party but so high in its councils that the Party's secret instructions bore Lattimore's Party symbol "XL." However, a vast number of papers throughout the country did not have Washington correspondents present at the hearings. Such papers were honest in reporting and editorializing that Communism's No. 1 enemy, Louis Budenz, by his sworn testimony, had "completely disproved McCarthy's description of Lattimore." Even to this day, many of those editors are unaware of the false wire service story which they headlined.

As I waited for the chairman to open the hearing that morning, I, of course, knew the left-wing elements of the press would twist and distort the story to protect every Communist whom I exposed, but frankly I had no conception of how far the dishonest news coverage would go. One young reporter later commented that "you have to

use a sieve to strain out the bias in the McCarthy stories published in many papers."[8]

An abrupt rap of the gavel stopped some of the chatter in the crowded room. Another rap and the room was quiet. The hearing was called to order. In accordance with my earlier request, I was sworn before starting my testimony. Then began the most unusual hearing which the Senate has ever witnessed. I was there, prepared to give the committee a carefully catalogued and painstakingly documented case of Communist infiltration of the State Department.

So unusual was the record of the first two days hearings that Senator Brewster had a study made of the written record and the tape recordings which showed that on the first day I was allowed to devote only 8 minutes to direct testimony and on the second day 9 minutes and 30 seconds. The rest of the time was used up by bickering and long statements by the Democrat members of the committee apparently for the benefit of the press.

Senators Hickenlooper and Lodge both objected to the unusual procedure. On one occasion, Senator Lodge said:

"Mr. Chairman, this is the most unusual procedure I have seen in all the years I have been here. Why cannot the Senator from Wisconsin get normal treatment . . ."[9]

At another point during the hearing, Lodge said:

"I do not understand why Senator McCarty cannot have the opportunity to present his statement and not be compelled to act as though he were in some sort of a kangaroo court . . ."[10]

Senators Lodge and Hickenlooper repeatedly attempted to persuade the committee to do what the Senate had ordered them to do—namely, investigate and report on Communist infiltration of government. They were in the minority, however, and were voted down each time by a straight vote of the three Democrat senators.

The blueprint which the committee had determined to follow was exposed late in the first day's session when Chairman Tydings, white-faced and tight-lipped, leaned across the table, shook his finger at me and said:

"You are in the position of being the man who occasioned this hearing, and so far as I am concerned in this committee you are going to get one of the most complete investigations ever given in the history of this Republic, so far as my abilities will permit."[11]

True to his word, Tydings had his staff of investigators spend their time investigating and attempting to discredit McCarthy rather than running down the valuable leads on treason which had been given them.

The investigation that Tydings promised did not end when Tydings was removed from office by an overwhelming vote of the people of Maryland. Since Tydings' defeat the investigation has been carried on by the Administration through the Gillette-Monroney committee whose staff has been running down every possible rumor about

[5] Tydings Committee Hearings, Pt. 1, April 20, 1950, pp. 487-558.
[6] Tydings Committee Hearings, Pt. 1, April 20, 1950, pp. 505, 506.
[7] Milwaukee Journal, April 20, 1950.
[8] Dave McConnell, New York Herald Tribune, May 15, 1950.
[9] Tydings Committee Hearings, Pt. 1, March 8, 1950, p. 9.
[10] Tydings Committee Hearings, Pt. 1, March 8, 1950, p. 17.
[11] Tydings Committee Hearings, Pt. 1, March 8, 1950, p. 6.

McCarthy since the date of his birth in search of smear material to be used in this year's campaign.

When Tydings made his threat that I had brought on an investigation of McCarthy and not an investigation of Communists in government, I heard a slight commotion at the press table behind me. Glancing around I saw Richard L. Strout of the *Christian Science Monitor*, shaking the hand of Rob Hall of the Communist *Daily Worker*.

I had never paid much attention to the *Christian Science Monitor*, but had always thought of it as the paper it had been 20 years ago—a respected paper, known for its wide coverage of foreign news. As I witnessed that comradely handshake between an American newspaperman and the reporter for the official Communist newspaper, there flashed across my mind the story of Gunther Stein, who had been the *Christian Science Monitor's* correspondent in China.[12] General MacArthur's intelligence headquarters had exposed the fact that Gunther Stein was a Communist and an "indispensable and important member" of the famous Sorge Communist spy ring.[13] Within 24 hours after the War Department released a report on the activities of this Communist spy ring, Gunther Stein disappeared. He remained incognito until the spring of 1950 when he was picked up by the French police as a Communist spy.[14]

At the time of Gunther Stein's exposure as an important member of the internationally famous Sorge Communist spy ring, I thought that Gunther Stein had cleverly deceived the *Christian Science Monitor* when they made him their China correspondent—that they did not know they were hiring a traitor to America to write the news on China for the *Christian Science Monitor's* readers. But now I began to wonder as I watched Strout of the *Christian Science Monitor* and Rob Hall of the *Daily Worker* cheek by jowl during the entire hearing and then read the venomous distorted parallel stories which they both wrote. Knowing that many fine, trusting, deeply religious people would get their picture of the evidence of Communists in government from the pen of Strout, I was disturbed. However, I was doubly disturbed with the thought that if a columnist for a paper like the *Christian Science Monitor* could so closely follow the Communist line, no publication and no institution in the entire country could be secure from Communist infiltration.

The committee displayed the greatest amount of frustrated rage when, regardless of how they tried, they could not force from me the names of any people in government who were giving me information. I patiently explained to them over and over and over that under no circumstances could I or would I violate the confidence of those loyal people who were risking their jobs in order to disclose the extent to which the Communist conspiracy was shaping our foreign policy. I explained to the committee that they were being used by the State Department because if I were to give the committee the name of a single State Department employee who had been helping me, he would lose his job immediately.

This was promptly labelled as an "irresponsible statement"[15] by the committee. What I said was fully confirmed over a year later, however, by Carlisle Humelsine,

the State Department's Security officer. On August 19, 1951, he appeared on a television program and, in answer to a question, stated:

"I don't know if anyone in the State Department is feeding Senator McCarthy information. If I catch anyone that is feeding him information, I am afraid they won't be in the State Department any longer."[16]

Perhaps the most astounding indication that the committee was being used as a "Committee for the Defense of Lattimore" occurred when Louis Budenz was called to testify in closed session after he told the committee he wanted to give them information on other State Department officials in addition to Lattimore. On my way over to hear Budenz' testimony I met Bob Morris, who was selected by the Republican members as their counsel after the Democrats on the committee finally consented to let the Republicans have one counsel. I asked him why he was not at the very important executive session to hear Budenz testify. His answer was, "Senator Tydings has decided that the Republican counsel should not be allowed to attend executive sessions."

I thought about the unusual precedent Tydings was setting. To my knowledge, this was the only time under either Democrat or Republican leadership that the Majority allowed its counsel to be present at secret sessions but excluded the Minority counsel.

I opened the door and stepped into the committee room.

I could hardly believe what I saw.

Sitting at the hearing table taking notes and listening to the secret testimony of Louis Budenz from which Republican Counsel Morris had been excluded, was none other than Owen Lattimore and his lawyer.

I drew up a chair to sit down.

Tydings interrupted the questioning of Budenz. "You needn't sit down, McCarthy," he said, "you can't stay here."

I pointed out to Tydings that it would be unusual to exclude me from the hearings—especially in view of the fact that the committee was taking the position that I alone had to present the entire case and that the committee had no obligation to use their investigators to run down the valuable leads which I had given them. I reminded Tydings that if I could not even hear the testimony of the witnesses I had asked them to call, my task would be made doubly difficult. Tydings' answer was that the committee could get along without me.

I asked Tydings whether he would like the opportunity of explaining to the press waiting outside the door, why he had invited Lattimore, who had already been named under oath as a Communist, to sit in and take notes at a hearing so secret that the Republican counsel was excluded. Tydings ordered me from the room.

Thus was set the pattern for the Tydings' committee "investigation."

---

[12] McCarran Committee Hearings on IPR, Pt. 2, August 23, 1951, p. 635.
[13] McCarran Committee Hearings on IPR, Pt. 2, August 8, 1951, p. 363.
[14] McCarran Committee Hearings on IPR, Pt. 2, August 8, 1951, P. 384.
[15] Tydings Committee Hearings, Pt. 1, March 9, 1950, p. 42.
[16] Meet The Press, August 19, 1951.

Senator Joe McCarthy receiving annual "Americanism Award" from Military Order of the Purple Heart, August 26, 1950, Worcester, Mass.

6

CHAPTER II

Round I—Wheeling, West Virginia

DURING the public phase of my fight to expose pro-Communists and Communist treason in government, a vast number of deeply disturbed Americans have asked a multitude of questions. They want the answers—documented and proved—so they may determine for themselves the true situation.

This book is my answer to those questions. This is my answer to every American who seeks to know the truth about my fight against pro-Communists and Communist treason in government. As you read the carefully documented answers to the questions those Americans have asked over the past two years, I am confident you will agree that this fight is your fight—your fight for your children and your children's children.

Here are all the important questions that have been asked by friends and enemies of my anti-Communist fight together with my answers.

I have often heard people say "I agree with Senator McCarthy's aim of removing Communists from Government, but I do not agree with his methods." Senator, why don't you use methods which could receive the approval of everyone?

I have followed the method of publicly exposing the truth about men who, because of incompetence or treason, were betraying this nation. Another method would be to take the evidence to the President and ask him to discharge those who were serving the Communist cause. A third method would be to give the facts to the proper Senate committee which had the power to hire investigators and subpoena witnesses and records.

The second and third methods listed above were tried without success. The President apparently considered any attempt to expose Communists in the government as a cheap political trick to embarrass him and would not even answer a letter offering him evidence of Communist infiltration. The result of my attempt to give the evidence to a Senate committee (the Tydings Committee) is well known. Every person I named was whitewashed and given a clean bill of health. The list included one who has since been convicted and others who have been discharged under the loyalty program.

The only method left to me was to present the truth to the American people. This I did. Even though the Administration has been fine-tooth combing my evidence for over 2 years, they have been unable to find a single item of that evidence that was untrue.

One of the safest and most popular sports engaged in today by every politician and office seeker is to "agree with McCarthy's aim of getting rid of Communists in government," but at the same time to "condemn his irresponsible charges and shot-gun technique." It is a completely safe position to take. The Communist Party and their camp followers in press and radio do not strike back as long as you merely condemn Communism in general terms. It is only when one adopts an effective method of digging out and exposing the under-cover, dangerous, "sacred cow" Communists that all of the venom and smear of the Party is loosed upon him.

I suggest to you, therefore, that when a politician mounts the speaker's rostrum and makes the statement that he "agrees with McCarthy's aims but not his methods," that you ask him what methods he himself has used against Communists. I suggest you ask him to name a single Communist or camp follower that he has forced out of the government by his methods.

I do not much mind the Communists screaming about my methods. That is their duty as Communists. They are under orders to do just that. But it makes me ill deep down inside when I hear cowardly politicians and self-proclaimed "liberals," too lazy to do their own thinking, parrot over and over this Communist Party line. By constant repetition they deceive good, loyal Americans into believing that there is some easy, delicate way of exposing Communists without at the same time exposing all of their traitorous, sordid acts.

Whenever I ask those who object to my methods to name the "objectionable methods," again I hear parroted back to me the Communist *Daily Worker* stock phrase "irresponsible charges" and "smearing innocent people." But as often as I have asked for the name of a single innocent person who has been "smeared" or "irresponsibly charged," nothing but silence answers.

When you hear a politician assuring you that "I am against Communism, but do not like McCarthy's methods," you might ask yourself this question: "Is this politician willing and eager to be against Communism on the speaker's stand but afraid to pay the high price in smear and abuse which is heaped upon anyone who really starts to draw blood from the Communist conspiracy?" During this fall's campaign, timid, cautious politicians who want to stay at the public trough regardless of the cost to the nation and those who would protect Communism and corruption in government will parrot over and over the same stock excuse. They will tell you how "vigorously" they "condemn" Communism. With equal vigor they will tell you that they condemn McCarthy for taking off his gloves and painfully digging out, one by one, the Administration-protected Communists.

The last 20 years have proved that even the most eloquent speeches against Commun*ism generally,* are as ineffective as speeches against crime *generally* by a prosecuting attorney who fails to dig out and convict the dangerous criminals.

When I launched the public phase of this fight at Wheeling, West Virginia, on February 9, 1950, I discussed, among others, the case of John Stewart Service. At the time I was discussing the Service case with the people at Wheeling, Service was in India. He had just arrived in that country. His task was to advise the State Department on a policy toward India. India was then facing a threat from Communism as serious as was China when Service represented the State Department there. I discussed point by point how John Service had contributed to the disastrous policy which sold 400 million Chinese to Communism. Had I merely discussed in general terms how disastrous our policy in China had been or how seriously India was threatened by Communism, Service obviously would not have been recalled, nor would he have been slowed down one iota in his planning.

For the last six years we have been losing the war against Communism at the rate of 100 million people a year. Anyone watching our civilization plunge so rapidly toward the abyss of oblivion, must conclude that we are losing the war to Communism for one of two reasons. We are losing either because of stumbling, fumbling idiocy on the part of those allegedly leading the fight against Communism or because, like Hiss, they are "planning it that way."

I have maintained that regardless of whether our defeat is because of treason or because of incompetence, those doing the planning should be removed from power if this nation and our civilization are to survive. My efforts have been in that direction and will continue to be so.

Have those who have criticized your "methods" of fighting Communists demonstrated any other method of exposing treason?

In answering this question let us consider the most recent attack upon my "methods." On the date this manuscript goes to the printer, May 18, 1952, the press carries the story of four attacks upon "McCarthyism" and "McCarthy's methods." The attacks, according to the press, were made before the National Convention of the Americans for Democratic Action by four men who are asking the American people to place them at the helm of this government—candidates for President.[17] The candidates were Kefauver, Humphrey, Harriman, and McMahon. Each with apparently equal vigor condemned McCarthy's method of exposing Communists. All four of these men who ask to be elected President know that 10 of those whom I originally named before the Tydings Committee and who were cleared by that committee have since either been convicted or removed from the State Department under the loyalty program. (See pg. 13).

Therefore, the following questions should be asked those candidates for President:

(1) If elected President will you reinstate and return to positions of power those who were exposed and forced out of the State Department by McCarthy?

(2) Can you name one person whom you have exposed and had removed from government because he was either a Communist or a loyalty or security risk?

(3) Despite the opposition of the vast power of your party which had been in control of the federal government, Senator McCarthy has forced out of high position 10 of those whom he originally named. Three of you are on Senate Committees controlled by your party. You

have the power to subpoena. You know the names of the Communist traitors as well as McCarthy does. There are still nearly six months before the November elections. This gives you time to prove that you can remove more Communists and loyalty and security risks by your method than McCarthy has removed by his. He has challenged you to do that. Will you accept that challenge?

(4) If with your combined efforts you are unable in the next six months to remove from government one Communist or loyalty or security risk as compared to McCarthy's record of 10, then are not the American people entitled to conclude that you are attacking McCarthy's fight against Communists because of either stupidity or dishonesty?

Why did you take your case of Communists in government to the people rather than to the President or the Congress?

The Democrat Administration obviously did not—or would not—recognize the fact that the Communist Party, in order to achieve its objective most effectively, was employing the technique of infiltrating our government so as to shape our foreign policy. No action was being taken to remove Communist elements from government. Instead those who made American policy dovetail with Soviet aims were promoted up the scale to positions of greater power.

The Democrat Party was not only unwilling to act—it also effectively tied the hands of Congress and prevented it from acting. Time and again members of Congress and Congressional committees had been prevented from getting at the truth by the President's order forbidding any government employee from giving Congress information concerning loyalty matters. The difficulty a Congressional committee had in obtaining the facts when faced with the President's blackout order was rather well demonstrated when General Charles Willoughby appeared before the McCarran Committee on August 9, 1951. General Willoughby had been chief of General Douglas MacArthur's intelligence for more than 10 years. Willoughby was being asked about three individuals who had been accused of Communist activities, and who according to Willoughby "were hired in the United States [by the State Department] and unloaded on Tokyo." Willoughby's testimony follows:

GENERAL WILLOUGHBY: "Mr. Chairman, as a citizen, I am naturally most desirous to assist this important committee. However, as a federal officer, I am expected to observe Army orders and Presidential directives.

"I invite your attention to a Department of Army circular letter dated August 21, '48, on the subject, 'Release of Personnel Records and Information.' I quote:

"'No information of any sort relating to the employee's loyalty and no investigative data of any type, whether relating to loyalty or other aspects of the individual's records, shall be included in material submitted to a Congressional commitee.'

"The provision of the Presidential directive of March 13, 1948, is intended to apply to records

17 Washington Star, May 18, 1952, p. A-4.

of former employees a well as persons now in the federal service.

"These people, Bisson, Farley, Grajdanzev, fall under the category of former employees.

"Still quoting the regulation:

'Any individual who may appear as a witness before a Congressional committee will respectfully decline to testify concerning the loyalty of any person or as to the contents of any investigative files and will state that he is forbidden to answer such questions by pertinent directives of the Army.' "

SENATOR WATKINS: "I take it, General, that the order of that directive is not classified?"

GENERAL WILLOUGHBY: "No. The basis is the Presidential directive of 13th of March, 1948."[18]

On February 9, 1950, I went to Wheeling to launch the public exposure of Communists in government. Less than a month before, Dean Acheson had publicly announced, "I do not intend to turn my back on Alger Hiss." What clearer signal could have been given to the other traitors and potential traitors in government? They were assured of support from the highest officials in our government.

Truman had previously viciously condemned the House Committee on Un-American Activities for exposing Alger Hiss. He called the investigation a "red herring"—not once, but six times. With this background it would obviously have been a waste of time to take the evidence of treason to the President. As pointed out, the President had tied the hands of Congress by his blackout order. This left only one place to take my case—to the boss of the President and the Congress, the American people.

I was convinced the American people had to be told the truth and given the facts about the enormity of the impending disaster so that they could force the removal of those responsible. Otherwise, we would have to pay the price that must be paid by those who wait too long.

I was convinced that if the American people were given the facts, they would insist upon a housecleaning of the State Department, and that if that housecleaning were not forthcoming, they, the people, would do a thorough housecleaning at the ballot boxes.

Will you explain your use of the number 205 and 57 in your Wheeling speech?

At Wheeling I discussed a letter which Secretary of State Byrnes wrote in 1946 to Congressman Adolph Sabath.[19] In that letter Byrnes stated that 284 individuals had been declared by the President's security officers as unfit to work in the State Department because of Communist activities and for other reasons, but that only 79 had been discharged. This left a balance of 205 who were still on the State Department's payroll even though the President's own security officers had declared them unfit for government service.

In the same speech at Wheeling, I said that while I did not have the names of the 205 referred to in the Byrnes letter, I did have the names of 57 who were either members of or loyal to the Communist Party. The following day I wired President Truman and sug-

gested that he call in Secretary of State Acheson and ask for the names of the 205 who were kept in the State Department despite the fact that Truman's own security officers had declared them unfit to serve. I urged him to have Acheson tell him how many of the 205 were still in the State Department and why. I told the President that I had the names of 57. I offered those names to the President.[20] The offer was never accepted. The wire was never answered.

The Tydings Committee reported that you said you had the names of 205 and not merely the names of 57 when you spoke in Wheeling. What are the facts?

This question is best answered by Daniel Buckley, an investigator for the completely unfriendly Gillette-Monroney Committee which is investigating Senator Benton's charge that I should be expelled from the Senate because of my fight against Communists. Buckley lost his job with the committee because of his efforts to get to the truth about the "numbers game." The committee sent him to Wheeling to get evidence on this question of the numbers used in my Wheeling speech. The affidavits which he obtained from a large number of witnesses confirmed my report of what was said.

In a public statement released to the press on December 27, 1951, Buckley said:

"My job in Wheeling, I thought was to find the facts, to find whether, as Senator Benton charged, Senator McCarthy had said that he had a list of 205 Communists in the State Department, or whether, as Senator McCarthy maintained, he had said he had a list of 57 individuals either members of or loyal to the Communist Party.

"While in Wheeling, I conscientiously interviewed a large number of witnesses who were in a position to know what Senator McCarthy had actually said. Every one of these witnesses, save one, supplied information which cast grave doubt and suspicion on Senator Benton's story and substantially corroborated Senator McCarthy's account of the facts."

After conducting this investigation in Wheeling, Buckley stated that he returned to Washington and filed his report. He declared that Millard Tydings, who was no longer a member of the Senate, thereupon phoned him and questioned him about his findings.

When he advised Tydings that the witnesses had confirmed my statements about the use of the number 205 and 57, Buckley stated:

"Senator Tydings became highly indignant and irritated. I soon found myself on my way back to Wheeling, this time accompanied by our chief investigator for the unusual purpose of double checking on my original report."

Buckley reported as follows on that second trip to Wheeling:

"The information I developed on the second Wheeling trip did more than merely cast grave doubt and suspicion on Senator Benton's story. The newly

18 McCarran Committee Hearings on IPR, Pt. 2, August 9, 1951, pp. 387-388.
19 Congressional Record (Unbound), Feb. 20, 1950, p. 2044.
20 Congressional Record (Unbound), Feb. 20, 1950, p. 2062.

unearthed evidence demolished Senator Benton's charge in all material respects and thoroughly proved Senator McCarthy's account of the facts to be truthful."[21]

Why has the opposition insisted upon playing this "numbers game" even after all the facts about what you said at Wheeling, West Virginia, were fully known to them?

This juggling and playing with numbers has apparently been for the sole purpose of confusing the issue and distracting attention from the all-important question: Are there still Hisses in the State Department betraying this nation?

A great deal of light is shed on this numbers game by former Senator Tydings' speech on the Senate floor on July 20, 1950,[22] and his actions subsequent thereto. On that date, Tydings told the Senate that he had a recording which would prove that I had deceived the Senate about this question of numbers. He did not play the recording.

On August 4, 1950, a few weeks after Tydings' speech, I spoke to the Senate. I discussed the numbers game being played by Tydings—his juggling of the figures 205, 57, and 81. I pointed out that this question of what McCarthy had said about the numbers 205 and 57 now became very important, because either, as Tydings stated, he had a recording which proved that McCarthy did not speak the truth, or Tydings was deliberately lying to the Senate and to the country. As I pointed out to the Senate at that time, it therefore became of the greatest importance to discover who spoke the truth. In that way the Senate and the country could better evaluate the entire Communist fight which, unfortunately, instead of being a contest between Communism and America, had become a fight between McCarthy and the Administration.[23]

I suggested that while the Senate could not force Tydings to play the recording, perhaps the press could shame him into playing this recording by constantly asking him to do so. Various members of the press did this, but while Tydings referred to the recording a number of times thereafter, especially during his campaign, it was never played.

Will you explain your use of the figure 81?

On February 20, 1950, without naming names, I gave the Senate a resume of the facts from the files of 81 individuals—including the 57 referred to at Wheeling.

While I strongly felt that the 57 were either Communists or at least completely loyal to the Communist Party, the 81 included cases which were marginal. All their files suggested unfitness for government jobs. However, I felt that some might be able to prove their loyalty. I therefore called for a careful investigation in closed session by a Senate committee.[24]

To again summarize the numbers used:

205—Number of State Department employees referred to in a letter of Secretary of State James Byrnes. They were declared unfit for government service by the Pres-

ident's board but were not discharged. Neither the Congress nor the American people have been advised who those people were or whether they are today employed by the government.

81—Cases which McCarthy presented to the Senate in a speech on February 20, 1950. This list included the 57, plus additional cases of less importance against whom the evidence was less conclusive.

57—State Department employees described by McCarthy in a speech in Wheeling, West Virginia, as either members of or loyal to the Communist Party.

Incidentally, the State Department's Security Officer, Carlisle Humelsine, and the Chairman of the State Department Loyalty Board, Conrad Snow, admitted under rigorous cross-examination that 54 out of 57 cases of State Department employees charged with disloyalty, resigned while their cases were pending before a loyalty panel. The other three, who were found to be disloyal, have appealed their cases to Dean Acheson.[24-A]

Were all of the names given to the Tydings Committee?

All except the 205 mentioned in Secretary Byrnes' letter.

Why did you not give the names of the 205 mentioned in the Byrnes' letter to the Tydings Committee?

As I explained at Wheeling and in my wire to the President, I did not have the names of those mentioned in the Byrnes letter. However, I urged the Tydings Committee to subpoena Secretary Acheson and obtain those names. This was never done.

Do you claim there are only 57 Communists or individuals doing the work of the Communist Party in the State Department?

Obviously not. I have no committee or agency to pass upon the approximately 28,000 State Department employees.

I have no power to subpoena witnesses or records. I have a very limited staff of investigators. Nevertheless, I have been able to dig out the facts to show that 57 are either Communists or doing the work of the Communist Party. Therefore, it is safe to assume that there are many more Communists about whom I have no information.

Is this fight against Communists in government a fight against the Democrat Administration?

No, only against those in the Administration who have joined forces to protect Communists in government. If America is to win this battle, all loyal Democrats and Republicans must join forces against the Communist conspiracy.

Unfortunately, the Administration branch of the Democrat party feels that having coddled and protected Com-

21 New York Times, Dec. 28, 1951, p. 8.
22 Congressional Record (Unbound), July 20, 1950, pp. 10861-10872.
23 Congressional Record (Unbound), August 4, 1950, p. 11990.
24 Congressional Record (Unbound), February 20, 1950, pp. 2049, 2053, 2055.
24A Senate Appropriations Committee Hearings, March 25, 1952, p. 385, 395.

munists in government over the past years, it must now for political reasons avoid having them exposed. For the Administration to label the Democrat party as the protector of Communists is extremely unfair to the millions of Americans who have long voted the Democrat ticket. Certainly, those Democrats dislike Communists as much as the average Republican. [All thinking Democrats and Republicans must admit that we are paying today—in lives in Korea and in taxes from every week's payroll —because we completely failed to win the peace following World War II and that since then we have followed a foreign policy that is in the interest of international Communism, not America.]

A FEW OF THOSE WHO HAVE BEEN REMOVED FROM IMPORTANT
GOVERNMENT POSITIONS SINCE THE WHEELING SPEECH

(International News Photo)
Oliver Edmund Clubb, jr.

(International News Photo)
Edward Posniak

(International News Photo)
John Stewart Service

(AP Photo)
Stephen Brunauer

(International News Photo)
William Remington

CHAPTER III

What Has Been Proved?

ALL of those you named before the Tydings Committee were cleared by that committee. Since then have any of them been removed from the government on the grounds that they were either disloyal or bad security risks?

Yes, following is a partial list:

John Stewart Service

Service was dismissed from the State Department on December 13, 1951, on orders from the Loyalty Review Board which reversed the State Department's previous clearance.

Edward Posniak

Posniak, after having been cleared by the State Department Loyalty Board in November, 1948, resigned after I exposed his record. He was subsequently called for questioning before a Grand Jury.

Esther Brunauer

Mrs. Brunauer has been suspended from a high State Department job where she was handling secret material.

Stephen Brunauer

Brunauer, an admitted former member of the Young Communist League, was suspended from his job as head of the Navy's high explosives section where he was engaged in top secret work. He resigned before the Navy's Loyalty Board could complete questioning him and dispose of his case.

Peveril Meigs

Meigs was allowed to resign from the State Department with a clear record. He then obtained a job with the Military Establishment. He was discharged from that job under the Loyalty Program.

Hans Lansberg

Lansberg had been allowed to resign from the State Department with a clear record. He then secured a position as an Economist with the Department of Commerce. The Secretary of Commerce ordered Lansberg discharged under the Loyalty Program. The Loyalty Review Board, upon appeal, affirmed the action of the Secretary of Commerce, and Lansberg was removed from his position on May 25, 1951.

Oliver Edmund Clubb

Clubb, Director of the State Department's Division of Chinese Affairs, was cleared by the Tydings Committee, but the State Department Loyalty Board unanimously ruled against Clubb. Dean Acheson, however, overruled his own Loyalty Board and gave Clubb a clean bill of health, after which Clubb immediately resigned to accept a life pension of $5,800.*

William Remington

Remington was convicted in connection with his membership in the Communist Party and sentenced to 5 years. Remington was on the Commerce Department's payroll but working closely with the State Department, handling secret material. When his case was presented to the Tydings Committee, that committee failed to hear the evidence and cleared him. Remington was later indicted by a Grand Jury. Evidence presented at his trial showed that he had supplied secret government documents to a Soviet courier. He was convicted and sentenced to 5 years. His conviction was set aside on technical grounds. He has since been reindicted on 5 counts.

V. Lorwin

Lorwin was suspended under the State Department's Loyalty Program (according to a letter received from the Chairman of the Civil Service Loyalty Review Board in June, 1951).

William T. Stone

Stone was ordered removed under the State Department Security Program while he was assistant to Assistant Secretary of State William Benton (now Senator Benton). However, Benton failed to remove Stone in accordance with that order. On February 2, 1952, Stone resigned after the Civil Service Commission Loyalty Review Board had selected a panel to rehear his case.

The list is growing from month to month. It should be remembered that it took ten years to get rid of Hiss after he had been named as a Communist spy.

What has happened to Ambassador Jessup and the State Department's Far Eastern expert John P. Davies, who were named by you?

A subcommittee of the Senate Foreign Relations Committee found Ambassador Jessup unfit to represent this country and rejected his nomination as U. S. Delegate to the United Nations. Nevertheless, after Congress adjourned, President Truman gave Jessup an interim appointment as U. S. Delegate to the U. N. As this is written, Jessup is the State Department's Ambassador-at-Large.

John Patton Davies was cleared by the State Department Loyalty Board. His case has since been referred to the Attorney General by the McCarran Committee.

You have referred to the State Department Loyalty Board and the Civil Service Commission Loyalty Review Board. Will you explain the difference?

The State Department Loyalty Board consists of a panel of State Department employees selected by Dean Acheson or his assistant. Their task is to hear the evidence and pass judgment upon their fellow State Department employees who, as a result of investigations by the FBI and

---

*While I gave the Tydings Committee information on Clubb, he was not one of the 81 cases.

other government agencies, are suspected of being disloyal or security risks.

The Civil Service Commission Loyalty Review Board is, as the name implies, a loyalty board set up by the Civil Service Commission. It has no connection with the State Department. Its function is to review loyalty cases which have been passed upon by the loyalty boards within various departments, such as State Department, Treasury Department, and Department of Agriculture.

This review board has power only to review loyalty cases. It has no power to review security cases.

Why were the people who were removed from the State Department as a result of your evidence all cleared by the State Department's Loyalty Board?

This is best answered by the following excerpts from a transcript of a meeting of the Civil Service Loyalty Review Board on February 13 and 14, 1951:

CHAIRMAN BINGHAM: ". . . *The State Department . . . has the worst record of any department in the action of its Loyalty Record.* The Loyalty Board in all the cases they have considered in the State Department has not found anyone—shall I say guilty—or not found anyone disloyal under our rule. It is the only board which has acted in that way . . ."

CLARK: "What are you going to do when the attorney who is presenting the charges acts as though he were the attorney for the incumbent? I read 100 pages of a record where the three members of the [State Department] board were acting as attorneys for the employee . . ."

MELOY: "Oh, you're talking about the State Department. They're taking the attitude that they're there to clear the employee, and not to protect the government. We've been arguing with them since the program started." [Emphasis mine] [25]

Since the above Loyalty Review Board meeting in February of 1951, the State Department Loyalty Board has found three cases of disloyalty in the State Department. [26] All three have appealed their cases to Dean Acheson.

What is your answer to the State Department's attempted ridicule of your evidence on the ground that your cases are "old cases?"

It is true that many of the cases were "old cases" in the sense that the evidence of their Communist activities extended over many years. They should have been dismissed years ago. The fact that a State Department official has a long record of Communist activities over many years certainly does not make him less dangerous than the case of a new Communist arrival in the State Department. It would indeed be an odd district attorney who would scoff at and refuse to prosecute a bank robber because he was an "old case"—because he had been plying his trade over a period of many years. If old cases of Communists should be ruled out, then the House Committee on Un-American Activities should not have exposed Alger Hiss and he should not be in jail today. Information about Hiss' espionage activities was brought to Dean Acheson's attention more than ten years ago. [27]

William Remington's case could be considered an old

case. When I first named him before the Tydings Committee he was holding an $11,000 a year job even though his file showed Communist connections and activities over a long period of time. At that time he was on the Commerce Department payroll working closely with the State Department. A House Committee had already done an excellent job of exposing Remington. Senator Ferguson had also exposed many of Remington's activities. When Ferguson investigated the Remington case in 1948, the President refused to release loyalty data to the committee. The President's Loyalty Review Board then "cleared" Remington.

When I brought the facts in the Remington case up to date and presented them to the Tydings Committee, columnists such as Marquis Childs shed crocodile tears for this "innocent" man, Remington, who had been previously cleared. The Tydings Committee labelled my evidence a "fraud and a hoax." This was an "old" case and according to one Washington columnist, "warmed-over bisquits."

Since then, however, a New York Grand Jury heard the evidence and indicted Remington on the ground that he had perjured himself when he said he was not a member of the Communist Party. For this he was then convicted, which conviction was set aside on technical grounds. Since that time he has been re-indicted on five counts of perjury in connection with Communist activities.

How many sex deviates have been removed from the State Department?

Ninety-one were forced to resign from the State Department prior to 1950, and 54 since that time.

The Senate Special Investigating Committee had this to say about those who were allowed to resign:

"In most of those cases these known homosexuals were allowed to resign for 'personal reasons,' and no information was placed in the regular personnel files of the State Department indicating the real reason for resignation nor was the Civil Service Commission informed of the true reason for the resignation. . . . *Due to the manner in which these cases were mishandled, 23 of those 91 State Department employees found their way into other departments of the government.*" [28]

Do you claim that the sex deviates removed from the State Department were all disloyal?

No, but all are considered security risks. One reason why sex deviates are considered by all intelligence agencies of the government to be security risks is that they are subject to blackmail. It is a known fact that espionage agents often have been successful in extorting information from them by threatening to expose their abnormal habits.

To illustrate the seriousness of this problem, let me cite from the Report of the Senate Special Investigating

[25] Congressional Record (Unbound), January 15, 1952, pp. 192-194.
[26] Senate Appropriations Committee Hearings on State Dept. Appropriation, March 25, 1952, p. 395.
[27] Hearings on Communist Espionage in the United States, House Committee on Un-American Activities, August 30, 1948, pp. 1291-1300.
[28] Report on Employment of Homosexuals and Other Sex Perverts in Government, Senate Committee on Expenditures in the Executive Departments, Subcommittee on Investigations, Dec. 1950, p. 11

Committee, the classic case of Captain Raedl who was chief of the Austrian Counter-Intelligence Service in the early part of World War I.

"Captain Raedl became chief of the Austrian counter-intelligence service in 1912. He succeeded in building up an excellent intelligence net in Russia and had done considerable damage to the espionage net which the Russians had set up in Austria.

"However, Russian agents soon discovered that Raedl was a homosexual and shortly thereafter they managed to catch him in the act of perversion as the result of a trap they had set for the purpose.

"Under the threat of exposure Raedl agreed to furnish, and he did furnish, the Russians with Austrian military secrets. He also doctored or destroyed the intelligence reports which his own Austrian agents were sending from Russia with the result that the Austrian and German General staffs, at the outbreak of World War I in 1914, were completely misinformed as to the Russians' mobilization intentions.

"On the other hand, the Russians had obtained from Raedl the war plans of the Austrians and that part of the German plans which had been made available to the Austrian government. Shortly after the outbreak of the war, Captain Raedl's traitorous acts were discovered by his own government and he committed suicide."[29]

In addition to the security question, it should be noted that individuals who are morally weak and perverted and who are representing the State Department in foreign countries certainly detract from the prestige of this nation.

The Special Senate Investigating Committee had this to say about the high percentage of sex deviates in government:

"[The homosexual has a] tendency to gather other perverts about him. Eminent psychiatrists have informed the subcommittee that the homosexual is likely to seek his own kind because the pressures of society are such that he feels uncomfortable unless he is with his own kind. Due to this situation the homosexual tends to surround himself with other homosexuals, not only in his social but in his business life. Under these circumstances, if a homosexual attains a position in government where he can influence the hiring of personnel, it is almost inevitable that he will attempt to place other homosexuals in government jobs."[30]

[29] Report on Employment of Homosexuals in Government, Senate Subcommittee on Investigations, Dec. 1950, p. 5.
[30] Report of Employment of Homosexuals in Government, Senate Subcommittee on Investigations, Dec. 1950, p. 4.

CHAPTER IV

Congressional Immunity

Have you ever made your charges against Communists in government without the protection of Congressional immunity?

Yes. Over the past two years I have made speeches from the Atlantic to the Pacific and from the Gulf of Mexico to the Canadian border exposing Communists and pro-Communists in government. I have repeatedly named names and documented cases. At such times there was no Congressional immunity—nor is there Congressional immunity attached to this book.

Why do Senators and Congressmen have Congressional immunity?

The answer to this question is found in the long struggle of the human race to establish a workable representative government. History records that legislative immunity was written into English law after "The Case of the Seven Bishops" which precipitated the Revolution of 1688. During that Revolution Parliament triumphed over King James II who had been ignoring the Parliament and trying to impose one-man rule upon England. Matters were brought to a head after James II ignored the Parliament and passed a law by proclamation. The King then required the clergy to read this law to their church members. Seven bishops protested and issued a petition to the King setting forth their reasons for objecting to this arbitrary procedure. The King immediately had the seven bishops arrested and charged them with "libelous and seditious" statements. When the court set the seven bishops free, the people of England cheered the court. The same day an invitation was sent to William and Mary to take over the throne of England. After this experience, the people became determined to make sure once and for all that their representatives should have the freedom to speak out against the government without fear of arrest for what they said. After William and Mary succeeded James II in 1688, the Bill of Rights was drawn up by the people. One of the rights provided for in that document was the right of the representatives of the people to speak freely against anything which they thought endangered the welfare or security of the nation and its people, without fear of reprisal. The new monarchs, William and Mary, signed that document.[31]

When our forefathers drew up the Constitution, they too considered this right a basic one and wrote it into the Constitution. It is today known as Congressional immunity. Its purpose is to make a Republic workable. If the people are to have a voice in government through their representatives, then those representatives must be free to speak out even though their remarks may embarrass and hurt the party in power and tend to remove that party from power.

It should be remembered that the provision for Congressional immunity was written into our Constitution not for the benefit of the individual Congressman or Senator, but for the benefit of the people of this country. This was made clear in a court decision in one of the first lawsuits testing Congressional immunity. The court stated:

"These privileges are thus secured, not with the intention of protecting the members against prosecutions for their own benefit, but to support the rights of the people, by enabling their representatives to execute the functions of their office without fear of prosecutions, civil or criminal."[32]

The real liberals of their day provided for Congressional immunity in the English Bill of Rights and the United States Constitution. The Communists and the phoney and deluded liberals of today would take from the people the right to hear all of the facts from their representatives. Unfortunately, the freedom of Senators and Congressmen to speak unpleasant and embarrassing truths without fear of prosecution in lawsuits is at times abused. Rather than remove this freedom of speech, it would seem wiser for the voters to remove those who abuse that freedom of speech.

Do you feel that you properly used Congressional immunity to expose Communists and pro-Communists in government?

The test is whether the facts which I gave to the Senate and the country were true. If it could be proved that the facts which I gave the Senate and the country were untrue, then, of course, the use of immunity was improper. If, on the other hand, the facts which I gave the Senate were all true, there should be no objection to my giving the country the truth under the usual rules of Congressional immunity.

Even though the opposition has at its command the vast power of the federal government, it has been unable to disprove any of the evidence on the Communists, fellow travelers, and well-meaning dupes of the Kremlin which I gave to the committee and the Senate. One by one, those whom I named before the Tydings committee are being exposed and removed from government. Were I being proved wrong on the cases of John Stewart Service, Owen Lattimore, Philip Jessup, Edward Posniak, William T. Stone, and others, then the argument that I should not have used Congressional immunity to expose them would have merit.

A Senator who is aware of treason but who refuses to expose the dangerous unpleasant facts for fear that he will be politically scarred and bloodied if he does, is actually guilty of a greater treason than the traitors themselves. Every Senator has the duty to use the means provided by the Constitution to protect the people who

---

[31] 1 William and Mary, Session 2, Chap. 2; Frederick George Marcham, A History of England, Revised Edition (New York, 1950), p. 484; William, Political History of England, Edited by William Hunt, Vol. 8, pp. 273, 278.
[32] Coffin v. Coffin (1808) 4 Mass. 1, 3 Am. Dec. 189.

have entrusted him with the task of manning the watch-towers of this nation.

Can newspapers freely publish the facts proving corruption and Communism in government without benefit of Congressional immunity?

This question was answered rather well by David Lawrence in his column of August 9, 1951, which follows:

"Senator Joseph McCarthy of Wisconsin, Republican, has given a public demonstration of the importance, as he sees it, of congressional immunity—and why he thinks the press, too, recognizes its advantages.

"Congressional immunity is the right of a member of Congress to say what he pleases on the floor or in a committee proceeding and yet to be free from prosecution for libel or slander by those individuals who may consider themselves unjustly attacked or subjected to ridicule.

"The Wisconsin Senator offered on a television program to make public the names of the 29 employees of the State Department who, he says, are now being investigated by the department's loyalty board in connection with charges involving 'security' risks.

"But promptly the moderator of the television program declined to have the names given, and Senator McCarthy said he understood and sympathized with the desire of the broadcasting company and the sponsor to avoid responsibility for such disclosures.

"So the Wisconsin Senator announced that he would meet the next morning at his office the reporters from the press associations and give them the names for publication. He said he not only would announce the names but would permit the reporters to give his own name publicly as their source or authority for the information. He made, however, one condition—that the press associations assure him in advance they would print the 29 names.

"The press associations declared that they would give no guarantees in advance that they would print anything about anybody and that, if Senator McCarthy issued the names, they would then decide on their own whether or not to publish them.

"Mr. McCarthy, of course, knew that, the moment the names were printed, all immunity vanished not only for him but for the press associations as well as all the newspapers served by them which printed the names. There is no certainty that the individuals would refrain from filing lawsuits against the newspapers and sue only the Wisconsin Senator, though the press would be jointly liable with him . . .

"But the purpose of the stunt was achieved. What Mr. McCarthy wanted to do was to emphasize the real reason for congressional immunity—to protect not only members of Congress but the newspapers and periodicals which desired to publish the information made available by members of Congress and governmental agencies. Without congressional immunity, many a scandal, like the recent revelations of the RFC, would appear in print in only a few publications ready to risk lawsuits. Nation-wide publicity on such wrongdoings would occur rarely . . ."[33]

Why do Communists object so strenuously to the use of Congressional immunity?

Part of the answer is found in the following testimony of Louis Budenz, former editor of the official Communist newspaper, the *Daily Worker*, and member of the national committee of the Communist Party:

"... the Communist Party—and this is something that everyone should know—agreed that after that period of 1945, that with the cold war beginning, all concealed Communists should sue anyone who accused them of being Communists, sue them for libel.

"As Alexander Trachtenberg [member of the Communist Politburo], who made the report, said, 'This is not necessarily for the purpose of winning the libel suit. It is to bleed white anyone who dares to accuse anyone of being a Communist, so that they will be shut up.' As a matter of fact, that became the policy.

"... this plan was very successful, those who might speak in organs, or in the press or over the radio of concealed Communists—that the Communists, as a matter of duty, were to sue them for libel . . . we have a very striking case of Mrs. McCullough . . . who, even if she wins the case, is going to lose $55,000 from the cost of the case."[34]

An example of what Budenz was discussing is William Remington's lawsuit against Elizabeth Bentley. Remington sued Miss Bentley after she named him as a Communist on a radio program.

In this lawsuit, Miss Bentley had no power to order the government through a subpoena to produce the files on Remington which contained full information about his Communist connections. It would have been useless to have subpoenaed and brought into court the individuals who had been fellow-Communists with Remington because (1) they could have availed themselves of the common Communist dodge of "I refuse to answer on the grounds my answer might tend to incriminate me," or (2) if they did choose to testify, Miss Bentley as a former Communist knew that they were bound "to practice trickery, to employ cunning, and to resort to illegal methods . . . to overlook or conceal the truth."[35]

Faced with this situation, Miss Bentley's co-defendant, the radio program sponsor, had no choice but to settle the case. It is reported that a $10,000 settlement was made.

A jury later convicted Remington of perjury in connection with his Communist activities. However, the program sponsor is still out $10,000, and Miss Bentley is out her attorney's fees.

If on that radio program Miss Bentley had named all of the Communists in her spy ring and all the other Communists with whom she had contact, each of them, under orders from the Communist Party, would have been obliged to sue her. Even if she had finally won all of the lawsuits, it would undoubtedly have bankrupted her, the radio program sponsor, and the radio network.

Instead of using Congressional immunity to name names publicly, why were not the names given in closed session of the committee? Could not the same results have been obtained in that fashion?

In answer to that question allow me to quote from a speech made by Senator Hickenlooper on April 5, 1950:

Senator Hickenlooper Tells Senate: Tydings Insisted on Public Disclosure of Names

"The Senator from Wisconsin [on February 20,

33 David Lawrence, Washington Star, August 9, 1951.
34 Tydings Committee Hearings, Pt. 1, April 20, 1950, p. 506.
35 Lenin, Should Communists Participate in Reactionary Trade Unions?, p. 13.

1950] repeatedly stated and restated on the floor of the Senate that he did not want to make names public, that he would not tell the names to the Senate in public . . .

"The junior Senator from Massachusetts and I, both at the first executive meeting of the subcommittee, suggested and proposed the procedure, that the subcommittee meet in executive session, call the Senator from Wisconsin before it, and ask him to disclose the names in private, together with whatever information he had in connection with the names; but the majority of the subcommittee said no, this must be brought out in public. So they held their first hearing, requiring the Senator from Wisconsin to come, in public, to name the names. I tell the Senate that, if it is not familiar with it, merely to keep the factual history of the publicity of those names accurate.

"I should like to say also that so far as I am concerned, while we did not have the machinery to set up a court of inquiry such as the Canadian spy-ring case called for, we did propose and urge that an inquiry in secrecy without naming names be made with the facts collected. But we were overruled, and the Senator from Wisconsin was required, or requested, to come before the committee in public hearing, with klieg lights, television, and all the rest of the fanfare of such an emotional occasion, there to bring out his cases, name names, and produce facts."[36]

Why was your advice that the names be taken in secret session not followed?

I cannot guess why the Democrat Majority Party in the Senate did not follow this advice.

The Majority leader, former Senator Scott Lucas, interrupted my February 20th Senate speech five times and insisted that the names be made public.

For example, on page 2046 of the *Congressional Record*, he had this to say:

"I want to remain here until he names them—that is what I am interested in."

Again, on page 2049, he said,

"Will the Senator tell us the name of the man for the record? We are entitled to know this. I say this in all seriousness."

Again, on page 2053,

"The Senator should name names before that Committee."

And again on page 2063, he said,

"Why does the Senator refuse to divulge names before the Senate?"

What was your answer to Senator Lucas' demand that the names be made public?

My answer was as follows:

"The names are available. The Senators may have them if they care for them. I think, however, it would be improper to make the names public until the appropriate Senate Committee can meet in executive session and get them. I have approximately 81 cases. I do not claim to have any tremendous investigative agency to get the facts, but if I were

to give all the names involved, it might leave a wrong impression.

"If we should label one man a Communist when he is not a Communist, I think it would be too bad. However, the names are here. I shall be glad to abide by the decision of the Senate after it hears the cases, but I think the sensible thing to do would be to have a proper committee go over the whole situation."[37]

If you felt it was wrong to name the names publicly, why did you do so under the orders of the Tydings Committee?

Because this is still a Republic and the majority rules.

Where in the record of the Tydings Committee did you object to giving the names in public?

On Page 17 of the Tydings hearings I stated:

". . . On the Senate floor I said that I would not divulge any names. I said I hoped any names that were divulged would be developed in executive session. Mr. Lucas, who is the leader of the majority party, demanded time after time on the Senate floor and publicly that I divulge names. I am now before the committee. In order to present the case I must give the names, otherwise I cannot intelligibly present it. If the committee desires to go into executive session, that is a decision that the committee and not I can make, but if I am to testify, I say it is impossible to do it without divulging names . . .

"I personally do not favor presenting names, no matter how conclusive the evidence is. The committee has called me this morning, and in order to intelligibly present this information I must give names. I think this should be in executive session. I think it would be better. However, I am here. The committee has voted to hold open sessions, so I shall proceed."

At that point I handed copies of my testimony on Kenyon to the press. After Tydings saw that the testimony had been distributed to the press he then offered to allow me to testify in executive session on the Kenyon case—a cleverly deceptive gesture because he knew there could be nothing secret about the evidence after some 50 newspapermen had been given copies of it.

After holding public sessions to hear the evidence on nine of my cases, the committee decided to hear the balance in closed session. However, the only case in which the committee allowed me to present evidence in closed session was the Lattimore case.

How about the claim that you have used Congressional immunity to smear innocent people?

This is the type of general statement which has been parroted over and over by such men as Drew Pearson, and publications such as *Time* Magazine, the St. Louis *Post Dispatch*, the Milwaukee *Journal*, as well as the official publication of the Communist Party, the *Daily Worker*.

This is the well-known and effective Hitlerian technique of shouting loud and often a lie that is so big that at least part of it will be repeated and finally come to be accepted as fact.

[36] Congressional Record, (Unbound), April 5, 1950, pp. 4957, 4958.
[37] Congressional Record (Unbound), Feb. 20, 1950, p. 2049.

All of those critics refuse to name a single "innocent" person whom they claim I have "smeared." If by exposing Communists and pro-Communists I have smeared them, then the district attorney who convicts a murderer and his accomplice is also guilty of "smearing innocent people."

Did you publicly name Lattimore as one of Russia's top agents?

No. Lattimore was named in a closed session of the Tydings Committee with the strict understanding that his name would not be made public by the committee until his case had been fully investigated.

At that time I urged the committee to consider the Lattimore case as a test case. I suggested that if the committee found my evidence on Lattimore true in every respect, then they could reasonably assume the accuracy of my evidence on the other cases. I suggested that if, on the other hand, my evidence against Lattimore proved untrue—if the charges against him were "irresponsible" —then they could assume that the evidence which I gave them about others in the State Department was equally unfounded. I told the Tydings Committee at that time that I was willing to stand or fall on the Lattimore case.

Who made public the fact that you had named Lattimore as one of Russia's top agents?

Drew Pearson made Lattimore's name public. According to Lattimore's book, Mrs. Lattimore wrote him that on the night of March 26, 1950, Drew Pearson's broadcast "really broke the story."[38] In his broadcast Pearson stated, "I am now going to reveal the name of the man whom Senator McCarthy has designated the top Communist agent in the United States . . . The man is Owen Lattimore." Pearson continued, "Now I happen to know Owen Lattimore personally, and I only wish this country had more patriots like him."[39]

Lattimore's book, *Ordeal by Slander*, reveals the fact that Abe Fortas, Lattimore's lawyer, invited Mrs. Lattimore to listen to the broadcast, knowing in advance that Pearson was going to make Lattimore's name public.[40] Thus it seems that the name was made public upon agreement between Lattimore's lawyer and Pearson for a definite purpose. Lattimore's "Ordeal by Slander," it would appear, was deliberately commenced by his good friend, Pearson, upon the advice of Lattimore's lawyer.

This was secret information until Pearson made it public. After having made it public, Pearson then started a running smear compaign against me for having "publicly smeared Owen Lattimore under the cloak of Congressional immunity."

Owen Lattimore has challenged you to make your statements about him away from the Senate floor so he could sue you. What is your answer to this?

I have offered to waive all immunity in the Lattimore case if he would consent to have the legal evidence in his FBI file made available in any lawsuit which he might start.

On page 483 of the Tydings hearings, he was asked by Senator Hickenlooper whether or not he was willing to have the legal evidence in his file made available. In his answer Lattimore refused to ask that his file be made available on the ground that "I should be asking for a favor and that I refuse to do."[41]

Did an Administration Senator, who repeatedly used Congressional Immunity to charge people with being crooks, racketeers, gamblers, and thugs, viciously attack you for having exposed Communists in government under the same immunity rules?

Yes. Senator Kefauver in his bid for the support of the left-wing and Communist-controlled elements of press and radio in his campaign for the Presidential nomination has conducted a running public attack on my exposure of Communists in government. He has been unable to find one single thing good for America in my fight against Communists. His parroting of the stock left-wing phrases against McCarthy has sounded like a broken record— phrases such as "irresponsible charges," "shot-gun technique," "smearing innocent people," ad infinitum. To date, of course, he has not named a single "innocent person" who was "hit by a stray bullet" nor a single "innocent person" who was "smeared." No mention is made of the fact that a sizable number of the "innocent" people who were "irresponsibly" charged by McCarthy have since either gone to jail or have been gotten rid of under the Loyalty Program.

Why do some Senators feel that it is proper to use Congressional immunity to accuse people of being dishonest and of being crooks and gamblers but improper to use the same immunity to expose traitors?

I cannot answer that question. It is safe, of course, for a politician to trumpet against and "expose" men long known and publicly recognized as racketeers.

Was Senator Kefauver offered a bribe to protect certain racketeering activities?

Yes, according to Kefauver's story in the *Saturday Evening Post* of April 7, 1951, pages 76 and 79.

Was the person who offered Kefauver this bribe to protect racketeers guilty of a crime?

In the *Post* article Kefauver says that the man offering the $100,000.00-plus bribe was not committing a crime. However, under federal law and the laws of each of the 48 states, it is a crime—a felony to bribe a public official.

In order to expose crime and convict criminals, is it not extremely important to expose and convict those who try to bribe public officials?

Obviously so.

In this connection, three things should be kept in mind:
(1) Unless he who is offering the bribe is guilty of

38 Owen Lattimore, Ordeal By Slander (Little, Brown & Co., 1950), p. 14.
39 Owen Lattimore, Ordeal By Slander, p. 46.
40 Owen Lattimore, Ordeal By Slander, p. 44
41 Tydings Committee Hearings, Pt. 1, April 6, 1950, p. 483, 484.

very serious wrong doing, he would not, as Kefauver said, offer a bribe "in six figures"—meaning $100,000 or more.

(2) Offering to pay a public official a huge bribe is a serious crime.

(3) Unless the criminal who makes the offer is exposed and prosecuted, he and other criminals and racketeers will rightly understand this as a green light to attempt to buy protection from other public officers.

Why has not Senator Kefauver who claims to be against crime ever exposed the name of the man who offered him this bribe to protect racketeering?

? ? ?

This racketeer, according to Kefauver's story, was offering a huge bribe to keep the Kefauver Committee from investigating him. In other words, he was trying to buy protection from the Senate Crime investigators. Did he get that protection or was he investigated?

Only Kefauver, the Crime Fighter, and the crook who offered him the bribe can answer this question. Kefauver has refused to disclose either the name of the individual or the racket in which he was involved. Kefauver's story merely shows that this racketeer was worried about being exposed by the Senate Crime Committee and that he tried to buy Kefauver off by offering (1) to contribute $100,-000 or more to the Democrat National Committee, or (2) to hire workers for Kefauver with "nobody knowing anything about it," or (3) to send out campaign material for Kefauver.[42]

Senator Kefauver in the *Saturday Evening Post* article admits that he refused to expose a man who offered him a bribe to ignore or whitewash racketeering. Obviously, Communist traitors have much more at stake than this bribing racketeer. They, of course, would pay a much higher price to have their activities covered up and whitewashed. Why does Presidential candidate Kefauver so bitterly condemn you throughout the country for refusing, where Communist traitors are concerned, to follow the same cover-up rule that he followed where this cheap racketeer was concerned?

I would prefer not to speculate as to Kefauver's motives.

---

[42] Saturday Evening Post, April 7, 1951, p. 79.

June 10, 1947

FROM: SENATE APPROPRIATIONS COMMITTEE

TO: SECRETARY OF STATE, GEORGE C. MARSHALL

It becomes necessary due to the gravity of the situation to call your attention to a condition that developed and still flourishes in the State Department under the administration of Dean Acheson.

It is evident that there is a deliberate, calculated program being carried out not only to protect Communist personnel in high places, but to reduce security and intelligence protection to a nullity.

Regarding the much-publicized MARZANI case, the evidence brought out at his trial was well known to State Department officers, who ignored it and refused to act for a full year.

MARZANI and several other Department officials, with full knowledge of the State Department, and with Government time and money, promoted a scheme called PRESENTATIONS, INC., which contracted with a Communist dominated organization to disseminate propaganda.

Security objections to these and other even more dangerous developments were rebuffed by high administrative officials; and there followed the substitution of unqualified men for these competent, highly respected personnel who theretofore held the intelligence and security assignments in the Department. The new chief of controls is a man utterly devoid of background and experience for the job, who is and at the time of his appointment was known to those who appointed him to be, a cousin and close associate of a suspected Soviet espionage agent. The next development was the refusal of the FBI, G-2, ONI and other federal investigative agencies to continue the whole hearted cooperation they had for years extended to the State Department.

On the file in the Department is a copy of a preliminary report of the FBI on Soviet espionage activities in the United States, which involves a large number of State Department employes, some in high official positions. This report has been challenged and ignored by those charged with the responsibility of administering the Department with the apparent tacit approval of Mr. Acheson. Should this case break before the State Department acts, it will be a national disgrace.

Voluminous files are on hand in the Department proving the connection of the State Department employes and officials with this Soviet espionage ring. Despite this, only two persons, one of whom is MARZANI, were released under the McCarran rider because of their subversive activity.

1. ████████████   6. ████████████
2. ████████████   7. ████████████
3. ████████████   8. ████████████
4. ████████████   9. ████████████
5. ████████████

are only a few of the hundreds now employed in varying capacities who are protected and allowed to remain despite the fact that their presence is an obvious hazard to national security. There is also the extensive employment in highly classified position of admitted homosexuals, who are historically known to be security risks.

The War and Navy Departments have been thwarted for a year in their efforts to carry out the German Scientist program. They are blocked by one man in the State Department, a protege of Acheson named ████████, who is also the chief instrument in the subverting of the over-all security program.

This deplorable condition runs all the way up and down the line. Assistant Secretary Braden also surrounded himself with men like ████████ and with ████████ who has a notorious international reputation. The network also extends into the office of Assistant Secretary Benton.

SUBCOMMITTEE OF
SENATE APPROPRIATIONS COMMITTEE

CHAPTER V

The Record of Dean Acheson

THE principal target of your criticism has been Dean Acheson. Will you give the record—not your opinion—to prove that Acheson has aided the Communist cause?

Following is the documented record of Acheson's aid to international Communism over the past 20 years.

On the opposite page there is reproduced a confidential memorandum from a subcommittee of the Senate Appropriations Committee in 1947 to the then Secretary of State, George Marshall. It will be noted that the Senate subcommittee warned that "under the administration of Dean Acheson" there was being carried out "a deliberate, calculated program . . . to protect Communist personnel in high places." The memorandum included the names of 10 State Department officials and warned that "the network extends into the office of the Assistant Secretary Benton [now Senator Benton]."

This warning was disregarded by Marshall.

Communist Russia Hires
Acheson and Pressman

Before Russia was recognized by the United States in 1933, Dean Acheson was paid by the Soviet Union to act as Stalin's lawyer in this country.[43] Lee Pressman, an admitted member of the Communist Party, also was on Stalin's payroll as one of his American lawyers.[44] Some of Acheson's duties were to appear before such agencies as the U. S. Tariff Commission.[45]

Felix Wittmer in the *American Mercury* asks:

"Just why among all the American lawyers, did the Soviet leaders hire these two: Acheson and Lee Pressman? It's easy to explain why they hired Pressman: he was a Communist and a member of the Ware cell organized for espionage in the government. The Soviet Union, of course, followed a general policy in all countries of hiring sympathetic lawyers. Then why did Stalin hire Acheson?"[46]

This has never yet been satisfactorily explained by our Secretary of State whose job it is to "fight" the Communist threat to this country.

Communist Infiltration of Government
Commences

Acheson first entered the government in 1933, when he was appointed Under Secretary of the Treasury. It was in 1933 also that the Communist Party began the systematic infiltration of our government under the direction of Harold Ware, son of Ella Reeve Bloor, the so-called "mother" of the American Communist Party. Alger Hiss, in those early days, was a member of the Ware cell. The far-reaching importance of this Communist cell in the U. S. government was described by Whittaker Chambers who said that its members have "helped to shape the future of every American now alive and indirectly affected the fate of every man now in uniform."[47]

After leaving the Treasury Department, Acheson served in the Attorney General's office for one year. In 1941 he entered the State Department.

Vouched for Hiss in 1941
When Told Hiss Was a Communist

Adolph Berle, the State Department official in charge of security, has testified that he notified Acheson (both before and after Acheson became Assistant Secretary of State) of a conversation he had in 1939 with Whittaker Chambers about Alger Hiss and his brother, Donald. Chambers had advised Berle that the Hiss brothers were underground Communists. Assistant Secretary of State Berle's notes on Chambers' knowledge of the Hiss brothers' Communist activities were headed "Underground Espionage Agent."[48] At the time Berle warned Acheson, Acheson ridiculed the fears of this State Department security officer and stated that he "could vouch for them absolutely."

Following is Berle's testimony before the House Committee on Un-American Activities:

"Specifically, I checked with Dean Acheson and later I checked when Acheson became Assistant Secretary of State [1941] and Alger Hiss became his executive assistant. That, to the best of my knowledge, was the first time when Hiss would have been in a position to do anything effective. Acheson said he had known the family and these two boys from childhood and could vouch for them absolutely."[49]

Ignored Reports on Hiss

Acheson ignored loyalty reports on Alger Hiss and continued to help him up the ladder of success. It is interesting to note that Hiss' meteoric rise in government began *after* Acheson was advised that Hiss had been named as an underground Communist.

Hiss moved up the ladder, first becoming attached to the Office of Far Eastern Affairs. Next he became Special Assistant to the Adviser on Political Relations; Special Assistant to the Office of Special Political Affairs; Deputy Director, Office of Special Political Affairs; and finally Director, Office of Special Political Affairs.[50]

In addition Acheson helped secure for Hiss the appointment as Executive Secretary of the Dumbarton Oaks Conference, which laid the foundation for the United Nations.

Sends Hiss to Yalta

At Yalta, Hiss was one of the chief advisers to the

[43] American Mercury Magazine, "Freedom's Case Against Dean Acheson," Felix Wittmer, April, 1952, p. 5; Congressional Record, May 16, 1933, p. 3484.
[44] House Un-American Activities Committee, Hearings on Communism in the United States, Pt. 2, August 28, 1950, pp. 2843-2901.
[45] American Mercury, April, 1952, p. 5.
[46] American Mercury, April, 1952, pp. 5, 6.
[47] Whittaker Chambers, Saturday Evening Post, "I Was The Witness," February 23, 1952, p. 22.
[48] Whittaker Chambers, Witness (Random House, 1952), pp. 466-469.
[49] Hearings on Communist Espionage in United States, House Committee on Un-American Activities, August 30, 1948, pp. 1291-1300.
[50] Letter from Department of State to Library of Congress. (Author has copy).

President, and with Gromyko of Russia and Jebb of England drafted major portions of the Yalta Agreement. It was at Yalta that China and Poland were sold out to Communist Russia and the stage was set for the present war in Korea. As Hiss said about his activities at Yalta:

"I think it is an accurate and not immodest statement to say that I helped formulate the Yalta agreement to some extent."[50-A]

In 1945, Hiss reached the heights when he was made Secretary-General of the United Nations Conference in San Francisco. There he presided during the drafting of the United Nations Charter.

"I Do Not Intend to Turn My Back on Alger Hiss"

In 1950, after serving Communist Russia well for many years as an agent, Hiss was convicted of perjury in connection with his espionage activities. Acheson then called a press conference and announced to the world that "whatever the outcome" of Alger Hiss' appeal, "I do not intend to turn my back on him."[51]

This statement is significant not because it expressed undying support for an old friend who was a convicted traitor. Acheson's statement was extremely important because it served public notice on every other "Hiss" in the State Department that he could bank upon the powerful backing of the Secretary of State if he were caught and accused or convicted of treason.

Donald Hiss, brother of Alger, who was also named by Chambers in 1939 as an underground Communist, remained in the State Department until 1945 when it was arranged for his transfer to the Acheson law firm. Donald Hiss is today a member of the Acheson law firm.

Acheson and Hiss Head Pro-Communist Group in State Department

On August 30, 1948, Adolph Berle, former Assistant Secretary of State, testified before the House Committee on Un-American Activities as follows:

". . . In the fall of 1944 there was a difference of opinion in the State Department . . . the intelligence reports which were in my charge indicated a very aggressive Russian policy . . . and I was pressing for a pretty clean-cut showdown then when our position was strongest. The opposite group in the State Department [the pro-Communist group] was largely the men—Mr. Acheson's group, of course—with Mr. Hiss as a principal assistant in the matter . . . I got trimmed in that fight and, as a result, went to Brazil and that ended my diplomatic career."[52]

Communist Party Campaign To Remove Anti-Communists from State Department

According to the testimony of Louis Budenz, former editor of the *Daily Worker* and a former member of the American Communists' national committee, the Communist Party mapped out a campaign in 1942 which "began with an attack on Mr. Adolph Berle . . . to clean the State Department of all anti-Soviet elements."[53] Berle

at that time was the official in charge of security matters in the department.

According to Budenz' testimony, word was sent out through the *Daily Worker* to all loyal Party members to attack and demand the resignation of "those who were considered to be against Soviet policy in the Far East."[54] As a result, there was unloosed a barrage of insidious smear attacks and an all-out attempt to discredit the anti-Communists in the State Department. This was done through Communist front organizations and by the "liberal" elements of press and radio.

The Communist Party, according to the testimony, also used men within the State Department to sabotage the work of the anti-Communists. In this they had the active assistance of Acheson's group. Budenz cited one example:

"The Communists relied very strongly on Service and John Carter Vincent in the campaign against Ambassador Hurley."[55]

Budenz testified that the Communist Party's opening attack—a speech delivered by Earl Browder to the Young Communist League on October 2, 1942—was "prepared through an arrangement with Lauchlin Currie [Administrative Assistant to the President who was named under oath as "a full fledged member" of a Communist spy ring][56] in order to smoke out the people who were opposed to Soviet policy in the Far East in the State Department."[57]

Following the reprinting of this speech in the *Daily Worker*, on October 4, Earl Browder, the head of the Communist Party in the United States met with Under Secretary of State Sumner Welles and Lauchlin Currie and secured from Welles a statement on State Department policy on China that was acceptable to Browder. Welles' memorandum to Browder, which was then published in the *Daily Worker* of October 16, stated:

"With regard to the specific charge that 'these officials continue the old policy of "war against the Communists" in China,' this government has had no such policy, either 'old' or new. *This Government has in fact viewed with skepticism many alarmist accounts of the 'serious menace' of 'Communism' in China.* We have, for instance, as is publicly and well known, declined to be moved by Japanese contentions that presence and maintenance of Japanese armed forces in China were and would be desirable for the purpose of 'combating Communism.' With regard to the specific charge that officials of this Government 'tell Chungking [headquarters of the anti-Communist government of China] it must continue to fight the Communists if it wishes United States friendship,' the simple fact is that no official of this government ever has told Chungking either that it must fight or that it must continue to fight the 'Communists'; this government holds no such belief . . ." (Emphasis mine)[58]

Asked what anti-Communist officials in addition to Berle

50-A Testimony before House Committee on Un-American Activities, 1948, quoted by The Freeman, Sept. 24, 1951, p. 817.
51 World Almanac, 1951, p. 208.
52 Hearings on Communist Espionage in United States, House Committee on Un-American Activities, August 30, 1948, pp. 1291-1300.
53 McCarran Committee Hearings on IPR, August 23, 1951, Pt. 2, p. 602.
54 McCarran Committee Hearings on IPR, Pt. 2, August 23, 1951, p. 602.
55 McCarran Committee Hearings on IPR, Pt. 2, August 23, 1951, p. 624.
56 McCarran Committee Hearings on IPR, Pt. 2, August 14, 1951, p. 423.
57 McCarran Committee Hearings on IPR, Pt. 2, August 23, 1951, p. 594.
58 McCarran Committee Hearings on IPR, Pt. 2, August 23, 1951, pp. 599, 600.

were slated for removal by the Communist Party, Budenz replied:

> "Joseph C. Grew, Under Secretary of State; Lt. Gen. Albert Wedemeyer, not technically with the State Department but connected at least diplomatically with the State Department relations; Eugene C. Dooman, who was head of the Far Eastern Division, if I remember correctly, at least he was in control of the details of far eastern policy; and Gen. Patrick Hurley, Ambassador to China, who particularly was under attack from the Communists."[59]

In all cases the Communist Party, with the aid of their friends within the department, was successful.

It is interesting that in almost every case the men singled out for removal by the Communist Party were in bitter conflict with Acheson, particularly over his Far Eastern policy.

Grew Resigns after Insisting on Prosecution in Amerasia Case

Joseph Grew was one of the State Department officials on the Communist black list. Budenz testified that "the Politburo laid plans against Mr. Grew" because:

> ". . . he didn't have the right policy in China, and secondly, as we approached the question of what to do with Japan, he favored a soft peace with Japan.
> "The Communists wanted a tough peace just as there was to be the Morgenthau plan in Germany. They didn't hesitate in their own discussions to show that this would tend to drive the Japanese into the hands of the Soviet Union."[60]

According to Freda Utley, author of *The China Story*, "so long as Grew was in charge of Far Eastern affairs at the State Department, the Communists had comparatively little influence there." To circumvent Grew, who stymied the pro-Communists' attempts to send their reports into the White House, Acheson had already made State Department official John Carter Vincent a special assistant in the White House to Lauchlin Currie[61] (named under oath as a Communist and as a member of a Communist spy ring respectively).

Grew's final anti-Communist act in the State Department came in 1945 when he insisted upon prosecution in the *Amerasia* case. The Washington *Daily News* has reported that Grew insisted on the arrests because he was under the "certain impression at that time that the case against the 6 persons arrested was so air tight as to make convictions all but assured."[62] According to Fred Woltman's newspaper series "The Amerasia Case," this assurance came to Grew from the FBI.[63] John Stewart Service was one of the State Department officials arrested in this case. The FBI had wire recordings of Service visiting the hotel room of Philip Jaffe (who has been named as a Soviet agent) and turning over to him military information which Service warned Jaffe was secret.[64] Soon after Grew insisted that the cases go to trial, he resigned from the State Department because of "bad health."

Communists Praise Acheson

Acheson then replaced Grew as Under Secretary of

State. Service was reinstated in his State Department job and later put on the board which had charge of placements and promotions of State Department personnel in the entire Far Eastern area.

The official publication of the Communist Party, the *Daily Worker*, had already praised Acheson on June 7, 1945, as "one of the more forward-looking men in the State Department." In the same article the *Daily Worker* stated that the real test of the President's concern over anti-Soviet policies would be "what he does about it, whether he removes those in the State Department responsible for anti-Soviet policies, whether he finds solutions for outstanding points of friction with the Soviet Union . . ." When Grew resigned and Acheson replaced him, *PM* (which John L. Lewis has described as the "uptown edition of the *Daily Worker*") wrote:

> "What the government seeks now is to develop a diplomacy based on a better appreciation of what the Soviet wants . . . That explains in part the search for liberals . . ."[65]

Removes Anti-Communist Who Opposed Him

The day after Acheson replaced Under Secretary of State Joseph Grew, he announced he was replacing Eugene Dooman, long-time Far Eastern expert, with John Carter Vincent.[66] It was little wonder, for Dooman, who was another anti-Communist official slated for removal by the Communist Party, had just run head-on into Acheson's vigorous attempts to inject the Lattimore line into postwar policy toward Japan.

This occurred during a meeting of the powerful interdepartmental committee representing the State, War and Navy Departments, known as SWINK. Dooman, who was chairman of the Far Eastern subcommittee of SWINK, had just made his report on proposed postwar policy toward Japan. At the end of that report, according to Dooman's testimony before the McCarran Committee, Mr. McCloy, chairman of the full committee, turned to Dean Acheson and said:

> "Dean, you are a great authority on Far Eastern matters. What do you think of what we have just heard?"

Acheson's answer was:

> "I have discovered that Far Eastern experts are a penny a dozen. And you can find some experts who will support any point of view that you care to have. And I, myself, do not go along with what we have just heard. I prefer to be guided by experts who think more along my point of view."

Dooman testified that Acheson from then on:

> ". . . quoted virtually textually from this *Solution in Asia* by Dr. Lattimore."[67]

Lattimore, in *Solution in Asia*, had advocated the

[59] McCarran Committee Hearings on IPR, Pt. 2, August 23, 1951, p. 604.
[60] McCarran Committee Hearings on IPR, Pt. 2, August 23, 1951, p. 604.
[61] Freda Utley, The China Story (Henry Regnery Company, Chicago, 1951), pp. 117, 118.
[62] Washington Daily News, June 7, 1950, p. 3.
[63] Fred Woltman, "The Shocking Story of The Amerasia Case," Pamphlet, Scripps-Howard, 1950, p. 14.
[64] Tydings Committee Hearings, Pt. 1, June 26, 1950, p. 1404.
[65] PM, October 7, 1945, p. 6.
[66] McCarran Committee Hearings on IPR, Pt. 3, September 14, 1951, p. 716.
[67] McCarran Committee Hearings on IPR, Pt. 3, September 14, 1951, p. 723.

straight Communist Party line on Japan, namely, that we should force a "hard" peace on Japan—remove the emperor, destroy all successful business, confiscate all private property, in short, reduce Japan to a weak state which would be ripe for Communist conquest.

In a government policy-making meeting, Professor William McGovern of Northwestern University heard Lattimore argue the Acheson-Lattimore case for a "hard" peace against Japan. Testifying under oath before the McCarran Committee, Professor McGovern said:

> "I was somewhat shocked and horrified, not only as to his [Lattimore's] views with regard to the emperor, but he wanted to have not only a strict and stern policy, but a bloody peace in Japan . . . he wanted to completely reduce Japan to beggary and impotence."[68]

The Acheson-Lattimore plan for Japan was the same as the plan masterminded for postwar Germany by Harry Dexter White, named under oath by government witnesses as having aided a Communist spy ring in Washington.

Shortly after Dooman opposed Acheson's attempts to inject the Communist Party line into postwar U.S. policy toward Japan, Dooman was removed by Acheson from the State Department. Acheson then promoted John Carter Vincent to Dooman's job.

State Department Document Altered to Conform to Communist Line

Once Vincent came into power as chairman of the subcommittee which was setting up postwar policy on Japan, he immediately set out to inaugurate policies for Japan which, according to the sworn testimony of Eugene Dooman, were the same as Russia dictated for satellite countries.[69]

Vincent's first act, according to Dooman's testimony, was to alter an official program entitled "U. S. Initial Post-Surrender Policy for Japan"—a program which had already been officially adopted by the government and telegraphed to General MacArthur "as firm United States Policy for Japan."[70]

The testimony was that the major surgery which Vincent performed on that already adopted policy was to inject into it the Communist Party objective of destroying and eliminating the capitalist class in Japan.

Following are some excerpts from Dooman's testimony, appearing on pages 718 to 720 of the McCarran hearings, in which he explains the changes made by Vincent:

DOOMAN: "The first thing that was done, and this was in 1946, was to levy a capital tax of from 60 to 90 percent on all property in excess of $1,000 . . . That almost at one stroke wiped out the capitalistic class . . . The next thing was to appropriate all land in excess of 5 acres held by any one owner."

SENATOR EASTLAND: "That was a Communist system, was it not? . . . they were following now the Communist system, were they not?"

DOOMAN: "Yes . . . Then all holdings by any one individual in any large corporation in excess of 3 per cent were confiscated . . . They were transferred to a government pool. And then the Japanese Government was ordered to sell those shares . . . [and] ordered

to disregard any relationship between the price offered and the real value . . . Practically the whole white-collar element in Japanese big business was removed at one stroke. Not because there was any record against them, but because they occupied certain positions . . . It was an attempt to destroy and eliminate the brains of Japanese business.

". . . The net result was then to destroy the previously existing capitalist class . . . Their places have been taken by hordes of black marketeers and . . . thugs of various kinds who have been engaged in illicit trade of various kinds and have then amassed this enormous fortune. The net result was to replace people who had traditionally had property with these black marketeers and thugs and blackguards of various kinds."

Service Recommends "Sympathetic Support" For Japanese Communists

In this connection there should be recalled the views on Japan of Acheson's protégé John Stewart Service. One of the State Department documents picked up by the FBI in the Amerasia offices was an official report on Japan by John Stewart Service. Following is an excerpt from that report, S187 with "Q" number 524:

> "The Japanese Communist Party is still small (Mr. Okano himself does not claim more than 'a few thousand members'), but it has the advantages of strong organization and loyal, politically experienced membership. If its policies as claimed, seek to achieve our own hopes of a democratic, non-militaristic Japan, we may wish to consider the adoption toward it of an attitude of sympathetic support."

Acheson and Vincent Attack MacArthur's Anti-Communist Policies in Japan

General Douglas MacArthur vigorously opposed the State Department's plans and its attempts to Communize or create a fertile ground for the Communization of Japan. He was viciously attacked by both Vincent and Acheson. Vincent accused MacArthur of violating State Department directives to use Japan for "building a bridge of friendship to the Soviet Union." The New York Times of September 20, 1945, printed the following story of Acheson's rebuke of MacArthur:

> "The State Department revealed today a decision for a social and economic revolution in Japan and emphasized that it would be carried out regardless of what might be said about slashing the American army of occupation.
>
> "Secretary Acheson said that the United States government and not General MacArthur was determining American policy toward Japan."

Communist Press Hails Acheson's Attack on MacArthur

For Acheson's public criticism of MacArthur's anti-Communist policies, the Communist Daily Worker applauded "the repudiation of General MacArthur by Dean Acheson of the State Department . . ."[71]

PM, the "uptown edition of the Daily Worker," hailed Dean Acheson's action with the following editorial:

68 McCarran Committee Hearings on IPR, Pt. 4, Sept. 28, 1951, p. 1016.
69 McCarran Committee Hearings on IPR, Pt. 3, Sept. 14, 1951, p. 718.
70 McCarran Committee Hearings on IPR, Pt. 3, Sept. 14, 1951, p. 717.
71 Daily Worker, Sept. 30, 1945.

"Acheson is the leader of the younger, more progressive men in the State Department."[72]

General Wedemeyer on Communist Black List

Another man on the Communist black list was General Albert Wedemeyer. He was scheduled to be removed from the scene, because, as Budenz testified:

". . . the Communists viewed General Wedemeyer as the enemy of the Soviet interests in the Far East."[73]

After Wedemeyer's return from China where he was sent on a special mission by the President, he submitted his report containing his recommendations on how China could be saved from Communist conquest. This report was steadfastly denied the Congress. When the Senate Armed Services Committee asked General George C. Marshall, "Why did you join in the suppression of the Wedemeyer Report on China?" Marshall replied:

"I did not join in the suppression of the Report. I personally suppressed it."[74]

Communists Select Ambassador to China

When Wedemeyer was scheduled to be Ambassador to China, Marshall and Acheson vetoed his appointment because the Chinese Communists objected. In July, 1946, Wedemeyer's appointment was on Truman's desk and Wedemeyer was awaiting his commission when Acheson sent for him to say that his appointment had been cancelled. He read Wedemeyer a telegram from Marshall saying. "The Communists are protesting violently." Upon the recommendation of Chou En-lai, Chinese Communist leader, Marshall and Acheson secured the appointment instead for Dr. Leighton Stuart, an educator who had at one time taught Chou En-lai.[75]

Ambassador Lane Next on Communist Black List

Arthur Bliss Lane was another intelligently anti-Communist State Department official on the Communist black list. Lane, like other anti-Communists in the department, had learned from bitter experience that Dean Acheson was a tough man to reckon with when the chips were down.

Acheson Grants Communists in Poland $90,000,000 U. S. Loan

In 1946 the Communist-controlled government of Poland requested a $90 million loan from the United States. Ambassador Lane protested strongly against this loan. "With the greatest earnestness of which I am capable," he cabled the State Department, "I beg the department not to approve the extension of any credits at this time."[76] Lane pointed out the terroristic activities of the Communists, the imprisonment of American citizens and the fact that much of the loan was slated to equip the Communist terror police. Nevertheless, Acheson granted the loan.

Acheson Law Firm Gets $50,000 Fee from Communist Loan

Acheson reluctantly admitted to a Senate committee that he, as Under Secretary of State, had the power of decision in the matter and was responsible for granting the loan. He further admitted that his own law firm had handled the private end of the negotiation for the loan, with Donald Hiss personally in charge, and that the Acheson law firm had received a fee of over $50,000 when the loan was granted by Acheson. He stated, however, that he personally received no part of the fee.[77]

Another Anti-Communist Purged

After the Polish loan was granted, Ambassador Arthur Bliss Lane resigned. He has since told the sordid story of how the State Department betrayed Polish and American interests in a book entitled, *I Saw Poland Betrayed*.

Acheson's action on the Polish loan could not have come as too great a surprise, however, because in 1945 he gave the world fair warning of what his policy toward Communist aggression would be.

Speaks to Communists At Madison Square Garden Rally

On November 14, 1945, Acheson traveled to New York City to address a rally at Madison Square Garden which was called for the purpose of welcoming to American soil the Red Dean of Canterbury, a loud supporter of Communist Russia.[79] The rally was sponsored by the National Council of Soviet-American Friendship, which more than a year before (March 29, 1944) had been cited as subversive by the House Committee on Un-American Activities. It has also been listed as subversive by the Attorney General (December 4, 1947, and September 21, 1948.)

On the speakers platform with Acheson were Paul Robeson, Corliss Lamont, Albert Fitzgerald, and Joseph E. Davies. Paul Robeson is the noted Negro singer, active in a vast number of Communist fronts, who has stated he would never bear arms against Soviet Russia. Corliss Lamont was so well known as a spokesman for Communist fronts that the House Committee on Un-American Activities stated in Appendix IX, page 1471, that when Lamont's name appeared on the speakers program for a suspected Communist front, that fact could be considered as part of the proof that the organization was in fact doing the work of the Communist Party. Albert J. Fitzgerald, who also appeared on the speakers platform with Acheson, was president of the Communist-controlled United Electrical, Radio and Machine Workers of America, which was expelled by the CIO for being Communist dominated. Joseph E. Davies, of *Mission to Moscow* fame, while Ambassador to Moscow, revealed confidential information to the Kremlin, according to the sworn testimony of Igor Bogolepov, former Red army Colonel.[80]

Such were Acheson's platform and speaking companions

[72] PM, September 21, 1945, p. 13.
[73] McCarran Committee Hearings on IPR, Pt. 2, August 23, 1951, p. 623.
[74] Hearings on Nomination of Gen. George C. Marshall as Secretary of Defense, Senate Armed Service Committee Hearings, Sept. 19, 1950, p. 22.
[75] Constantine Brown, Column of June 13, 1951, Washington Star, Russell Committee Hearings, Pt. 3, June 11, 1951, pp. 2311-2312.
[76] Arthur Bliss Lane, I Saw Poland Betrayed (The Bobbs-Merrill Company, 1948), p. 237.
[77] Hearings on Nomination of Dean Acheson as Secretary of State, Senate Foreign Relations Committee Hearings, Jan. 13, 1949, pp. 2-6.
[79] Daily Worker, Nov. 16, 1945, p. 8.
[80] McCarran Committee Hearings on IPR, April 7, 1952 (now being printed).

when he addressed the Madison Square Garden Rally of left-wingers and Communists.

Favors "Friendly Borders" for Soviet Union

In addressing this audience of Communists and Communist sympathizers, Acheson served public notice that we would approve Communist Russia's conquest or control of her neighbors. Acheson said:

> "We understand, and agree with them [Communist Russia] to have friendly governments along her borders is essential, both for the security of the Soviet Union and for the peace of the World."[81]

It is easy to understand how the "security" of Communist Russia has been enhanced by the enslavement of the people of Poland, Czechoslovakia, Hungary, East Germany, Rumania, Bulgaria, Yugoslavia, Albania, China, North Korea, Estonia, Latvia, and Lithuania. But even the most tortured reasoning cannot support the view that the terroristic Communist rule in those satellite countries has promoted the "peace of the world" or the security of America. Certainly, the people of those countries would not agree with Acheson. It would be impossible to over-estimate the awful and terrifying effect upon Russia's neighbors of this statement by the United States Secretary of State that we would not only abandon our friends along the borders of Communist Russia but actually approve of their conquest by Russia.

State Department Honors Communist Picket of Churchill

While going out of his way in 1945 to assure Communist Russia that her aggressive plans were acceptable to America, Acheson made it clear to Winston Churchill the following year that his Fulton, Missouri, speech warning the world of the Communist threat, was distasteful to him.

The Communist Party showed its disapproval of Churchill's Fulton speech by throwing a picket line around the Waldorf-Astoria Hotel when a dinner was later given there in Churchill's honor.[82] Acheson honored that picket line and showed his disapproval of Churchill's warning of the Communist threat, and according to the New York Times of March 15, 1946, "abruptly cancelled" the speech he was scheduled to give at the dinner.[83]

Turns His Back on Anti-Communist Governments

Acheson's attitude toward anti-Communist Spain stands in sharp contrast to his 1945 speech approving of Communist Russia's conquest or control of her neighbors.

When the United Nations proposed in 1946 that all UN members recall their ambassadors from Spain in protest to the "non-free" government of Spain, the United States voted in favor of the proposal. However, we retained an ambassador to Russia.

Acheson's attitude toward anti-Communist governments was further illustrated when, as Acting Secretary of State, he refused to see the anti-Communist representatives

of the Spanish Republican government, but granted an appointment to the pro-Communist elements of the Spanish government-in-exile.[84] According to the *Daily Worker* of December 21, 1945, Acheson also received Congressman Vito Marcantonio and Milton Wolff, head of the Abraham Lincoln Brigade which recruited Americans to fight illegally on the side of the Communists during the Spanish Civil War. He promised those visitors, according to both the New York *Times* and the *Daily Worker*, that he would intervene with Franco in behalf of imprisoned Communists in Spain.[85]

Civil Service Loyalty Review Board Says State Department Has Worst Record in Loyalty Cases

Acheson's record of intervening in behalf of State Department officials under suspicion of Communist activities is a long one. His protection of those whose activities caused Congress and even the government's top Loyalty Review Board to call for investigation, is recorded throughout his years in government in numerous government documents.

The official minutes of a secret meeting of the Loyalty Review Board on February 13 and 14, 1951, make note of this record which Acheson has made on Acheson.[86] At one point during the meeting of the board, Chairman Bingham said, "The State Department . . . has the worst record of any department in the action of its Loyalty Board . . . The State Department has not found anyone . . . disloyal under our rule." Additional excerpts from those minutes are quoted on page 14.

Halts Investigation by Un-American Activities Committee

The April, 1952, issue of *American Mercury* describes Acheson's assistance to Russian Foreign Minister Molotov's brother-in-law as follows:

> "When, in September, 1945, the House Un-American Activities Committee prepared to hold hearings relative to one Sam Carp, Acheson's office prevailed upon the committee to drop the proceedings. Carp, a filling station operator in Bridgeport, Connecticut, had been discovered dispensing large amounts of money under suspicious circumstances. But it developed that he was the brother-in-law of Molotov, the Russian foreign Minister, so Acheson got the case dropped . . ."[87]

Refuses to Fire Loyalty Suspects

In 1946 Acheson told a Congressional committee that many persons who had been listed as loyalty suspects or security risks were affiliated with "progressive organizations" and that he would not fire "progressives." Many of those "progressive organizations" have been cited as subversive and Communist by the Attorney General.[88]

---

[81] Daily Worker, Nov. 15, 1945, p. 3.
[82] New York Times, March 16, 1946, pp. 1, 3.
[83] New York Times, March 15, 1946, pp. 1, 3.
[84] Victor Lasky, "The Case Against Dean Acheson," Congressional Record, Dec. 6, 1950, p. 16338.
[85] Daily Worker, Dec. 21, 1945, p. 16; New York Times, Dec. 21, 1945, p. 5.
[86] Congressional Record (Unbound), Jan. 15, 1952, pp. 192-194.
[87] The American Mercury, April, 1952, p. 11.
[88] Congressional Record (Unbound), Dec. 6, 1950, p. 16336.

Was Lawyer for Lauchlin Currie, Who Was Named as Member of Soviet Spy Ring

In 1948 Acheson acted as the lawyer for Lauchlin Currie before the House Committee on Un-American Activities, after Currie had been named as a member of a Soviet spy ring in Washington.

While Currie denied that he was a Communist or an espionage agent he did admit that he used his powerful influence in government to save the government job of Gregory Silvermaster, also named under oath as a member of a Soviet spy ring.

While Acheson did not appear publicly at the hearing to represent Currie, he did personally go to the office of the House Committee on Un-American Activities and as Currie's lawyer discussed the case with the Committee staff.

Defends John Service

In 1950, after I brought the Service case up to date and presented the facts to the Tydings committee, Service was recalled from India by the Loyalty Review Board.

When I told the Tydings Committee that the Loyalty Review Board had ordered Service recalled, the State Department issued a statement saying that this was untrue. When I suggested that I was about to make public the Loyalty Board order providing for Service's recall, the State Department reversed itself, and admitted that the Loyalty Review Board had demanded Service's recall. Thereafter the following statement was authorized for release by Acheson:

"... I can't refrain from calling attention at this time to the spectacular way in which the so-called 'case' of John S. Service dramatizes the harmful results of such techniques as the Senator [McCarthy] is using in an effort to bolster up his attack on the Department—results that are harmful both in terms of the day-to-day conduct of the foreign relations of United States Government and in terms of human relations.

"Here, in the person of Jack Service, we have an able, conscientious, and—I say again, as I've already said many times before—a demonstrably loyal foreign service officer, a veteran of 17 years with the Department, and one of our outstanding experts on Far Eastern affairs.

"As I've recounted in considerable detail more than a month ago, when Mr. Service's name was first mentioned by Senator McCarthy, this isn't the first time that his loyalty has been questioned. On the same basis of implied 'guilty-by-association' that has been used in most of the other 'cases' thus far presented to the Senate subcommittee, he underwent a Grand Jury investigation back in August 1945, in connection with charges that he had transmitted classified material to unauthorized persons.

"He had the satisfaction at that time, though, of having the Grand Jury return a 'no true bill' and of being notified of his full reinstatement to the Department in a personal letter from then Secretary of State James F. Byrnes himself and also a similar letter from the then Under Secretary, Joseph C. Grew.

"As a matter of Departmental routine, Mr. Service's file has been reviewed 5 times during the ensuing 5 years, and in each instance the findings of the reviewing agents have been completely favorable.

"But now, as a result of Senator McCarthy's resuscitation of these dead, discredited, disproven charges against him, Mr. Service finds his character once more called into question, his name once more blazoned in headlines of the whole country's press, and his brilliant career as a diplomat once more interrupted so that he can be defended, and can defend himself, against such baseless allegations all over again."

"... it's a shame and a disgrace that he and his family should have to face, once again, such humiliation, embarrassment, and inconvenience; and I'd like to say that the sympathy and good wishes of the entire Department go out to them."[89]

The State Department Loyalty Board then held a secret hearing and cleared Service. However, after the Loyalty Review Board examined the evidence in the case, they ordered Acheson to discharge Service.

Acheson Law Firm Defends Loyalty Case Before Acheson Loyalty Board

One of the many loyalty cases defended by Acheson's law firm before Acheson's State Department Loyalty Board was that of Edward Posniak. Dean Acheson states that he is no longer a member of the firm but that his son is.

In 1948 Letters of Charges were filed against Posniak after the reports of 9 FBI investigators were presented to the State Department. Posniak thereupon retained Attorney Westwood of Acheson's law firm to represent him. Westwood succeeded in getting the charge against Posniak reduced before any evidence was taken. At the hearing he was cleared by a 2 to 1 vote of the State Department loyalty panel. After I gave the Senate a resume of the 9 FBI reports on Posniak,[90] his loyalty-security case was reopened and he was allowed to resign while his case was pending. He has since been before a federal grand jury, but as far as is known at the time this is written, no action has been taken on his case.

The acting chairman of the State Department loyalty panel which heard the Posniak case was Darrel St. Clair. St. Clair cast the deciding vote clearing Posniak. At the time this is written he is the chief clerk of the Senate Rules Committee and is helping to write a report on the Benton Resolution which asks that McCarthy be expelled from the Senate because of his activities in connection with exposing Communists and fellow travellers in the State Department.

Clears Clubb After State Department Loyalty Board Had Unanimously Ruled Against Clubb

Oliver Edmund Clubb was a top State Department official against whom the State Department Loyalty Board had ruled. Acheson overruled his own Loyalty Board, in early 1952. After being "cleared" by Acheson, Clubb resigned with a lifetime pension of $5,800 a year.

Clubb was chief of the China Division of the State Department. Evidence on Clubb was given to the Tydings Committee, but he was not called to testify, nor was any of the evidence checked by the committee. He was part

89 Department of State Bulletin, Vol. XXII, No. 560, March 27, 1950, pp. 479, 480.
90 Congressional Record (Unbound), July 25, 1950, pp. 11105-11114, 11120-11122.

of the group given a blanket clearance by the Tydings committee. He was later called before both the McCarran committee and the House Committee on Un-American Activities.

Following is the Washington *Times-Herald's* report of some of Clubb's testimony and of the contents of his diary:

"The diary revealed Clubb's meetings with the following persons:

"Whittaker Chambers, admitted spy for the Soviet Union in the 30s, whose testimony resulted in the conviction of Alger Hiss for prejury to conceal espionage.

"Agnes Smedley, identified by Maj. Gen. Charles A. Willoughby, Gen. MacArthur's intelligence chief, as a member of the celebrated spy ring headed by Richard Sorge, executed by the Japanese in 1944.

"Michael Gold, a well-known Communist writer and revolutionary.

"Lawrence Todd, Washington correspondent for *Tass*, Soviet News agency.

"Under prolonged questioning, Clubb admitted a long and friendly relationship with Owen Lattimore, State department consultant identified as a Soviet agent by Gen. Alexander Barmine, Russian intelligence agent; and John Carter Vincent, State department official repeatedly accused in Congress of pro-Communist operations.

"He also conceded an acquaintance with Philip Jaffe, center of the Amerasia stolen documents case of 1945 and other figures in that incident.

"When Clubb had been questioned secretly by the committee last March, he denied recalling a meeting with Chambers in the office of New Masses, a Communist magazine, in July 1932. Chambers had previously testified to this meeting.

"But Clubb later informed the committee that an entry in his diary had refreshed his recollection and that he had talked with Chambers on July 9, 1932, according to the diary. A subpoena was then issued for the entire diary but Clubb brought in only two volumes.

"Another diary entry dated in Washington, July 7, 1932, revealed Clubb's seeking out of Todd, the *Tass* correspondent . . . [Tass is the official Soviet newspaper which has been described, under oath, by a former Russian Army Intelligence Officer as a front for Russian espionage.]

" 'I went with Todd to the State department press room and was introduced to several journalists, among them, Drew Pearson,' the entry said. 'I had dinner at the Press club with Todd and also had dinner in Pearson's home with Lawrence Duggan of the Latin-American section . . .' [Duggan, who has been named as a Communist spy, either committed suicide or was murdered after it became apparent he would be called during the House investigation of the Hiss case.]

"Clubb said his relationship with Lattimore extended over a long period, beginning in 1929 or 1930 and extending to the present date. In 1935, Clubb was the certifying officer on an affidavit signed by Lattimore, who declared he had lost his passport at the headquarters of Communist leader Ten Wang in Inner Mongolia. Lattimore was then issued a new passport."[91]

The State Department's Loyalty Board held a hearing on Clubb, and on February 11, 1952, Acheson's publicity office called in the press. The head of the office announced that Clubb had been "cleared on both loyalty and security."

The following questions were asked of him by newsmen:

Q. "Did you say he was cleared of these charges?"
A. "Absolutely cleared, —cleared on loyalty and security."
Q. "If there were loyalty charges, this new standard was used and he was judged innocent?"
A. "That is right."
Q. "Mac, you say he was cleared on both loyalty and security charges, —then there were both charges against him?"
A. "He was cleared on both loyalty and security. It doesn't say charges. There is no question about either one and he was restored to duty."[92]

Clubb's clearance was headlined throughout the country. Clubb thereupon resigned, indicating that the reason for his resignation was that his usefulness in the State Department had been greatly impaired by the unfounded charges made against him.

Senator Homer Ferguson and I then revealed that Clubb had not been cleared by the State Department's Loyalty Board, but that the Loyalty Board by a verdict of 3 to 0 had ruled against him, and that this ruling was approved by Assistant Secretary of State Humelsine who is in charge of Security, but that Dean Acheson reversed his own Loyalty Board and his top security officer and ordered Clubb restored to active duty.

When questioned by the press as to whether his press office had attempted to deceive the American people or whether Senators Ferguson and McCarthy were in error, Acheson first refused to answer. Finally, on March 5, 1952, he called a press conference and admitted (1) that his own Loyalty Board had unanimously ruled against Clubb, (2) that his security officer, Humelsine, had approved of that ruling, and (3) that he, Acheson, had reversed the decision and cleared Clubb.

Acheson, however, refused to discuss his reason for clearing Clubb, stating, *"I did not study the record because as I have said I do not have time to do that."*[93]

Refuses to Fire William Stone
Even Though Security Office
Requested His Dismissal

Another typical case of State Department "clearance," is that of William T. Stone. On March 22, 1946, the State Department Security Office made the following recommendation on Stone:

"In behalf of the above-mentioned, it is recommended that action be instituted to terminate his services with the State Department immediately. It is suggested, to achieve this purpose, than an appropriate officer of the Department should inform Mr. Stone that *his continued employment in the Department is embarrassing to the Department* and he should be given an opportunity to resign. If he should not resign voluntarily, action should be immediately instituted under Civil Service Rule No. 3 to termi-

[91] Washington Times-Herald, August 21, 1951, pp. 1, 4.
[92] Record of State Department Press Conference of Michael McDermott, Special Assistant to the Secretary for Press Relations, Feb. 11, 1952, pp. 3, 4.
[93] Press Conference of Secretary of State Dean Acheson (No. 171), March 5, 1952, p. 3.

nate his service with the Department." (Emphasis Mine) [94]

Stone's immediate superior was William Benton (now Senator from Connecticut) who was at that time Assistant Secretary of State in Charge of International Information and Cultural Program.

Stone remained and was promoted.

Six years later, on February 2, 1952, Stone "voluntarily" resigned. His resignation came when his case was being considered by the Civil Service Commission Loyalty Review Board. I pointed out at the time that Stone's "voluntary resignation," coming at the time the Loyalty Review Board was considering his case, was for the purpose of saving the State Department the possible embarrassment of another Service case. Stone called me a liar and threatened to sue, saying that he had been cleared. The State Department also issued a statement that Stone had been fully cleared.

However, under cross-examination the State Department Security Officer, Humelsine, admitted before the Senate Appropriation Sub-Committee that Stone resigned after the Civil Service Loyalty Review Board (which had previously ordered Service fired after he was "cleared" by the State Department) had ordered a loyalty board panel to hear the evidence on Stone's case and had requested the State Department for additional investigation and information on Stone.[95]

It is impossible to know how many times and in how many cases the State Department has followed the same pattern of issuing false press releases and making misleading statements calculated to deceive the public as they did in this case.

Promotes Man Named as Member
of Communist Party

Haldore Hanson is another young man who was rapidly promoted under Acheson. He is now holding a vitally important position in the State Department high in the Point IV Program. In 1949 he was designated by Acheson as head of the Technical Staff of Point IV. As pointed out on page 76, Hanson was named under oath by a government witness as a member of the Communist Party. He had once been arrested with a Communist group in China according to his own book, *Humane Endeavor*. In that book he extolled the virtues of the Communist leaders and the Communist movement in China. He has never repudiated that book.

Vouches for Man Named
as Communist

Another of the men whom Acheson refused to turn his back upon was Harold Glasser. Glasser had been Acheson's technical adviser at the founding meeting of the United Nations Relief and Rehabilitation Administration, known as UNRRA. Glasser also was named under oath by a government witness as a Communist.[96] Thereafter Acheson wrote a letter of recommendation stating that Glasser "was a good working companion." Glasser used

this letter to obtain a high post in a New York charitable organization.[97]

Former Law Partner Attempts
to Smear FBI

A former law partner of Dean Acheson, Charles A. Horsky, circulated a petition in February, 1950, demanding a public investigation of the FBI and accusing the FBI of "lawless conduct, of illegal wire tapping, rifling private mail, destroying evidence, and advising false sworn testimony by FBI agents."[98] He did this after the Communist Party had launched its own anti-FBI campaign in which it constantly refers to the FBI as a "Nazi Gestapo" and as a "collector of . . . political garbage, rumors on the political thinking of millions of citizens . . . junk and filthy scandal." Acheson's former partner, Horsky, was of course "against Communism," but he was much more against the FBI's "lawless and illegal methods" of fighting Communism.

Punishes Anti-Communist Expert on
China and Russia

A State Department officer who would appear to be the direct opposite of Service, Clubb, Lattimore, Stone, etc., is Angus Ward. Ward slowly worked his way to an important post in the State Department. When the Communists took over in China he was the Consul General at Mukden. Being anti-Communist he was arrested by the Chinese Communists and held for 13 months until he was convicted by the Chinese Communists and ordered out of China.

After Ward returned to this country, he clearly and intelligently spoke out, warning the world of the terrors and dangers of Communist conquest. Instead of using Ward in the State Department in a position where his vast knowledge of China and Communism could be utilized to the benefit of China and the U. S., he was assigned by Acheson to a remote post in East Africa—Nairobi, Kenya —where there is no current Communist drive and where he can do the least amount of damage to the Communist movement.

Sends $17,000,000 Lend-lease to
Russia After the War

Two years after World War II had ended, Acheson insisted, over Congressional protests, that the United States deliver $17,000,000 of lend-lease to Russia. This included oil-refinery equipment, electric motors, locomotive parts and other machinery.[99] At this same time, under the Forrestal Plan, we were giving military aid to Greece and Turkey in their fight against Communism. Fortunately, the will of Congress prevailed.

94 Third Supplemental Appropriation Bill 1951, Senate Appropriations Committee, April 17, 1951, p. 408.
95 Senate Appropriations Committee Hearings on State Dept. Appropriations, March 25, 1952, p. 389.
96 Congressional Record (Unbound), Dec. 6, 1950, p. 16336.
97 Author has Photostat of letter.
98 Congressional Record (Unbound), Dec. 6, 1950, p. 16336.
99 Congressional Record (Bound), April 21, 1947, p. 3736; Congressional Record (Unbound), Dec. 6, 1950, p. 16338.

Calls Russian Communists
"Little Boys"

During a 1946 State Department lecture, Acheson told a group of college professors:

"I don't believe the Soviet leaders are bad men. They are like little boys who enjoy throwing brickbats at other people's greenhouses."[100]

Invites Soviet to Bikini Tests
and Recommends We Turn Atomic Secrets
Over to Russia

Perhaps this was the reasoning that prompted Acheson in that same year to invite Communist Russia to send observers to U. S. atomic bomb tests at Bikini.

Together with David Lilienthal, he prepared an Atomic Energy Report which recommended in effect that we exchange atomic knowledge with the Soviet Union. "When the plan is in full operation," the Acheson-Lilienthal Report stated, "there will no longer be secrets about atomic energy."[101]

Allows Soviet Espionage Agents
to Enter U. S.

Acheson's description of the Soviet leaders as "little boys who enjoy throwing brickbats at other people's greenhouses" cannot, however, explain all of his actions. It cannot, for example, explain why it was that he allowed foreign agents of the Soviet to enter and leave the United States freely for years, even though he was warned about their espionage missions. This fact was made public in November, 1951, by the McCarran Internal Security Committee.

Admits Soviet Agent to U. S. Who Stole
A-Bomb and Bacteriological Warfare Secrets

From 1948 to 1951 Colonel Otto Biheler was given visas by the State Department to enter this country and travel between the U. S. and Mexico, Canada, and Czechoslovakia. This was done despite warnings that Biheler was a "high ranking member of the counter-intelligence corps of Czechoslovakia and had a notorious record of Communist activity abroad."[103] According to Senator O'Conor, Chairman of the Senate subcommittee that investigated this matter, Biheler was a "key figure in the Communist espionage apparatus in the United States ... engaged in the procurement of information concerning atomic energy, the uranium stock of the United States and bacteriological and chemical warfare."

Senator O'Conor also stated that:

"In April, 1950, he is reported to have been the mastermind behind a plot to effect the assassination of Major Carlos y Paz-Tejuda, Chief of the Army of Guatemala, and is reported to have given the instructions to two Soviet nationals in Guatemala to effect the assassination."[104]

Allows Professional Killer for
Communist Russia to Enter U. S.

Another such case was that of Jiri Stary, head of a Czechoslovakian spy ring. Senator Pat McCarran on November 21, 1951, described Stary as "a man trained in 'silent killing' by a Communist spy school, [who] has been harbored in the United States for more than two years ... a director of an espionage network ... in charge of the discipline of Czechoslovakian nationals who stray from the Communist influence."[106]

There was also a Communist espionage agent attached to the UN Information Section with a long record of "Communist associations and of indicated espionage services for the Soviet Union in southeastern Europe." "Despite this record," Senator McCarran said, "the State Department has consented, time and again, to her accreditization as a press correspondent by the United Nations and has evaded a request of the Immigration Service to order her deported."[107]

State Department Breaks Promise and
Forces Deportation of Anti-Communist
Who Worked for U. S.

While those known agents of the Soviet were being allowed to enter and leave the United States freely under Acheson's administration of the State Department, in 1947 Acheson refused entry to Dr. Karl von Kleczkowski. Kleczkowski had been recruited in the Balkans for anti-Communist counter-espionage work for the U. S. by Governor George H. Earle of Pennsylvania, wartime undercover representative of the President. Earle promised Kleczkowski and his wife asylum in the U. S. in return for their anti-Communist work. However, when the Kleczkowskis arrived in the U. S. aboard an army plane, the State Department denied them entrance. Governor Earle charged that Communist influences in the State Department sought their deportation. Acheson accused them of being "dangerous aliens," and the Kleczkowskis were deported to South America.[108]

You have said that Acheson followed the Communist Party line in Asia. What was the major aim of Communism in Asia?

The major aim of international Communism in Asia was stated by Lenin decades ago. It has been restated at Comintern meetings year after year. That aim was the creation of a Red China as a necessary prelude to the creation of a Red Asia and then a Red Pacific prior to the assault upon America. As Lenin said, "He who controls China can control the world."

Who were Acheson's advisers on China?

Acheson, who said he preferred "to be guided by experts who think ... along my point of view,"[109] selected the following men as his advisers and policy-makers on China:

(1) Alger Hiss, on whom Acheson declared he "would

[100] American Mercury, April, 1952, p. 3.
[101] Congressional Record (Unbound), Dec. 6, 1950, p. 16338.
[103] Press Release of Senator Herbert O'Conor, Nov. 8, 1951; Testimony taken in Executive Session, Senate Subcommittee on Internal Security, Nov. 7, 1951.
[104] Press Release of Senator Herbert O'Conor, Nov. 8, 1951; Testimony taken in Executive Session, Senate Subcommittee on Internal Security, Nov. 7, 1951.
[106] Press Release of Senator Pat McCarran, Nov. 21, 1951; Testimony taken in Executive Session, Senate Subcommittee on Internal Security, Nov. 19, 1951.
[107] Congressional Record (Unbound), Oct. 17, 1951, pp. 13591-13593; Press Release Senator Pat McCarran, Oct. 17, 1951.
[108] Congressional Record (Unbound), Dec. 6, 1950, p. 16336.
[109] McCarran Committee Hearings on IPR, Pt. 3, Sept. 14, 1951, p. 723.

not turn his back" even after Hiss was convicted of perjury in connection with Soviet espionage;

(2) Owen Lattimore, who has been named under oath as a member of the Communist Party and as a Soviet agent;

(3) Lauchlin Currie, who has been named under oath as a "full-fledged member" of the Silvermaster spy ring;

(4) John Stewart Service, who was arrested in connection with the *Amerasia* espionage case, then cleared of disloyalty charges by Acheson, but finally dismissed on orders of the Loyalty Review Board;

(5) John Carter Vincent, who has been named under oath as a member of the Communist Party, but who was recently cleared of disloyalty charges by Acheson;

(6) John P. Davies, who was accused by General Hurley of operating behind his back to support the Communists and who, in his official reports to the State Department, adopted the thinking of Agnes Smedley, a known Communist agent, whom he described as one of the "pure in heart" in China; and

(7) Edmund Oliver Clubb, who was ordered discharged by the State Department loyalty board which decision was reversed by Acheson.

The names of all of the "experts" chosen by Acheson to form our policy toward China are too numerous to list in this book. Many of them were supplied to the State Department by the Institute of Pacific Relations, which has been labeled by Senator Pat McCarran as an organization "taken over by Communist design and made a vehicle for attempted control and conditioning of American thinking and American policy with regard to the Far East."[110]

What part did the Yalta Agreement play in the Communist conquest of China?

The Yalta Agreement contained two major provisions insofar as China was concerned: (1) surrender of Manchuria to Russia, (2) arrangements for the United States to arm and equip a Russian army. At the time of the Yalta Agreement Chiang Kai-shek was not informed that we were offering control of Chinese territory to Stalin. The loss of Manchuria meant that the Chinese Communists were given a gateway to Russian arms and supplies in their war against him.

In return for those concessions, Stalin "promised" to enter the Pacific War at some undetermined time.

The Yalta Agreement was confirmed at Potsdam by Truman against the urgent advice of fifty of the Army's top intelligence officers. On April 31, 1945, three months before the Potsdam Conference, those fifty high-ranking Army officers reported to General Marshall, who was the military adviser at both Yalta and Potsdam, as follows:

"The entry of Soviet Russia into the Asiatic war would be a political event of world-shaking importance, the ill effect of which would be felt for decades to come . . . [it] would destroy America's position in Asia quite as effectively as our position is now destroyed in Europe east of the Elbe and beyond the Adriatic.

"If Russia enters the Asiatic war, China will certainly lose her independence, to become the Poland of Asia; Korea, the Asiatic Rumania; Manchukuo, the Soviet Bulgaria. Whether more than a nominal China will exist after the impact of the Russian armies is felt is very doubtful. Chiang may well have to depart and a Chinese Soviet government may be installed in Nanking which we would have to recognize.

"To take a line of action which would save few lives now, and only a little time—at an unpredictable cost in lives, treasure, and honor in the future—and simultaneously destroy our ally China, would be an act of treachery that would make the Atlantic Charter and our hopes for world peace a tragic farce.

"*Under no circumstances should we pay the Soviet Union to destroy China.* This would certainly injure the material and moral position of the United States in Asia." (Emphasis Mine.)[111]

Thus the treason which Hiss advised at Yalta was confirmed and brought to full bloom at Potsdam against the advice of Army Intelligence.

While the State Department was trying to sell the idea that the Chinese Communists were "agrarian reformers" and not really Communists, were Chinese Communist leaders denying that they were Communists?

This is perhaps best answered by Mao Tse-tung, the leader of the Chinese Communists, in his book *The New Democracy*, published in 1940 and sold in the *Daily Worker* bookshop in New York City. Mao said:

"We cannot separate ourselves from the assistance of the Soviet Union."
"No matter who you follow so long as you are anti-Communist, you are traitors."

What part did General Stilwell play in the Communist conquest of China, and who were his advisers?

In China, Stilwell was surrounded by a group of foreign service officers supplied by the State Department, including John Stewart Service, since ordered discharged under the loyalty program, and headed by John Paton Davies, whose case has been referred to the Attorney General.

The ground for Communist conquest was cultivated from 1942 to 1944 by General "Vinegar Joe" Stilwell (a close friend and protege of General George C. Marshall.) Stilwell's bitter hatred of Chiang, the leader of the anti-Communist forces of China, is well-known and seems matched only by his infatuation with the Chinese Communists.

Agnes Smedley, although not a State Department employee, was part of that tightly knit group which was so close to Stilwell. For example, Davies who was referred to as "Stilwell's Secretary of State," referred to Smedley as "one of the pure in heart." Writers, such as Freda Utley, who visited China reported the mutual admiration between Smedley and Stilwell. Smedley has been exposed by General MacArthur's Intelligence Headquarters as an important cog in a Communist international

[110] Interview with Senator Pat McCarran, U.S. News and World Report, Nov. 16, 1951, p. 27.
[111] Russell Committee Hearings, Pt. 4, June 21, 1951, p. 2916.

spy ring which was headed by Richard Sorge who was later convicted of being a Communist spy and hanged by the Japanese.

A letter which Stilwell wrote a friend while in China casts much light on his attitude toward the Communists. The letter reads in part as follows:

"It makes me itch to throw down my shovel and get over there and shoulder a rifle with Chu Teh."[112]

Chu Teh, with whom Stilwell, the American Commander in China, wanted to "shoulder a rifle" was then the Commander-in-Chief of the Chinese Red Armies. He is now Commander-in-Chief of the Red Armies warring with us in Korea.

General Claire Chennault, of Flying Tiger fame, has told part of the story of Stilwell's activities in China in his book, *Way of a Fighter*. On page 317 Chennault, in describing how Stilwell in the spring of 1944 sent a mission to Communist headquarters in Yenan, had this to say:

"The American mission to Yenan was hardly established before Stilwell's Chungking staff began to proclaim loudly the superiority of the Communist regime over the Chungking government. No secret was made of their admiration for the Communists, whom, they said, were really only 'agrarian reformers,' and more like New Dealers than Communists. The hue and cry charging the Generalissimo with 'hoarding lend-lease arms' to fight the Communists was raised with renewed vigor . . .

"Then Yenan Communists shrewdly tickled Stilwell's vanity with many flattering appreciations of his military prowess and clinched him as an ally by shrewdly letting it be known that they would be delighted to have him command their armies. Stilwell never gave up his hopes of commanding the Chinese Red armies . . . Since it was still official American policy in the summer of 1944 to support the Chungking government, it was a common joke (in Chungking) that Stilwell's headquarters were developing a private foreign policy with John Davies as secretary of state.

"During this period there was a strong group of left wingers in the Far Eastern Division of the State Department who used Stilwell's sympathy for the Chinese Communists and his violent antipathy to the generalissimo as a lever to shift American policy in favor of the Communists . . ."[113]

The tremendous hatred which Stilwell had for Chiang Kai-shek, the anti-Communist leader, is described in John T. Flynn's book, *While You Slept*. On page 164 he quotes what Stilwell entered in his diary after he had personally delivered a message apparently instigated by Marshall and sent by Roosevelt to Chiang. The message was understood by both Chiang and Stilwell as an ultimatum demanding Stilwell be put in "unrestricted command" of all Chinese forces. Stilwell describes Chiang's reaction to the message in the following language:

"At long last . . . FDR has spoken plain words . . . with a firecracker in every sentence . . . I handed this bundle of paprika to the Peanut and then sank back with a sigh. The harpoon hit the little bugger right in the solar plexus and went right through him. It was a clear hit. But beyond turning green and losing the power of speech, he did not bat an eye."

General Patrick Hurley, who was present when Stilwell delivered Roosevelt's ultimatum to Chiang, gave a detailed account of the incident in his testimony before the Russell Committee. Hurley stated that after Stilwell's temporary victory he expressed his feelings in a poem.

Hurley stated, ". . . that night, when I saw Stilwell, . . . he read it to me with great glee, it was supposed to be humorous."

"I've waited long for vengeance—
    At last I've had my chance.
I've looked the Peanut in the eye
    And kicked him in the pants.
The old harpoon was ready
    With aim and timing true,
I sank it to the handle
    And stung him through and through.
The little bastard shivered,
    And lost his power of speech.
His face turned green and quivered
    As he struggled not to screech.
For all my weary battles,
    For all my hours of woe,
At last I've had my innings
    And laid the Peanut low.
I know I've still to suffer,
    And run a weary race,
But Oh; the blessed pleasure!
    I've wrecked the Peanut's face."[114]

The contents of the message which Stilwell delivered have been inserted in the record of the Russell Committee on Pages 2867 and 2868. They ordered Chiang to appoint Stilwell Commander-in-Chief of all the Chinese armies. But Stilwell's gloating was premature. On this point John T. Flynn quotes Admiral Leahy as follows:

"The Generalissimo 'was willing and anxious to meet Roosevelt's wishes' that an American officer command all Chinese forces. But he insisted that 'it must be one in whom I can repose confidence . . . The officer must be capable of frank and sincere cooperation, and General Stilwell has shown himself conspicuously lacking in these indispensable qualifications.' "

Flynn then goes on to say:

"Admiral Leahy writes that Marshall even after this made an effort to dissuade Roosevelt but without success. Stilwell himself committed his sentiments to another poem about his downfall in unprintable English (though it appears in his posthumous papers) and disappeared from the scene."[115]

After Stilwell left China, those whom the State Department had selected as his advisers remained on to continue the job.

Thus was the soil carefully cultivated by Stilwell and his staff for the disastrous Marshall Mission to China which finally ripened into the Communist conquest of China and eventually into the Korean war.

112 Daily Worker, Jan. 26, 1947, p. 7.
113 General Claire Chennault, Way of a Fighter, p. 317.
114 Russell Committee Hearings, Pt. 4, June 21, 1951, p. 2872; Joseph W. Stilwell, The Stilwell Papers (William Sloan Associates, 1948), p. 334.
115 John T. Flynn, While You Slept (The Devin-Adair Company, New York, 1951), p. 165.

Service and Davies were both named by you before the Tydings Committee. You claimed they helped to betray China. Will you give the facts?

Since I gave the cases of Service and Davies to the Tydings Committee, Service has been discharged from the State Department upon orders of the Loyalty Board; Davies' case has been referred to the Justice Department by the McCarran Committee.

Both Service and Davies spent considerable time in China as State Department officials. In their recommendations to Washington both followed the Communist Party line.

For example, on November 7, 1944, Davies submitted a memorandum to the State Department stating that the Communist Party in China was "a modern dynamic popular government." At the same time he referred to the anti-Communists as "feudal." "The Communists are in China to stay. And China's destiny is not Chiang's but theirs," said Davies.[116] As if predicting the argument to be used seven years later in the Korean debate, Davies warned that the United States might become involved in a war with Russia if we continued to support the anti-Communist government of China.[117] On December 12, 1944 he urged that we supply the Chinese Communists with arms—a proposal which Dean Acheson two years later requested Congress to approve.[118]

Service Labels Communists "Democratic"

Acheson's protégé, John Stewart Service, reported from China that the Chinese Communists were "moderate and democratic."[119] The anti-Communist government he described as ". . . a decadent regime which by its existing composition and program is incapable of solving China's problems."[120]

In describing the Communist movement in China, Service, on October 9, 1944, reported:

"It has improved the economic condition of the peasants by rent and interest reduction, tax reform and good government. It has given them democratic self-government, political consciousness and a sense of their rights. It has freed them from feudalistic bonds and given them self-respect, self-reliance, and a strong feeling of cooperative group interest. The common people, for the first time, have been given something to fight for."[121]

Service made no mention of the fact that more Chinese starved and were beheaded under Communist control than under any comparable period in China's ageless history.

In his dispatches, Service argued against aid to the anti-Communists. But he was not blind to the fact that the life of the anti-Communists depended upon our assistance. "The Kuomintang," he reported on October 10, 1944, "is dependent on American support for survival."[122]

Both Service and Davies, were charged by Ambassador-to-China Hurley with supporting the Communists and sabotaging his anti-Communist policies in China. Hurley stated that Davies had one day flown off to Yenan to tell Mao Tse Tung, the Communist leader, that Hurley, our Ambassador (an anti-Communist), did not represent the American viewpoint.[123] Hurley had John Service recalled from China because, according to Hurley, his pro-Communist activities were disrupting Hurley's anti-Communist program in China. Later Hurley objected because men like Service whom he had asked to have recalled from Asia were returned to Washington and promoted.[124]

In 1945 Service was arrested in the *Amerasia* case which involved the theft of hundreds of secret and other classified documents found in the office of the magazine, *Amerasia.* Service admitted giving secret government documents to Philip Jaffe,[125] the editor of the magazine, who has been named by a government witness as a Soviet agent.[126]

Did Hiss play a part in the betrayal of China?

In 1944 Hiss was Special Assistant to the Director of the Office of Far Eastern Affairs. He later was director of the Office of Special Political Affairs, which office was responsible for the development and coordination of American foreign policy.

Thereafter Hiss was sent to Yalta where he, Gromyko of Russia, and Jebb of England drafted major portions of the Yalta Agreement which so greatly contributed to the betrayal of China.

Two years ago you named Vincent as one of those whom you considered bad for America and good for Communist Russia. What, if any, part did he play in the China picture?

John Carter Vincent worked with Hiss on the China phase of our foreign policy. In 1947 Vincent was under such heavy Congressional attack for his pro-Communist views and activities that Acheson removed him from the Washington scene by sending him to Switzerland. In 1950 when Vincent was again under fire, Acheson sent him to Tangiers.

Back in 1943 Vincent was appointed Assistant in the Far Eastern Division of the State Department and at the same time Special Assistant to the President's Administrative Assistant, Lauchlin Currie, who has been named under oath as a member of a Communist spy ring.[127]

The following year he and Owen Lattimore accompanied Henry Wallace to China and assisted in drawing up the Wallace Report which recommended that we withdraw any support we had been giving the anti-Communists and give our support to the Chinese Communists. During this visit to China, Vincent and Lattimore were toasted at a dinner by Sergei Godlize, high Soviet official, as

116 White Paper on United States Relations With China (The Department of State, 1949), p. 573.
117 Utley, The China Story, p. 112.
118 White Paper on China, pp. 574, 575.
119 White Paper on China, p. 566.
120 White Paper on China, p. 573.
121 White Paper on China, p. 566.
122 White Paper on China, p. 574.
123 Utley, The China Story, p. 110.
124 (Released names of Service and Acheson in Oct., 1945); White Paper on China, p. 582.
125 Tydings Committee Hearings, Pt. 1, June 22, 1950, p. 1283.
126 Tydings Committee Hearings, Pt. 1, April 20, 1950, p. 491.
127 McCarran Committee Hearings on IPR, Pt. 2, Aug. 14, 1951, p. 423.

the men "on whom rests great responsibility for China's future."[128]

In 1945 Vincent was made head of the Far Eastern Division of the State Department. Together with Service and Davies, Vincent contended Chiang should be forced to stop fighting the Communists and take them into his government. This was the basis of the Marshall Mission to China and of State Department policy toward China which General MacArthur has described as "one of the greatest blunders in American diplomatic history for which the free world is now paying in blood and disaster and will in all probability continue to do so indefinitely."[129]

In September, 1946, when General MacArthur issued a warning against the danger of Communism in Japan, Vincent publicly rebuked MacArthur and was quoted in the New York *Herald-Tribune* as accusing MacArthur of initiating an anti-Communist campaign.

When in December of 1946 Russia violated a provision of the Yalta agreement and the Sino-Soviet Treaty of 1945 by ordering an American Naval vessel out of the port of Darien, Vincent authorized a statement that Russia was acting within her rights.[130]

Lauchlin Currie has been described as a member of a Communist spy ring. What if any influence did he exert on State Department policy in China?

Lauchlin Currie, another member of the Acheson China group, has been named under oath by Elizabeth Bentley, (a former Communist who has been of great value to the government) as a member of the Silvermaster spy ring. Asked under oath if Currie was a full-fledged member of the Silvermaster spy ring, Miss Bentley replied, "Definitely."[131] The House Committee on Un-American Activities in a pamphlet entitled *The Shameful Years*, states that "Miss Bentley has stated that all individuals working in the apparatus were under the direction of the NKVD [the Russian Secret Police]."[132]

Miss Bentley, who was formerly a courier for a Soviet spy ring in Washington, testified as follows about Currie's assistance to the ring:

SENATOR FERGUSON: "Can you give us any information on what you received through Currie?"
MISS BENTLEY: "Most of it was Far Eastern. There was the time when he relayed the information that the Soviet code was about to be broken."
MR. MORRIS: "Broken by whom?"
MISS BENTLEY: "The United States authorities."
MR. MORRIS: "He discovered that the United States authorities had broken the code, and he relayed it to you?"[133]

Miss Bentley explained that Currie had advised her the Soviet code was about to be broken and that she relayed this information to her "Russian head."

MR. MORRIS: "Was that a highly classified fact at the time?"
MISS BENTLEY: "Definitely. I don't know enough about Government labelings, but it was certainly something you wouldn't pass around."[134]

According to her sworn testimony, Currie was always willing to help members of the spy ring—"bailing them out when they were in trouble, when they were being fired for disloyalty, or when they needed help to get a job."[135]

In addition, Currie was able to exert considerable influence on our Far Eastern policy through his friendship with Acheson and Hiss and through Vincent, who was assigned to Currie's White House office. It was through Currie's office that the Acheson group reached the White House with the pro-Communist reports and dispatches from China which anti-Communist Joseph Grew tried to pigeonhole in the State Department. The testimony before the McCarran Committee showed that Currie has worked closely with the Communist-front Institute of Pacific Relations.

Following is a letter written by E. C. Carter, head of the Communist-front IPR, to Joe Barnes, one-time head of the New York office of OWI, who has been named under oath as a Soviet agent:

"New York, N.Y., October 27, 1942.
"JOSEPH BARNES, Esq.
New York, N.Y.
"DEAR JOE: Recently in Washington Lauchlin Currie expressed to me the hope that some day soon when you are in Washington you would give him the privilege of a private talk. As you know, he is an intimate friend and admirer of Owen Lattimore and has himself made two visits to Chungking. You and he would find a great deal in common, not only in matters Chinese, but in affairs elsewhere. I do hope that you can see him soon.
"His office is in the State Department Building, but you reach him through the White House exchange.
"Sincerely yours,
"EDWARD C. CARTER."[136]

Has the Communist Party admitted that the State Department was following the Communist line on China?

Yes. For example, Earl Browder, General Secretary of the Communist Party until 1945, testified before the Tydings Committee as follows:

SENATOR HICKENLOOPER: "Now then, you have testified here, as I understand your testimony, . . . that you worked ceaselessly over a period of years, perhaps beginning in the thirties and continuing up until at least 1942, for the adoption of a definite policy on the part of the United States toward China, and the Chinese Communists."
MR. BROWDER: "That is correct."
SENATOR HICKENLOOPER: "And you were working on that policy as a Communist policy, were you not? That was the policy of the Communists that you were working on."
MR. BROWDER: "That was the policy of the Communist Party."
SENATOR HICKENLOOPER: "Then I believe that you said that in 1942, that policy upon which

128 Henry Wallace, Soviet-Asia Mission (Cornwall Press, Inc., 1946), p. 172.
129 General Douglas MacArthur by Clark Lee and Richard Henschel, (Henry Holt & Co., 1952), p. 127.
130 Utley, The China Story, p. 119.
131 McCarran Committee Hearings on IPR, Pt. 2, Aug. 14, 1951, p. 423.
132 The Shameful Years, Thirty Years of Soviet Espionage in the United States, House Committee on Un-American Activities, Dec. 30, 1951, p. 59.
133 McCarran Committee Hearings on IPR, Pt. 2, Aug. 14, 1951, p. 423.
134 McCarran Committee Hearings on IPR, Pt. 2, Aug. 14, 1951, p. 423.
135 McCarran Committee Hearings on IPR, Pt. 2, Aug. 14, 1951, p. 423.
136 McCarran Committee Hearings on IPR, Pt. 2, Aug. 14, 1951, p. 425.

you had been working was adopted as the policy of the United States toward China."

MR. BROWDER: ". . . I would say that the central points of that policy . . . were identical with the policy of the Communist Party."

SENATOR HICKENLOOPER: ". . . the substance of the important views advocated by the Communist Party up to 1942, were in fact adopted by the State Department, toward the Communists in China at about 1942—is that correct?"

MR. BROWDER: "In October 1942."

SENATOR HICKENLOOPER: "So, to that extent, regardless of the necessities of the situation or the explanations, you were successful or success met your efforts in getting that policy established?"

MR. BROWDER: "The policy which we had advocated was substantially incorporated into the policy of the United States Government."[137]

This statement of Browder's was confirmed by Louis Budenz, former editor of the *Daily Worker* and member of the Communist national committee.

Asked whether the Communist Party tried to influence the Far Eastern policy of the United States, Budenz replied:

"Yes, sir; that was one of our main assignments from the international Communist organization . . . Successes were reported on a number of occasions."[138]

Do you think Acheson realized he was following the Communist Party line in Asia?

Either he knew what he was doing or he was incompetent beyond words. As late as November, 1945, William Z. Foster, head of the Communist Party of the United States, notified the world that China was the prime target of the Soviet Union. He said:

"On the international scale, the key task . . . is to stop American intervention in China . . . The war in China is the key of all problems on the international front."

Less than a month after this Communist proclamation, Marshall embarked upon the "Marshall Mission to China." The testimony before the Russell Committee was that this mission was an Acheson-Marshall-Vincent project. Before Marshall went to China the Communists occupied a very small portion of China. Their Army numbered less than 300,000 badly equipped troops. When Marshall returned from China to be rewarded by Truman with an appointment as Secretary of State, the Communist-controlled area had greatly increased and the Communist Army had grown from 300,000 badly equipped troops to an Army of over 2,000,000 relatively well-equipped soldiers.

What about the State Department's excuse that we withdrew aid from Chiang Kai-shek because his government was corrupt?

Chiang Kai-Shek had been engaged in conflict and warfare since 1927—first with the Communists, then with Japan, then simultaneously with the Communists and Japan, and after Japan's defeat, again with the Communists. During that time, all the disruption of war

beset Chiang's Government. Under the circumstances it would be a miracle if there were no corruption or incompetence in his government.

But if corruption and incompetence are grounds for turning an administration over to the Communists, then Earl Browder should be President of the United States, Harry Bridges should be Secretary of Labor, and Alger Hiss should be Secretary of Defense.

What about Acheson's claim that we gave Chiang Kai-shek every help which he could utilize, including $2 billion worth of aid since the end of World War II?

That is untrue. Acheson made this claim in a letter to Senator Pat McCarran on March 14, 1949, in arguing against any further aid to anti-Communist China, which according to Acheson, "would almost surely be catastrophic."

Of the phony $2 billion figure, $335,800,000 was for repatriating Japanese soldiers in China and transporting Chinese Nationalist armed forces to accept the surrender of the Japanese. Even President Truman declared that those expenditures should properly have been charged to World War II. The $2 billion also included UNRRA payments, part of which went to Red China.[140]

Nationalist China was also charged for war materials never received—no one will ever know how much. For example, 120,000 tons of ammunition were dumped in the Bay of Bengal shortly after Japan's surrender, and China's Lend-Lease account was charged at the rate of $1,000 per ton for this ammunition. (See pages 39, 40.)

China was charged unreasonably high prices for the material we did deliver. Some slight idea of the fantastic prices we charged China can be obtained from the following figures quoted on page 47 of Freda Utley's book, *The China Story*:

	"Surplus" price to other nations	List Price	Price to China
Bazookas	$3.65	$36.25	$162.00
Rifles, .30-caliber	5.10	51.00	51.00
Rifle ammunition (per 1,000 rounds)	4.55	45.55	85.00
Machine-gun ammunition (per 100 rounds)	4.85	45.85	95.00

And so runs the sordid story of the dishonest bookkeeping which is the basis for Acheson's claim that China fell to the Communists despite our "two-billion-dollar" generosity. Left-wing radio commentators and newspaper columnists have parroted this attempted deception.

The year 1949 marked the Communist conquest of China. Will you list a few of the events which might help explain that victory?

Certainly. Following are a series of a few of the events which took place in 1949. They illustrate how Acheson

137 Tydings Committee Hearings, Pt. 1, April 27, 1950, p. 686, 687.
138 McCarran Committee Hearings on IPR, Pt. 2, Aug. 23, 1951, p. 593.
140 Utley, The China Story, pp. 32-49.

made it impossible for the anti-Communists in China to withstand the determined drive of the Communists.

Event No. 1

Senator Pat McCarran, an intelligently courageous anti-Communist fighter, introduced a bill on February 25, 1949, to provide aid to our anti-Communist friends in China.

Event No. 2

On March 1, 1949, the Communist Party of New York State directed all of its members to write their Congressmen and Senators and demand:

"... an end to all forms of American intervention in China and of plans to aid elements and remnants of the Kuomintang."

Continued aid to the anti-Communists, the Communist directive stated, would cause "frictions and misunderstandings."[141]

Event No. 3

On the same day the Communist directive was issued, Drew Pearson reported that the Secretary of State thought the anti-Communist leaders of China were cheap petty crooks and thieves. Acheson, according to Pearson, said that much of the past aid which America had given the anti-Communists "wasn't used to fight Communism, but went into the pockets of Chiang Kai-shek's lieutenants." The Chinese embassy patiently replied to this attack by saying that they could not believe the Secretary had actually said this because the great bulk of American aid to China had been spent and distributed under direct American supervision.[142]

Event No. 4

On March 13, 1949, Acheson wrote Senator Tom Connally, chairman of the Senate Foreign Relations Committee, that McCarran's Aid to China Bill:

"... would only prolong hostilities and the suffering of the Chinese people and would arouse in them deep resentment against the United States."[143]

In arguing against aid to the anti-Communists, Acheson said, "the outcome . . . would almost surely be catastrophic."

The anti-Communist government, Acheson wrote, "does not have the military capability of maintaining a foothold in South China against a determined Communist advance."

Acheson then went on to state that aid to China since V-J Day had reached a point "over $2 billion."[144]

Event No. 5

After making an analysis of all aid to China since V-J Day, Senator McCarran released a statement to the press on April 17, 1949, declaring that Acheson's letter was both "inaccurate and misleading." McCarran went on to state: "The State Department Division of Far Eastern Affairs is definitely soft to Communist Russia." Senator McCarran pointed out that "realistic analysis

shows that post V-J Day effective military aid has totaled only $110 million—not the $2 billion implied in the Secretary's letter."[145]

Event No. 6

On May 10, 1949, General Claire Chennault, a military man of many years experience in China, set forth his views in his "Summary of Present Communist Crisis in Asia." They were far different from those of Mr. Acheson's in Washington. While Acheson felt that the anti-Communists did not have the "military capability of maintaining a foothold in South China," General Chennault stated that some 150 million people in southern and western China—described by Chennault as "hardy mountaineers with a tradition of warlike defense of their native provinces against all invaders"—could supply "effective resistance to the Communist advance." Chennault wrote:

"Both the people and their leaders are prepared to resist the Communists and will in any case resist whether we help them or not. *But what we give in aid will make the difference between a hopeless and an effective resistance.*"

A few months later Acheson was to claim in his letter of transmittal of the *White Paper* that the anti-Communists had lost because "its troops had lost the will to fight, and its government had lost popular support."[146]

Event No. 7

On December 23, 1949, the State Department announced it had refused a permit for a New York firm, the Driggs Engineering Company, to ship 100,000 Springfield rifles "for the defense of Formosa." The company was acting as an agent for the Chinese Nationalists.

This was not a request for money. Chiang had the funds to pay for the rifles. It merely involved the granting of a permit by the State Department so the rifles could be shipped.

Did Acheson and Marshall recommend that we aid the Chinese Communist army?

Yes. This was recommended after the war with Japan had ended.

On June 19, 1946, Acheson appeared before the House Foreign Affairs Committee and requested that the United States Government arm 10 Chinese Communist divisions.[147]

At that time, Acheson reported that General Marshall had agreed to assign 69 U. S. officers and 400 tons of American equipment to train the Chinese Communist armies.

Ten months previously the war with Japan had ended. Acheson did not say who was to be fought by this American-equipped Communist army.

Is it true that Marshall, under State Department instructions, signed an order cutting off not only

141 McCarran Committee Hearings on IPR, Pt. 1, July 25, 1951, pp. 55-57.
142 Congressional Record (Unbound), March 5, 1949, p. 1937.
143 Congressional Record (Unbound), April 22, 1949, p. 5005.
144 Congressional Record (Unbound), April 22, 1949, p. 5005.
145 Press Release of Senator Pat McCarran, April 17, 1949; New York Times, April 17, 1949, p. 25.
146 White Paper on China, p. XIV.
147 House Foreign Affairs Committee, Hearings on H.R. 6795, June 19, 1946.

arms to our friends in China, but also all ammunition so that the arms they had would be useless?

Yes. The embargo on all arms and ammunition to China began in 1946 and continued into 1947.

Those were crucial years, and China's plight was so bad that even the New York *Times* reported on June 22, 1947, that the guns of the anti-Communists were so worn and burned out that "bullets fell through them to the ground."

The Communists, on the other hand, were kept well supplied by the Russians. Admiral Cooke has so testified before the McCarran Committee.

SENATOR FERGUSON: "What effect would the arming of the Nationalists have had as far as the Communists were concerned?"

ADMIRAL COOKE: "Of course, the Communists were being very well supplied in Manchuria by the Russians from arsenals and from captured Japanese guns and ammunition. We were practically certain that was going on, and, of course, in our *White Paper* reported from our diplomatic representatives in Moscow that it was going on."

SENATOR FERGUSON: "So we knew that the Communists were getting arms and ammunition and also it was our policy . . . to put an embargo on the Nationalists?"

ADMIRAL COOKE: "That is right."[148]

During the time that arms were completely denied the anti-Communists, as above stated, Acheson urged the House Committee on Foreign Affairs that we arm and train Communist divisions.[149]

Did the truces between the anti-Communist Chinese and the Chinese Communists which were arranged by Marshall help the Communists or our friends, the anti-Communists?

After Marshall arrived in China he succeeded in arranging four truces—four cease-fire orders. In each case, as I have documented in my book, *The Story of General George Marshall—America's Retreat From Victory*, the truce played into the hands of the Communists. It gave them time to rebuild their forces, and in each case denied the anti-Communists a military victory which was within their grasp. This same truce technique, incidentally, is now being used in Korea against us.

To illustrate the significance of those truces demanded by Marshall: When Chiang's anti-Communists were about to take Kalgan Mountain pass, which lead into Russian-controlled Manchuria, Marshall, on the request of the Communists, demanded a truce. Chiang Kai-shek in reply to Marshall's demand said that:

"It was absolutely essential to the national welfare that the government gain control of Kalgan and that the occupation of that city by the government would do much to prevent further military action by the Communists."[150]

When Chiang refused to leave Kalgan to the Reds, Marshall threatened to have himself recalled from China —which carried the threat of United States abandonment of China. Chiang thereupon yielded to Marshall's demands.

The fact that the Marshall-arranged truces helped deliver China into Communist hands was testified to by Admiral Cooke before the McCarran Committee.[151] Admiral Cooke was chief of staff to Admiral Ernest King during World War II. He served as chief strategic and policy adviser to Admiral King during the entire war, and later participated in the formulation of U. S. policy on the Far East when the war was brought to an end. Cooke commanded the 7th Fleet stationed in Chinese waters and then commanded all U. S. combat forces in China when General Wedemeyer returned to the U. S. His testimony that the Marshall truces helped deliver China into Communist hands is, therefore, the opinion of a real expert both on the Far East and on military matters.

Do you claim that General Marshall, who has long worked with Acheson, was knowingly working for the Communist cause in China?

As I stated in my book, *The Story of General George Marshall—America's Retreat from Victory*, I cannot delve into the mind of Marshall. I can only present the facts to the American people. Whether Marshall knowingly betrayed China or whether he honestly thought that he was helping China, the results are equally disastrous for America.

What about your charge that the United States dumped into the ocean 120,000 tons of ammunition which had been earmarked for China?

This is true. It is documented.

Following is the story of the attempt of the State Department and the left-wing press to keep those facts from the American people. First let me quote my speech of October 10, 1950, in San Diego, California:

"When the war with Japan ended, there was stored in India—as a way station to China—hundreds of millions of dollars' worth of lend-lease arms and ammunition.

"For months, Liberty ships were being loaded with those mountains of ammunition. Loaded they left the port and returned empty, time after time, to be reloaded and leave again. 120,000 tons of ammunition those ships took from the ports of India, yet every day during this period the artillery of Chiang Kai-shek remained silent for lack of ammunition.

"Why? Because under State Department expert planning, the orders were—dump this ammunition 200 miles at sea, dump it in the Bay of Bengal.

"All of the vast amount of ammunition which was destroyed by us is still carried on the Administration's books as aid which we gave China.

"When I heard this story of 120,000 tons of ammunition being dumped in the sea, I could not believe it. We sent investigators over to check and we found that it was true. Finally, we got a letter from Major General Edward F. Witsell. General Witsell admitted that this ammunition actually was dumped in the Bay of Bengal. But, of course, there was the usual double-talk, and the claim that the ammuni-

---

[148] McCarran Committee Hearings on IPR, Pt. 5, Oct. 19, 1951, p. 1496.
[149] House Foreign Affairs Committee, Hearings on H.R. 6795, June 19, 1946.
[150] White Paper on China, p. 190.
[151] McCarran Committee Hearings on IPR, Pt. 5, Oct. 19, 1951, p. 1592.

tion was corroded—as though a rusty bomb wouldn't kill a Communist as dead as a shiny bomb."

Milwaukee Journal Lies to Readers in an Attempt to Discredit Anti-Communist Fight

Several months later the left-wing Milwaukee *Journal* ran an editorial entitled, "How Big Can a Lie Get?" That editorial is reproduced herewith:

Milwaukee Journal Editorial

How Big Can a Lie Get?

Nobody is much surprised any more at Senator McCarthy's careless use of what he calls "facts," but he can still startle you with his ability to multiply misinformation.

How big can a lie get? There's a good answer in a story about a statement by McCarthy on page 42 in today's Journal.

Just before election McCarthy hysterically told a Washington audience (and Wisconsin audiences as well) that 120,000 tons of ammunition the United States had earmarked for the Nationalist regime in China had, under "state department planning," been deliberately dumped by our army into the Indian ocean—a waste of billions of dollars.

Peter Edson, highly reputable Washington correspondent, was flabbergasted and looked up the record. Ammunition was dumped, all right, back in 1945—120 tons of it, not 120,000 tons. It was dumped *after* the Chinese Nationalists had authorized its destruction because it had been damaged and corroded and was dangerous to have around.

How big can a lie get? McCarthy can multiply it 1,000 times and assess it as "billions of dollars" without the bat of an eyelash. Read Mr. Edson's story and see Senator McCarthy's method in action—inventing untruths and multiplying them to infinity.

Senate Investigating Committee Report

I already had a letter from General Witsell admitting that the ammunition which had been earmarked for Chiang Kai-shek was dumped in the ocean. Nevertheless, in order to nail down the lie I wrote to the Chief Counsel of the Senate Special Investigating Committee and asked him to check into this matter for me. His answer to my request is reproduced on the opposite page.

Did not the United States send a sizable military mission to aid Chiang Kai-shek?

Yes, *but*, as Ambassador Bullitt said: "Nearly half of the 1,500-man military 'mission' was composed of fellow travelers and Communist sympathizers."[152]

Since the fall of China has Acheson ever admitted that his China policy was a failure?

No. There is no indication that Acheson considers the loss of China to Communism a "failure." Instead, he hailed it as "a new day which has dawned in Asia."

About a month after the Communist conquest of China had been completed, Acheson declared in a speech before the National Press Club in Washington:

". . . what we conclude, I believe, is that there is a new day which has dawned in Asia. It is a day in which the Asian peoples are on their own and know it and intend to continue on their own. It is a day in which the old relationships between East and West are gone, relationships which at their worst were exploitation and which at their best were paternalism."

Nine months after the Communist conquest of China, Acheson, on September 10th, during an interview over a CBS television program, said:

"We do not think that any part of Asia is lost to the free world."

Owen Lattimore, who has been referred to as the State Department's Architect of Far Eastern Policy, had this to say after the Communist victories in China:

"Through Asia today there prevails an atmosphere of hope, not despair . . .
"What they see opening out before them is a limitless horizon of hope—the hope of peaceful, constructive activities in free countries and peaceful cooperation among free people."[153]

On December 7, 1949, less than a month before Acheson described the Communist conquest of China as the dawning of a new day, Radio Moscow had this to say about the Communist victory:

"The Chinese people have dumped Chiang Kaishek into the garbage can of history. The same fate awaits the United States puppets in other countries. Inspired by the grand historical victory of the Chinese people, the people of Indonesia and Viet Nam, the Philippines, Southern Korea and Burma, are intensifying their national liberation struggle. The democratic movement is gaining ground and strength in Japan where people refuse to be tools in implementation of the plan cooked up by Wall Street."

A report to the State Department, stamped secret, dated March 8, 1950, and entitled "Current Soviet Tactics," contains the following:

"Recent Soviet press and official statements have been marked by a new note of confidence in the advance of world-wide Communist revolution, emphasizing the theme that Communism is now moving at an accelerated pace for a final victory over capitalism everywhere . . .
"While Soviet propaganda has consistently echoed the classical Marxist-Leninist dogma that capitalism is doomed to destruction, the line is now being followed that the end of the capitalist world is 'approaching with unprecedented rapidity.' The heavy

152 Utley, The China Story, pp. 41, 42.
153 Owen Lattimore, The Situation in Asia (Little, Brown and Company, Boston, 1949), p. 238.

JOHN L. MC CLELLAN, ARK., CHAIRMAN

JAMES O. EASTLAND, MISS.   JOSEPH R. MC CARTHY, WIS.
CLYDE R. HOEY, N. C.   IRVING M. IVES, N. Y.
GLEN H. TAYLOR, IDAHO   KARL E. MUNDT, S. DAK.
HERBERT R. O'CONOR, MD.   MARGARET CHASE SMITH, MAINE
HUBERT H. HUMPHREY, MINN.   ANDREW F. SCHOEPPEL, KANS.
A. WILLIS ROBERTSON, VA.   ARTHUR H. VANDENBERG, MICH.

WALTER L. REYNOLDS, CLERK

SUBCOMMITTEE:
CLYDE R. HOEY, CHAIRMAN

HERBERT R. O'CONOR, MD.   JOSEPH R. MC CARTHY, WIS.
JAMES O. EASTLAND, MISS.   KARL E. MUNDT, S. DAK.
JOHN L. MC CLELLAN, ARK.   MARGARET CHASE SMITH, MAINE

FRANCIS D. FLANAGAN, CHIEF COUNSEL
HOWELL J. HATCHER, CHIEF ASSISTANT COUNSEL

United States Senate

COMMITTEE ON
EXPENDITURES IN THE EXECUTIVE
DEPARTMENTS

SENATE INVESTIGATIONS SUBCOMMITTEE
(PURSUANT TO S. RES. 52, 81ST CONGRESS)

January 16, 1951

Honorable Joseph R. McCarthy
United States Senate

Dear Senator McCarthy:

In accordance with your previous oral request, the staff of this Sub-committee has made preliminary inquiries of the Army concerning the alleged dumping of United States and Chinese Lend-Lease ammunition in the India Burma Theatre shortly after the end of World War II. In response to your letter of January 9, wherein you asked to be specifically advised as to the amount, type, and condition of the ammunition which was destroyed, please be advised that the following information was furnished to us by the Army.

An unspecified amount of ammunition was on hand in the India Burma Theatre after the cessation of hostilities at the end of World War II. Some of this material was Chinese Lend-Lease ammunition, some was United States stock, and the remainder was American ammunition earmarked for Lend-Lease to China. It was stated that some of the ammunition had deteriorated, although no specific information as to the amount or extent of deterioration was furnished to the Subcommittee, nor has the Subcommittee made any inquiries concerning the amount of deteriorated ammunition on hand at that time.

Some of the above mentioned ammunition stocks were demilitarized on land. However, due to the lack of experienced personnel and the danger involved in demilitarizing ammunition it was found that this was a formidable task. Furthermore, while demilitarizing ammunition at the Kanchrapara Ammunition Depot an explosion occurred which took the lives of nine Americans and fifty-five Indians. Under these circumstances, it was decided to dump the remainder at sea.

In response to your specific inquiry the Subcommittee has not been informed as to the amount of ammunition which was demilitarized prior to the decision to dump the material at sea, nor have we been advised as to the specific types of ammunition involved. However, the Army has stated that approximately 120,000 short tons of this ammunition at an estimated value of 120 million dollars was dumped in the Bay of Bengal under the supervision of the Army.

The above information was furnished to us by the Department of the Army and no independent inquiry has been made by the Subcommittee staff in connection with this matter.

Very truly yours,

F. D. Flanagan
Chief Counsel

play being given by Soviet propaganda to the 'peace front' suggests that it is serving as the chief propaganda facade for the program of world revolution . . .

"*The Communist conquest of the mainland of China and the conclusion of the Soviet-Chinese treaty of alliance constitute the greatest advance which Soviet imperialist expansion has achieved since the war, and this advance is no doubt a major factor behind the attitude of confidence which appears to characterize the current Soviet outlook.*"[155]

The above report was made to Acheson. However, he was subsequently to state, at the height of the UN debate over Korea, that:

". . . the Soviet Government may not be inherently and unalterably committed to standing in the way of peace, and that it may some day accept a live-and-let-live philosophy."

How did Acheson explain the sell-out of China?

He attempted to explain it in the *White Paper*, which was edited by Ambassador-at-large, Philip Jessup.

The *White Paper* obviously misstates the facts. Professor Kenneth Colegrove of the Political Science department at Northwestern University testified before the McCarran committee that the *White Paper* "was one of the most false documents ever published by any country."[156] Even that was an understatement.

In regard to Acheson's letter of transmittal of the *White Paper*, Professor Colegrove said:

"That letter of transmittal was thoroughly dishonest, especially the paragraph of the letter that says that . . . the United States had left nothing undone that might have saved him [Chiang Kai-shek] and kept the Communists from winning the victory . . . That obviously was a lie."[157]

Senator McCarthy, why do you concern yourself so much with the betrayal of 400 million Chinese who have been sold behind the Iron Curtain? In what way does that concern your people of Wisconsin and the people of the United States?

The Communist conquest of China concerns the people of Wisconsin because, for one thing, it means that the Communists were able to send thousands upon thousands of Chinese soldiers into Korea to kill American boys— some of them were Wisconsin boys. This not only concerns the mothers, fathers, and the wives of Wisconsin, but the mothers and fathers from every state in the union. The war in Korea is only one of the stepping stones to Communist world conquest. Another stepping stone will be Indo-China. And after Indo-China, the Philippines.

In this connection, it should be remembered that America has had a consistent over-all year to year, decade to decade foreign policy—a sound, long-time foreign policy —starting with Secretary of State John Hay's "open door" policy in China and followed by every Democrat and Republican President up to the time that Dean Acheson assumed command of our foreign policy.

Simply stated, that long-time foreign policy was to maintain a free, friendly China which completely protected our Pacific backdoor. Neither the Democrats nor

Republicans of this nation ever voted a change in that long-time successful foreign policy. No Democrat or Republican convention ever went on record for a change in that policy.

The abandonment of that foreign policy has already had a disastrous effect on America. The Korean war has cost us over 107,000 casualties. As to the future effect of the loss of China, let me quote General Douglas MacArthur, America's No. 1 expert on the Far East:

"It is my own personal opinion that the greatest political mistake we made in a hundred years in the Pacific was in allowing the Communists to grow in power in China . . . I believe we will pay for it for a century."[158]

Perhaps the best answer to the question: "In what way does the betrayal of China concern the people of Wisconsin," was given by Lenin when he said: "*He who controls China will control the world.*"

Most Americans know the significance of Formosa. I don't. Will you tell me about it?

Formosa is an island about 250 miles long and 70 miles wide. It is located about 100 miles off the coast of Communist-held China. Prior to World War II the Japanese spent vast amounts of money and effort to make Formosa the most important air and naval base in the western Pacific. From it was launched the air attacks upon the Philippines at the beginning of World War II. It served as a Japanese submarine and surface ship base for years.

When the anti-Communist forces were defeated in China in 1949 they retired to Formosa. As of today there are roughly 600,000 friendly anti-Communist Chinese soldiers on the island of Formosa. Those soldiers represent the only sizable anti-Communist Asiatic military force in all of the Pacific area. The significance of Formosa is well covered by the quotation from General MacArthur in answer to the next question.

You have said that Acheson represents the pro-Communist point of view and that MacArthur represents the American point of view. In what way and to what extent do they differ about Formosa?

I shall let General MacArthur and Secretary Acheson answer that question.

On December 23, 1949, Acheson sent the following secret memorandum to all overseas State Department officials telling them to prepare for the fall of Formosa and to pass the word that no aid would be sent to the anti-Communists on Formosa. When the memorandum was made public, Acheson admitted he was responsible for it. The message said:

"American criticism of American policy over Formosa has come largely because of *a mistaken popular conception of its strategic importance to the United States defense in the Pacific.* The loss of the Island is widely anticipated, and the manner in which civil and military conditions there have deteriorated under the Nationalists adds weight to the expecta-

[155] Author has photostatic copy.
[156] McCarran Committee Hearings on IPR, Pt. 3, Sept. 25, 1951, p. 922.
[157] McCarran Committee Hearings on IPR, Pt. 3, Sept. 25, 1951, p. 923.
[158] Russell Committee Hearings, Pt. 1, May 3, 1951, p. 32.

tion. *All available material should be used to counter false impressions that the retention of Formosa would save the Chinese Nationalist Government,* or that its loss would seriously damage American interests. Formosa is exclusively the responsibility of the Chinese government. *Formosa has no special military significance.*" (Emphasis Mine.)[159]

General MacArthur discussed the military significance of Formosa in a message to the National Encampment of the Veterans of Foreign Wars. After first outlining our chain of Pacific Island defenses, he had this to say:

"Our line of defense is a natural one and can be maintained with a minimum of military effort and expense.

"It envisions no attack against anyone nor does it provide the bastions essential for offensive operations, but properly maintained would be an invincible defense against aggression. *If we hold this line we may have peace—lose it and war is inevitable.*

"The geographic location of Formosa is such that in the hands of a power unfriendly to the United States it constitutes an enemy salient in the very center of this defensive perimeter, 100 to 150 miles closer to the adjacent friendly segments—Okinawa and the Philippines—than any point in continental Asia.

"At the present time there is on Formosa a concentration of operational air and naval bases which is potentially greater than any similar concentration of the Asiatic mainland between the Yellow Sea and the Straits of Malacca. Additional bases can be developed in a relatively short time by an aggressive exploitation of all World War II Japanese facilities.

"An enemy force utilizing those installations currently available could increase by 100 percent the air effort which could be directed against Okinawa as compared to operations based on the mainland and at the same time could direct damaging air attacks with fighter-type aircraft against friendly installations in the Philippines, which are currently beyond the range of fighters based on the mainland. Our air supremacy at once would become doubtful.

"As a result of its geographic location and base potential, utilization of Formosa by a military power hostile to the United States may either counterbalance or overshadow the strategic importance of the central and southern flank of the United States frontline position.

"Formosa in the hands of such a hostile power could be compared to an unsinkable aircraft carrier and submarine tender ideally located to accomplish offensive strategy and at the same time checkmate defensive or counter-offensive operations by friendly forces based on Okinawa and the Philippines.

"This unsinkable carrier-tender has the capacity to operate from ten to twenty air groups of types ranging from jet fighters to B-29 type bombers as well as to provide forward operating facilities for short-range coastal submarines.

"In acquiring this forward submarine base, the efficacy of the short-range submarine would be so enormously increased by the additional radius of activity as to threaten completely sea traffic from the south and interdict all set lanes in the Western Pacific. Submarine blockade by the enemy, with all its destructive ramifications, would thereby become a virtual certainty.

"Should Formosa fall and bases thereafter come into the hands of a potential enemy of the United States, the latter will have acquired an additional

'fleet' which will have been obtained and can be maintained at an incomparably lower cost than could its equivalent in aircraft carriers and submarine tenders.

"Current estimates of air and submarine resources in the Far East indicate the capability of such a potential enemy to extend his forces southward and still maintain an imposing degree of military strength for employment elsewhere in the Pacific area.

"Historically, Formosa has been used as a springboard for just such military aggression directed against areas to the south. The most notable and recent example was the utilization of it by the Japanese in World War II. At the outbreak of the Pacific War in 1941 it played an important part as a staging area and supporting base for the various Japanese invasion convoys. The supporting air forces of Japan's Army and Navy were based on fields situated along southern Formosa." (Emphasis Mine.)[160]

In testifying before the Russell Committee on May 3, 1951, MacArthur as usual was consistent. He said:

"I believe that from our standpoint we practically lose the Pacific Ocean if we give up or lose Formosa . . . Formosa should not be allowed to fall into Red hands."[161]

Acheson, who on December 23, 1950, instructed State Department personnel that "Formosa has no special military significance," testified on June 2, 1951 under oath before the Russell Committee that:

"I never had the slightest doubt about the fact that it [Formosa] was of strategic importance."[162]

You have stated that Acheson practically invited the Communists to take over South Korea and Formosa. What is the basis of that statement?

On January 20, 1950, a month after Chiang was driven off the mainland of China and onto Formosa, Acheson made a very significant speech before the National Press Club in Washington. He first hailed the Communist victory in China as "a new day which has dawned in Asia." Acheson then went on to outline those areas of the Pacific which if attacked would be defended by the United States. He made it clear that the United States would not come to the defense of either Formosa or Korea—an engraved invitation to the Communists to move on South Korea and Formosa. This invitation was accepted by the Communists six months later when they invaded South Korea.

On April 3, 1950, three months after Acheson's Press Club speech, he threatened to withdraw all economic aid from South Korea if its budget were not balanced.[163] South Korea's budget was unbalanced because of the money being spent on the military. Acheson's ultimatum, in effect was that unless South Korea ceased preparing to defend herself from the imminent Communist invasion, all U. S. economic aid would be withdrawn.

The aid which Acheson was going to withdraw was the balance of the $150 million of economic aid which had been requested by the State Department to "contain Communism." Lattimore had approved of the economic aid in

159 Russell Committee Hearings, Pt. 3, June 1, 1951, pp. 1667-1669.
160 Russell Committee Hearings, Appendix, Pt. 5, Aug. 17, 1951, pp. 3477-3480.
161 Russell Committee Hearings, Pt. 1, May 3, 1951, p. 53.
162 Russell Committee Hearings, Pt. 3, June 2, 1951, p. 1805.
163 Department of State Bulletin, Vol. XXII, No. 563, April 17, 1950, p. 602.

an article in the *Compass* of July 17, 1949, as a means of *allowing the South Koreans to fall without having it appearing that we pushed them.* A sizable number of Congressmen voted against the economic aid on the ground that it would be useless unless military aid were also granted to South Korea. It will be recalled that without State Department approval the sum of $10,300,000 military aid was voted for South Korea. As set forth on page 62, the State Department saw to it that none of the military aid was granted except the sum of $200 which was spent to load some wire on a ship on the West Coast.[164]

Acheson's threat to cut off economic aid to South Korea unless she balanced her budget by reducing military expenditures becomes doubly significant when viewed in relation to the sabotage of the Congressional military aid plan. Acheson, of course, did not order the South Koreans in so many words to reduce their military spending. However, as Acheson was fully informed, the major part of the budget was for military spending. Therefore, if the budget was to be balanced, South Korea had to greatly impair her defense program.

How can you intimate that Acheson invited the Communists to take over South Korea in view of the fact that the State Department approved sending American troops into Korea to fight the Communists?

If we were trying to win the war in Korea, this question could not be answered. However, the Administration spokesmen testifying before the MacArthur Ouster Hearings agreed that we could not risk winning the war or Russia might enter the war. When questioned as to our objective in Korea, the answer was: To kill enough Chinese Communists so that they will get sick of the war and call it off.

The Acheson-directed Administration has taken steps which make it difficult, if not impossible, to win that war. For example, when the United Nations called upon its members to supply fighting forces in Korea, the only member other than the United States which offered a substantial number of soldiers was China, whose troops are located on Formosa just a stone's throw from Korea. Acheson rejected that offer of troops.

General MacArthur, testifying at the investigation into his firing, gave an example of an unbelievable assist which Washington gave the Chinese Communists during the war. MacArthur told how, when the Chinese Communists started to pour men and weapons across the Yalu River bridges to kill American men, he ordered our air force to bomb those bridges. MacArthur stated that his order was countermanded from Washington.[165] It is impossible to even guess how many Americans died as a result of Washington's insistence that the Yalu River bridges be kept intact so the Chinese Communists could swarm into North Korea. Only after MacArthur "protested violently" was he allowed finally to bomb the bridges.

The Racin story is another example of shooting American soldiers in the back from Washington. Racin is a city in North Korea which was used as a staging point and supply depot for the Communist armies. MacArthur testified that he and the head of the air force in Korea agreed that Racin was an important military objective and should be bombed. Again the State Department said "No!"[166] No one can possibly estimate how many Americans died because of that "fantastic favoritism of war" to the enemy.

MacArthur also urged that he be allowed to bomb the enemy's air bases from whence came their planes to kill our men in Korea. He also asked permission to destroy the enemy's supply lines in Manchuria—the bridges, the railroad tunnels, the rail lines—in order to keep the Chinese Communists and their military supplies out of Korea. The State Department refused to allow him to do this on the theory that if we fought back effectively we might make the enemy angry and he would exert more effort against us. This reasoning would be difficult to explain to the families of the 107,371 United States casualties* of the Korean war. It would be difficult to convince the mothers of the dead, that their boys were killed by friendly bullets.

In discussing this situation MacArthur said:

"Now that China is using the maximum of her force against us is quite evident; and we are not using the maxium of ours against her in reply.

"The result is—we do not even use, to the maximum, the forces at our disposal, the scientific methods, and the result is that for every percentage you take away in the use of the Air and the Navy, you add a percentage to the dead American infantrymen.

"It may seem emotional for me to say that, but I happen to be the man that had to send them into it. The blood, to some extent, would rest on me; and with the objectives, I believe I could stop them. It seems terrific to me that we should not attempt something.

"The inertia that exists! There is no policy. There is nothing. I tell you, no plan or anything.

"When you say merely, 'we are going to continue to fight aggression,' that is not what the enemy is fighting for.

"The enemy is fighting for a very definite purpose —to destroy our forces in Korea."[167]

When our troops were ordered into Korea, the anti-Communist Chinese air force located on Formosa had 200 to 250 planes. That air force was doing a fairly good job of blockading the Communist ports of China. Chiang's anti-Communist army numbered about 600,000. The military forces on Formosa had immobilized the 3rd and 4th Chinese Communist field armies on the mainland of China opposite Formosa. Whether they could have moved across the 100 miles of water against Formosa was questionable in view of the fact that Chiang's air force had prevented their assembling any sizable amount of shipping in the area.

This situation was certainly a favorable one for us and an unfavorable one for the Communists. But the United States 7th Fleet was ordered to change the situation. It was ordered (1) to break Chiang's blockade of the Communist ports of China, (2) to prevent any assault by

*As of this writing.
[164] Congressional Record (Bound), August 16, 1950, p. 12600.
[165] Russell Committee Hearings, Pt. 1, May 3, 1951, p. 20.
[166] Russell Committee Hearings, Pt. 1, May 3, 1951, pp. 17, 18.
[167] Russell Committee Hearings, Pt. 1, May 3, 1951, p. 68.

Chiang's anti-Communist forces on the mainland of China, and (3) to prevent any attack on Communist shipping by Chiang's Navy. The fleet was also ordered to prevent any attack on Formosa by the Communist troops.

According to General MacArthur's testimony at the MacArthur Hearings, the fact that our 7th Fleet was ordered to protect the Communist mainland from any attacks by Chiang's forces released the 3rd and 4th Chinese Communist Field Armies for action in Korea.

Testimony before the MacArthur hearings was to the effect that this order to the 7th Fleet to break the blockade of the Communist ports resulted in huge amounts of war material flowing into Communist China. The testimony was that $40 million worth of material moved through one Communist port in one month after our 7th Fleet broke Chiang's blockade.[168]

Another result of the order to the 7th Fleet was described by former Ambassador William Bullitt on April 8, 1952, when testifying before the McCarran Committee. He was asked about Chiang's Navy.

> SENATOR WATKINS: "They do have a Navy?"
> MR. BULLITT: "Oh, yes. As a matter of fact, it has been quite an efficient force, although it is forbidden to act in any way by fiat of our government which has given orders to our fleet to prevent it from stopping the Communist supply ships going up to Korea. They sail right by Formosa, equipped with Soviet munitions put in the Polish Communist ships in Gydnia. They come all the way around and go right by Formosa and sail past there taking those weapons up to be used to kill American soldiers in Korea, and by order of our government the Chinese Navy is flatly forbidden to stop them on their way up there."
> SENATOR WATKINS: "Would the Chinese Navy have the power, except for that order, to intercept them and capture them?"
> MR. BULLITT: "Certainly, without question, without question."[169]

Have any American boys been killed because the 7th Fleet is protecting the Communist coastline of China?

In answer to that question let me quote a statement made by General MacArthur during his testimony at the MacArthur hearings. MacArthur stated that after the 7th Fleet began to protect the Communist coastline, the 3rd and 4th Red Field Armies were released from coastline duty and then "showed up in North Korea" where they fought and killed American soldiers. MacArthur testified:

> "As soon as it became know these troops had moved up north and were attacking me—the Third and Fourth Field Armies—I recommended to Washington that the wraps be taken off the generalissimo, that he be furnished such logistical support as would put these troops in fighting trim, and that he be permitted to use his own judgment as to their use. The slightest use that was made of those troops would have taken the pressure off my troops. *It would have saved me thousands of lives up there—even a threat of that.*
> "We were at that time with the 7th Fleet supporting my fighting line and doing everything else in Korea that was possible, bombarding and everything

else, at the same time with the other hand they were holding back these troops, which, if they had been used, or even threatened to be used, would have taken pressure off my front.
> "It was at that time that I made the recommendation that the generalissimo's troops be brought into play against the common enemy."[170]

Could Russia as a member of the United Nations have vetoed the use of UN troops in Korea?

Yes.

Is there any logical explanation of why Russia didn't veto the use of UN forces in Korea?

The only explanation I can think of is that Russia knew that her friends in our government would not let us win that war.

Russia has gained much in the Korean war up to this time. There has been siphoned from America billions of our wealth and the blood of over 100,000 of our young men. Much of our air force has been destroyed. Our economy has been disrupted, and we have been forced nearer to a semi-socialistic state.

In addition, every other nation within the path of Communist conquest has been taught a bitter lesson— the lesson that if she resists Communist aggression, her fate will be the same as that of Korea; namely, destruction. General MacArthur witnessed that destruction. This is what he had to say when he testified before the Senate Committee investigating his ouster:

> "The war in Korea has already almost destroyed that nation of 20 million people.
> "I have never seen such devastation.
> "I have seen, I guess, as much blood and disaster as any living man, and it just curdled my stomach, the last time I was there. After I looked at that wreckage and those thousands of women and children and everything, I vomited.
> "Now are you going to let that go on, by any sophistry of reasoning or possibilities? They may be there, but this is a certainty.
> "What are you going to do? Once more, I repeat the question: What is the policy in Korea?
> "If you go on indefinitely, you are perpetuating a slaughter such as I have never heard of in the history of mankind."[171]

There is nothing new about this pattern of conquest by terror. Genghis Khan was a past master at it. Early in the 13th century when his Mongolian hordes swept through the mountain passes out upon the eastern plains, his orders were to cut down every living thing that stood higher than the hub of a wagon wheel in any city or village which dared to resist him. This was done as a lesson and a warning to other lands in his path of conquest. Hitler, likewise, attempted to destroy the entire Jewish race and the Polish nation because they dared to resist him. This time, however, the United States is aiding Communist Russia in a campaign of conquest by terror, by insisting that the war be fought only in the country which we are allegedly helping. Not a single

168 Russell Committee Hearings, Pt. 1, May 3, 1951, p. 52.
169 McCarran Committee Hearings on IPR, April 8, 1952 (now being printed).
170 Russell Committee Hearings, Pt. 1, May 3, 1951, p. 22.
171 Russell Committee Hearings, Pt. 1, May 3, 1951, p. 82.

bomb must be dropped upon the land of the enemy. In Korea, according to the Administration, we dare not win but will continue a killing contest with two vast armies rolling back and forth across that unhappy land and destroying every city and village—destroying a whole race of people.

Thus we are doing much to convince any other nation which might be inclined to resist Communism that the cost of United States-UN "protection" is too high—that Russian conquest is far less painful than Acheson's brand of "liberation."

You state that we have aided Communism in Asia. How could this be done without the American people knowing it?

The best answer is perhaps contained in an article written by Owen Lattimore for the Sunday *Compass* on July 17, 1949. This, in my opinion, is the most revealing and sinister picture of the State Department's *modus operandi* that I have ever seen.

In it he points out that the State Department's big problem in China was how to allow China to fall to the Communists without having it appear that we pushed her.

In discussing South Korea, he said:

"The thing to do, therefore, is to let South Korea fall but not to let it look as though we pushed it. Hence the recommendation for a parting grant of $150,000,000."

It will be noted that there was no recommendation for military aid—merely economic aid. It was, in effect, the Marshall Plan for South Korea—no military aid but unlimited economic aid in order to fatten the goose before the Communists took over.

Acheson Asks Economic Aid Only for Korea

Acheson had very dutifully come before a Congressional committee and made a glowing speech on how $150,000,000 of economic aid should be given if we were to "contain" Communism in Korea. This was done, knowing, of course, that Communist Russia was supplying the North Koreans from the arsenals of Manchuria and that *economic* aid would, as Lattimore said, let them fall but keep the American people from knowing we pushed them.

Congress Earmarks Military Aid for Korea

Some Republican House members pointed out the ridiculousness of giving only economic aid to South Korea and no military aid while the North Koreans were building up their military forces. They were castigated and pilloried by the left-wing press as "opposing the fight against Communism."

The Congress—not upon the recommendation of the State Department—then appropriated and earmarked $10,300,000 for military aid for South Korea. This was months before the North Koreans moved. Whenever any Congressman or Senator tried to find out how the $10,-300,000 was being spent and what military equipment was being sent to Korea, he was told that the information must be withheld "in the interest of national security."

Sabotage

Finally, however, months later, after the North Koreans invaded South Korea, it was discovered that of the $10,300,000 only $200 had been spent—for wire which had been loaded aboard a ship on the west coast but which never arrived in Korea.[172]

Communist Line on China Applied to Korea

When the North Koreans started to cut through the South Korean army, the same cabal of Communist camp-following news and radio commentators who had sold the American people on the idea that the anti-Communist Chinese had not been willing to fight, took up the hue and cry that the South Koreans were well-armed and well-equipped but did not have the will to fight.

They would have gotten away with this, except that when American troops moved into Korea, American newspapermen also moved in with them. Honest reporting showed that the South Koreans had only a police force equipped to keep order in South Korea. For example, while they had American bazookas, they had no bazooka ammunition. The South Korean "air force," which left-wing writers talked about, consisted of five planes. None of them were combat planes.

Thus the stage had been set, but the Communist plans were disrupted by Truman's last-minute decision that he had to prove to the American people before the election that he was truly anti-Communist—the first apparent, but not real, doublecross of Stalin. Acheson and the rest of Hiss' friends in the State Department promptly set about the task of nullifying Truman's decision by preparing the infamous order to the 7th Fleet, by tying MacArthur's hands, and by the decision that was to control so many of our actions in the war—namely, that we could not risk a victory in Korea or we might make Russia mad.

Do the facts prove that Acheson followed Lattimore's advice of "let them fall but not to let the American people know we pushed them?"

According to Ambassador Patrick Hurley, "secret diplomacy enabled pro-Communists . . . in the American State Department to distort the truth and mislead the people."[173]

Acheson withheld from the American people and the Congress the warnings and advice of real *American* experts on China whom he ignored, such as General Hurley and General Wedemeyer. He also falsely denied he was following the advice of men such as Henry Wallace[174] Owen Lattimore.[175]

At the very time he was withholding from the Congress and the American people the reports of anti-Communist experts, and either denying or withholding the

[172] Congressional Record, (Bound), August 16, 1950, p. 12660.
[173] Washington Times-Herald, Feb. 18, 1947.
[174] Press Conference of Dean Acheson, Aug. 24, 1945; White Paper on China, p. 56.
[175] Tydings Committee Hearings, Pt. 2, Appendix, pp. 1839-1840.

fact that he was following the advice of pro-Communists, Acheson, on March 20, 1947, was assuring Congress:

"The Chinese government . . . is not approaching collapse. It is not threatened by defeat by the Communists. The war is going on much as it has for the last twenty years."[176]

On February 24, 1949, in answer to fifty-one Republican members of the House who asked, "What is our policy for China?", Acheson said we would have to "wait until the dust settles" before deciding upon a policy. Acheson did not mention that his policies had already determined exactly how the dust would settle.

After a Red dust had settled over China, Acheson, on August 5, 1949, released the *White Paper*, and declared in the letter of transmittal:

"Nothing that this country did or could have done within the reasonable limits of its capabilities could have changed that result [the Communist victory in China]."

Acheson, who in 1947 declared there was no danger of Communist conquest of China and in 1949 said it was too late to fight Communism in China, has never explained when it was—between March 20, 1947, and August 5, 1949—that he discovered Communism was a serious threat to China.

Do you feel that Acheson is knowingly working toward the triumph of Communism? In other words, do you feel that he is a traitor?

I cannot plumb Acheson's mind to discover what prompts him, but his actions have resulted in great damage to America.

I do not know whether he is in the same category as his great friend, Alger Hiss, or whether all his blunders were honest mistakes. The thought occurs, however, that if Acheson were honestly mistaken, at some time he would make a mistake in America's favor.

What about Europe? Do you think that Acheson has aided Communism in Europe as well as in the Far East?

I do not *think* Acheson aided Communism in Europe, I know he did. The record is clear on that point.

While Alger Hiss and other State Department officials played important roles in the sell-out of Poland, it was Acheson who played the leading role. It was Acheson who helped secure for Alger Hiss his appointment as an adviser to the President at Yalta. The Yalta agreement has been described by former Ambassador to Poland Arthur Bliss Lane as "the deathblow to Poland's hopes for independence and for a democratic form of government."[177]

It was Acheson who, over the protests of his own ambassador to Poland, granted a $90 million United States loan to the Communist-controlled government of Poland, thus supplying the Communist Secret Police with the weapons to control Poland.

It was Acheson who, over the protests of China and Britain, agreed to the Soviet aim of making the United

Nations Relief and Rehabilitation Administration, an innocent-looking relief organization (known as UNRRA), into a tool for Soviet conquest.

At the time each of those acts took place, urgent objections were made by both Americans and Poles who recognized in each the pattern of Communist conquest.

Arthur Bliss Lane, who was present when the Yalta Agreement was signed, spoke out and said:

"As I glanced over it, I could not believe my eyes. To me, almost every line spoke of a surrender to Stalin."[178]

After Yalta came Potsdam, when Truman met with Stalin and agreed to the Yalta betrayal of Poland. Jan Ciechanowski, ambassador of the anti-communist government of Poland, has told of his last days in Washington just before the die was cast.

"During this last stage of my official mission in Washington, I did my utmost to persuade the State Department that it was clearly in the interest of the United States at least not to grant full *de jure* recognition to the so-called Polish provisional government [the Communist-controlled government] . . . Despite all my insistent efforts, I found it impossible to get any consideration at the State Department for this suggestion."[179]

Even before Yalta our State Department was doing its part to Communize Poland. Stanislaw Mikolajczyk, prime minister of the anti-communist Polish government and leader of the Polish Peasant Party, tells of his vain pleas to the State Department to stop pro-Communist broadcasts into Poland by the Office of War Information, which was headed by Elmer Davis.

"We finally protested to the United States State Department about the tone of the OWI broadcasts to Poland. Such broadcasts, which we carefully monitored in London, might well have emanated from Moscow itself. The Polish underground wanted to hear what was going on in the United States to whom it turned responsive ears and hopeful eyes. It was not interested in hearing pro-Soviet propaganda from the United States, since that duplicated the broadcasts sent from Moscow . . .

"I mentioned . . . the tone of OWI broadcasts to Poland. They had been following the Communist line consistently, which made our job more difficult.

" 'It's unwise to adopt this approach to the Polish people,' I told the Under Secretary. 'If you continue to call Russia a "democracy," you may eventually regret that statement, and your people will condemn you.

" '*Your government once called Poland "the inspiration of the nations," but now the OWI calls the Communist forces just that.*' " [Emphasis mine.][180]

The Polish Prime Minister concluded his appeal to the State Department by saying, "Poland just does not want to become another Red satellite."[181]

The question naturally arises as to whether the State Department was aware of the Communist rule of terror

176 House Foreign Affairs Committee, March 20, 1947.
177 Arthur Bliss Lane, I Saw Poland Betrayed, p. 306.
178 Lane, I Saw Poland Betrayed, p. 80.
179 Jan Ciechanowski, Defeat in Victory (Doubleday & Company, Inc., New York, 1947), p. 383.
180 Stanislaw Mikolajczyk, The Rape of Poland, pp. 25, 58.
181 Mikolajczyk, The Rape of Poland, p. 59.

at the time it was initiating Communist propaganda in Poland and acceding to Communist demands.

This is best answered by considering the situation in Poland when Acheson granted the Communist-controlled government a $90 million United States loan. In March, 1946, U. S. Ambassador to Poland Arthur Bliss Lane learned that the State Department planned to grant a $50 million loan to the Communist-controlled government. He cabled his protests, but on Easter morning he learned that the loan was to be increased to $90 million. Lane immediately cabled again, urging that United States funds not be granted until ". . . the terroristic activities of the Security Police come to an end, and freedom of the press is restored, and American citizens are released from Polish prisons."[182]

But, as Lane has said, "My advice was in vain."[183]

Much of the $90 million U. S. loan was to be used to equip the UB, the Communist Secret Police—or "Security" police as they called themselves—in Poland. The activities of the Secret Police and the conditions in Poland when the loan was granted by Acheson are described by Stanislaw Mikolajczyk, leader of the Polish Peasant Party, who was in Poland at that time. He describes the Communist "campaign of terror" at that time as follows:

"On January 26 [1946], in the village of Gorniki Nowe, near Zamosc, twenty-five Security Police appeared at the farm of Jan Senderek, a Peasant Party member. His brother Stanislaw opened the door at their knock and was promptly annihilated by gunfire. When their hysterical mother kept crying, 'What have you done to my son?' the police answered, 'Be satisfied your other son is still alive.' Jan was taken from the house, mauled for two weeks in a Security Police station, then released, a physical wreck.

"Shortly thereafter in Grojec, near Warsaw, the Security Police seized five citizens, including a local judge, took them outside the town, shot them and shoveled them into a single grave.

"One man, however, lived. Knowing the butchering methods of the NKVD [the Communist Secret Police], this man dropped at the first rifle fire, pretending to be dead. He was buried alive in the pit with the others. Terribly wounded, he clawed his way up through the dirt and out of his tomb. He made his way to Warsaw, where he gave me a firsthand account of the shooting and named several of the assassins.

"I took these horrifyingly macabre facts to the next cabinet meeting, confronted the Communists with them, and demanded that the investigating commission be put to work immediately. The only result I obtained was this: the Peasant Party [anti-Communist] in the Grojec district was one of the first of thirty-six district organizations later dissolved by official decree."[184]

And what about the government to which Acheson gave a $90 million United States loan?

Mikolajczyk writes:

"The government [to which Acheson granted the loan in April, 1946] took no official notice of our congress [anti-communist] or its resolutions for several days. Then it acted. Through its controlled So-

cialist Party it sent word to the party that either we must join the government bloc by March 1, 1946, or face political annihilation."[185]

Less than two months later the $90 million loan was granted to this terroristic Communist government in Poland.

While the Russian-trained "Security" Police in Poland shot down private citizens on their doorsteps, imprisoned American citizens and carried on a rule of terror throughout Poland, Dean Acheson agreed to have Communist Russia and one other representative control the distribution of UNRRA food and relief in Poland and the entire European region.[186]

The power to control the distribution of food at that time was the power to control and direct hungry people. Arthur Bliss Lane in his book, *I Saw Poland Betrayed,* has told how this food, which was so desperately needed by the war-torn, starving areas of Poland, was used by the Communists as a political weapon. He tells how American-supplied food was withheld from all those who opposed Communism.[187]

In his book, *Defeat in Victory,* Jan Ciechanowski, former Polish ambassador to the U. S., tells the part Acheson played in this picture. About the time that Stalin defeated Hitler at Stalingrad and began to turn his attention away from the war at hand and toward his plans for world conquest, Acheson together with the representatives of Russia, Britain, and China, held a series of "top secret" meetings to plan the creation of the United Nations Relief and Rehabilitation Administration, known as UNRRA. Since the United States was to pay the major portion of the bill for UNRRA food and relief, Acheson held the position of greatest power in those meetings.

"The story as it unfolded at those five fateful meetings at the State Department," writes Ciechanowski, "has too great bearing on the present world setup to be left untold."

Here is the story of how UNRRA was turned into a tool for Soviet conquest and how it was used to subjugate the people of Poland.

At the first of those five meetings at the State Department, Acheson proposed that UNRRA be controlled by only four powers—Communist Russia, the United States, China, and Great Britain. China and Britain both protested, saying that all countries contributing to and receiving aid from UNRRA should have a voice in its affairs. Russia, however, agreed with the Acheson proposal. Russia then added a new twist. The veto of any one of the four powers could block any proposal made by the other three. China strongly protested and urged that the democratic rule of the majority be used. "Mr. Acheson," Ciechanowski writes, "then declared his support of the Soviet suggestion, while Lord Halifax [the British representative] did not appear to oppose it."

On March 24 Acheson finally secured the agreement of China and Britain for both Soviet proposals. Next the Soviet demanded that no outsider be permitted to enter

[182] Lane, I Saw Poland Betrayed, p. 237.
[183] Lane, I Saw Poland Betrayed, p. 237.
[184] Mikolajczyk, The Rape of Poland, pp. 153, 154.
[185] Mikolajczyk, The Rape of Poland, p. 153.
[186] Ciechanowski, Defeat in Victory, p. 256.
[187] Lane, I Saw Poland Betrayed, pp. 214-215, 224.

Russia to handle UNRRA aid to the Soviet or be permitted in any way to regulate food and relief sent to Russia. When China and Britain finally agreed with Acheson on this point, "Litvinoff's triumph was complete," writes Ciechanowski.

But even this was not enough. Russia then demanded that of the two officials who were to control UNRRA in the European region, one should be a Soviet official. Britain asked why Russia should be concerned with having a Soviet official distribute food for the entire European region since, unlike any other nation, it would have exclusive control over the aid going to its own country, Russia. The Communists replied that Russia "had a real interest in the measures to be undertaken elsewhere in Europe."

And what was Acheson's reaction when the Russians thus put their cards on the table? Acheson was representing the country which was to pay practically the entire cost of UNRRA. Ciechanowski reports: "Mr. Acheson curtly expressed the hope that the British government would be able to accept the Soviet proposal." Throughout the five meetings Ciechanowski states that "the Soviet demands were steadily supported by Mr. Acheson on behalf of the United States."[188]

Arthur Bliss Lane, who was in Poland as our ambassador at this time, tells how the Soviet used the power given them at those meetings in Acheson's office to distribute food in Poland "for their own political advantage." Schools, orphanages, and churches opposed to the Communist rule of terror, received no UNRRA aid. It was little wonder, for Acheson had made the rules and the director of the first UNRRA mission to Poland—appointed, despite the strong protests of Ambassador Lane, by UNRRA Director General Herbert H. Lehman, now Senator from New York—was a Soviet official.[189]

How do you explain your statement that Acheson is aiding Communism in Europe when he has made so many speeches urging that we fight Communism in Europe and that we send American troops to Europe?

Hiss also publicly proclaimed his love for the American flag. I can perhaps best answer this question by quoting from a speech which I made in the Senate on this subject on March 14, 1951.

"I realize that some of my good friends feel that the problem in Europe can be settled merely by the decision of whether we shall send an additional six or eight or ten American divisions to Western Europe. Would that it were that simple. Keep in mind that the group which is doing the planning for Western Europe is the identical group which has been doing the disastrous planning for Asia—the same group that did the planning for the sellout of Poland and China. Again without concerning ourselves over whether their actions are the result of treachery or incompetence, let's look at the unquestioned facts. Those facts speak for themselves.

Eisenhower's Hands Tied

"Those who have confidence in General Eisenhower as a great soldier should realize that Eisenhower's hands are also tied by the same crowd that has tied the hands of MacArthur in the East, and if good-natured Ike isn't careful, he is going to be taken for an awful ride. You know a good soldier does not have time to learn the ways of crooked, backroom diplomacy, and if he has spent enough time soldiering to be the good soldier that Eisenhower is, he cannot cope with unprincipled, crooked, clever diplomats. It is difficult for a soldier of integrity who has not had time off to study the ways of traitors to bring himself to believe that people in high positions could be actually disloyal to this nation.

Failure to Make West German Troops Available For Defense of Western Europe

"The Senate will recall that when the General appeared before the Joint Session of the Congress, he said he was unable to discuss the use of German manpower until the policies of the situation were cleared up by the diplomats. And for five years those diplomats have done nothing to clear up the situation. Periodically our State Department talks of rearming Western Germany to counter the army built up by the Russians in East Germany. But it is nothing but talk—words apparently planted to lull the American people into a sense of security that we are going to do something in West Germany to counter the threat of what Russia has been doing in East Germany. Clever administration of sleeping tablets, if you please!

Two Wells of Manpower for Defense of Europe

"When Eisenhower went to Europe to plan the defense of Western Europe, he wasn't even allowed to visit one of the greatest potential sources of manpower for a Western European Army—a country that has long been dedicated to fighting Communism—namely, Spain. I am not going to argue that Spain has or has not the kind of government of which we should approve. The point is we cannot make over that Spanish government. I am not going to argue that we should or should not love the 48 million people of Western Germany. But it takes no argument, it follows as the night follows the day, that there is no way on God's earth to defend the richest prize for which Communist Russia is aiming—the industrial heart of Europe—unless we use those two great wells of tough anti-Communist manpower, Western Germany and Spain. The talk of doing otherwise is either the talk of those who know not what they say or the talk of traitors planning a phony defense.

"Let Them Fall, but Don't Let American People Know We Pushed Them"

"When I hear Administration spokesmen urging that the solution to the whole problem lies in drafting and sending to Europe another six, eight or ten American divisions, there is called vividly to my mind an article which appeared in the *Compass* on July 17, 1949. The *Compass*, incidentally, is not *exactly* a *conservative* paper. It contains an article by that great expert on the Far East, the adviser to two Presidents and the man long referred to as the Architect of our Far Eastern Policy, the man who was called upon to give secret advice to our Roving Ambassador Philip Jessup before he started to rove.

"Let me read it to you and see if it doesn't give you an idea of what may be happening insofar as West-

188 Ciechanowski, Defeat in Victory, pp. 251-257.
189 Lane, I Saw Poland Betrayed, p. 143.

ern Europe, as well as Asia, is concerned.

"Here Mr. Lattimore, the State Department's adviser, praises the State Department for having succeeded in allowing China to fall to the Communists without letting it appear to the world that we have shoved her. He then goes on to state and I quote: 'The thing to do, therefore, is to let South Korea fall but not to let it look as though we pushed it. Hence the recommendation of a parting grant of $150 million.'

"The picture in Western Europe, gentlemen, is much the same. We are preparing to allow Western Europe to fall without having it appear that we pushed her. It matters not whether we send one American division or ten. It matters not whether Eisenhower is the most brilliant military genius the world has ever produced. He cannot defend Western Europe without the manpower of Spain and Western Germany. It just is not in the cards.

Communist Victory Inevitable Unless Immediate Reversal

"If we continue with the same type of planning, and argue over whether six divisions or ten or twenty American divisions should be sent to Europe and neglect the important question of utilizing the manpower of our allies, then Communist victory in Western Europe is just as certain as Communist victory was in China.

Amount of Time Left to Rearm Western Europe

"There are those who say if we start to rearm Western Europe that the Russians will promptly move in. This may well be. However, there is one condition which exists today which discourages that —a condition which may not exist a few years hence. As of today our long-range bombers using the atomic bomb could wipe Russian industry off the face of the earth. I do not believe Russia will move while that condition continues.

"We also know, of course, that Russia with a vast number of captured German scientists, is working feverishly to perfect that guided missile of the air, a missile which will track and destroy planes in the air. If and when this is accomplished—and it is only a matter of time—our atom-carrying bombers will act as no deterrent to Soviet Russia. They will be useless.

"My estimate of the situation is that we have a limited time to rearm Western Europe—the time during which it will take the Russian scientists to perfect a defense to our atom-carrying bombers. When that they have, they will be able to move on the ground unless in the meantime we have built up in Europe ground forces of sufficient power to deter them.

Armies of Western Europe Potentially Stronger Than Soviet Russia

"Now there are those who say that it is impossible for Western Europe to compete with the land armies of Russia. Gentlemen, this just is not true. Remember that German armies nearly destroyed Russia in the last war and now, with the exception of the 10 million Germans under Russian domination, we have not only Germany, but also Spain, France, the other small European nations and England.

"It seems that the time is long past due to build up in Western Europe, not an American Army, but a Western-European Army for peace. If this is done, peace may well be prolonged for another 15 or 20 years. In the meantime, Communism may rot from the inside out to the end that a peaceful world will then be possible.

"With the manpower of our friends in Asia and the manpower of our friends in Europe and the industrial capacity of this Nation, we are far more powerful still than the Communist countries. But we may not be more powerful tomorrow or the next day. If they take over Western Europe, if they take over Japan, then they will be far stronger in productive capacity, raw materials and manpower.

Aggression in Cause of Freedom and Justice

"There are those who say we should do nothing aggressive. This just does not make sense. There is no reason why free men should not be aggressive in the cause of freedom and justice.

Necessity of Recreating A Free Democratic China

"We should be aggressive in giving all-out aid to Chiang Kai-shek, to the end that China may again be a free, friendly, and a neutral China, that the peace of the Pacific may be assured.

Necessity of Recreating A Free Democratic Poland

"Aid should be given to anti-Communist forces in the Russian satellite nations—especially the anti-Communist forces in Poland when the opportunity presents itself, to the end that there may again be in Europe the stabilizing influence of a free, independent, democratic Poland. Now I do not propose to send American troops into China or Poland. But I do propose that we give the anti-Communist forces in those countries necessary aid when the opportunity presents itself, so that they themselves can strike the chains from the wrists and ankles that should never have borne them except for the actions of our planners.

SUMMARY

Phony Planning for Phony Defense

"In summary, I propose that we stop the phony planning for a phony defense of Western Europe and American interests. I propose that we restate our aims and then follow through with policies that will achieve those aims rather than what we have been doing in the past—namely, stating great and desirable aims and then putting into effect policies designed to accomplish the direct opposite result of those aims . . .

Must Make Use of Four Great Untouched Wells of Manpower

"Regardless of whether we send two or six or ten or twenty divisions to Europe, we are doomed to fail unless we promptly make use of the four great wells of manpower which we are now deliberately ignoring —namely, the manpower of Japan, the manpower of the anti-Communist Chinese, the Spanish, and the 48 million West Germans.

Use of American Troops

"In closing let me make it clear that I do not object to using American divisions in Europe. America has a heavy interest in keeping Western Europe from falling under Communist control. I do not object, that is, if we plan a real defense of Western Europe and not a phony defense under which those American troops will be condemned to death or permanent slavery in some Siberian prison camp.

"Before we send more American troops into Western Europe, we must reverse the Administration's virtual ban upon the use of Western German and Spanish soldiers in the defense of Western Europe. Then and only then can we hope for a real and not a phony defense of Western Europe."[190]

If you could replace Acheson, what would you most want in a Secretary of State?

Intelligent concern for America. Our State Department must be led by a man who thinks as an American, who represents America, and who will not allow himself, either through ignorance or design, to further the Communist cause.

[190] Congressional Record (Unbound), March 14, 1951, pp. 2461-2475.

Ambassador-at-Large Philip Jessup and Secretary of State Dean Acheson.

CHAPTER VI

Ambassador Philip C. Jessup

You have stated that Philip Jessup is unfit to hold his job as Ambassador-at-Large and delegate to the United Nations because of his "affinity for Communist causes." What evidence did you present to the Senate subcommittee on Jessup?

Following are highlights of the evidence that was submitted in the Jessup case:

1. Photostats showing his connection with six organizations officially cited as fronts for and doing the work of the Communist Party. The citations were either by the Attorney General or by legislative committees.

2. Photostats of some of the checks totaling $60,000 of Communist money contributed to the Institute of Pacific Relations, which was headed by Jessup for a number of years. The uncontradicted evidence before the McCarran committee shows that the institute was largely run by Jessup, Owen Lattimore, and Communist Frederick V. Field.

3. Sworn testimony before various Congressional committees identifying as members of the Communist Party and as espionage agents a sizable number of individuals on Jessup's staff and writers hired by the IPR while Jessup was chairman of the Pacific and American councils of the IPR.

4. Excerpts from Jessup's writings showing he followed the Communist Party line in taking the inconsistent position of urging that we send arms to the Communist elements in Spain and later that we withhold arms from England and France during the Hitler-Stalin pact.

5. Testimony given under oath by Jessup in the second Hiss trial showing his continued support of Hiss after the facts on Hiss' Communist activities were made known in the first trial, together with Jessup's sworn testimony before the Tydings committee in which he continued to support Alger Hiss after his conviction.

6. Reproduction of a petition signed by Jessup in which Jessup followed the Communist Party line and recommended that the United States stop manufacturing atomic bombs, and destroy atomic-bomb material by dumping it into the ocean. This was at a time when atomic spies, such as Fuchs, were stealing our atomic secrets and passing them on to Russia who was even then manufacturing atomic bombs.

7. Reproduction of letters from IPR files and excerpts from sworn testimony showing Jessup's close relationship with Communist Frederick V. Field and his support of Field in his Communist activities.

8. Reproduction of a letter showing that an *Amerasia* defendant, Andrew Roth, who was named as a Communist, was "rated very highly by Jessup."

9. Reproduction of sworn testimony showing that Jessup urged that Red China be recognized.[191]

After hearing your evidence on Jessup, what action did the Senate Committee take?

After hearing my evidence and a considerable amount of additional evidence, the Senate subcommittee recommended against Jessup's confirmation as delegate to the United Nations. The Senate did not confirm Jessup.

What did the President do after the Senate subcommittee found that Jessup was unfit to serve as the United States delegate to the United Nations?

After the Senate left Washington, the President reappointed Jessup as delegate to the United Nations, where he served during the entire conference, 12 weeks and 5 days, without Senate confirmation.

You stated that the Senate did not confirm Jessup for his United Nations job. Was this because the Senate did not have time to vote on Jessup, as Jessup has claimed?

No. Jessup was one of 10 individuals nominated by the President as delegates to the United Nations conference in Paris. Nine of the 10 were confirmed by a vote of the Senate. The Democratic leaders, however, refused to bring Jessup's name to the Floor for a vote because after an informal poll they found that Jessup could not secure enough votes for confirmation.

On January 17, 1952, Russian Foreign Minister Vishinsky speaking at the UN meeting in Paris had this to say about Jessup: "I learned the other day with some dismay that 37 Senators had asked the United States Government if it would dismiss Mr. Jessup from here because he was rather sympathetically inclined toward an un-American way of thought . . . I must express my sympathy for Mr. Jessup."[192]

Of what significance was Ambassador Jessup's Defense of Alger Hiss?

Jessup testified in Hiss' behalf at both the Hiss trials. In 1950 when Jessup was questioned on this by Senator Hickenlooper before the Tydings Committee, he stated he saw no reason to change his testimony as to Hiss' reputation for integrity, truthfulness, honesty and loyalty.[193]

This tied in closely with Acheson's action in calling a press conference after Hiss was convicted and announcing to the press and the country that he would never turn his back on Alger Hiss, even after Hiss was convicted of perjury in connection with the treason which may well

[191] Senate Foreign Relations Committee, Hearings on Nomination of Philip Jessup, Sept. 27, 1951, pp. 1-39; Oct. 2, 1951, pp. 41-102, 108-142.
[192] New York Times, January 18, 1952, p. C-5.
[193] Tydings Committee Hearings, Pt. 1, March 20, 1950, p. 267.

have signed the death warrant of a vast number of American boys.

Official Approval Given Hiss is Signal to Others

If Acheson and Jessup as private individuals were merely proclaiming their friendship for and loyalty to a convicted traitor, it would not be too disturbing. Unfortunately, however, the picture is much more sinister. Here we have the Secretary of State and the State Department's No. 2 man publicly proclaiming, in effect, that they would never desert and turn their backs upon any other Hisses in the State Department.

In my opinion, this was giving a green light to every Red in our government.

It is of more than passing significance that as late as Sunday, October 21, 1951, Jessup under constant questioning over the television program "Meet the Press," refused to repudiate Alger Hiss.

Does the fact that a person was affiliated with a Communist front organization prove that he is disloyal or in sympathy with the Communist cause?

No. One of the principal and rather successful aims of the Communist Party has been to trick loyal and well-known Americans into believing that various Communist fronts were good American organizations and to induce them to loan their names unknowingly to the Communist cause.

As one of our top intelligence officers testified: "While membership in one Communist front does not prove disloyalty, the conditions of his membership should be carefully checked to make sure that the individual in question unknowingly joined." But as he said, "If you find a man in our State Department whose task it is to fight Communism and to know all the workings of the Communist Party—if you find that he joins and sponsors or is affiliated with a number of Communist fronts, then you can assume that he is either so naive that he should be removed from his job or that he is loyal to the Communist cause."

Another Congressional witness said:

"Let's put it this way, if you find that a young man belongs to a Lutheran Young Men's Society, you can assume that he believes in the principles of the Lutheran Church. If a young lady belongs to a Methodist Young Women's group, you can assume that she believes in the principles of the Methodist Church. Or if a young man belongs to the Knights of Columbus or the Holy Name Society it is safe to assume he believes in the teachings of the Catholic Church. Likewise, if it is found that a government employee is affiliated with a number of organizations which are doing the work of the Communist Party, it can safely be assumed that he believes in the teachings of the Communist Party, or is so stupid as to be dangerous handling secret material."

You showed Ambassador Jessup's affiliation with 6 different organizations that had been officially named as fronts for and doing the work of the Communist Party. Who named them as Communist fronts?

Either the Attorney General or legislative committees. Citations were given in each case. The Attorney General cites an organization as a Communist front only after a thorough investigation by the FBI.

How can you blame a State Department official for joining a Communist front before it was cited as a Communist front?

The legislation providing for the public labeling of organizations doing the work of and serving as fronts for the Communist Party was for the benefit of the uninformed and not for men like Jessup who claim to lead the fight against Communism and who either know or should know the workings of the Communist Party.

In this connection it should be remembered that the Communist Party itself was not officially cited as a subversive organization until 1947. But certainly this should not be used by State Department officials as an excuse for having been active in the Communist Party prior to 1947.

You have stated that a sizable number of people employed on the staff of Ambassador Jessup, or hired as writers, while he was head of the Institute of Pacific Relations have been named as Communists or Soviet agents. Can you give the facts on this?

Throughout the time that Philip Jessup was chairman of the Pacific and the American Councils of the Institute of Pacific Relations, this organization was not only accepting Communist money to support its projects but also was employing Communist writers, Communist research workers, etc. Sixty officials and writers of the IPR have been named under oath as members of the Communist Party.

Following are a few of the 60 officials and writers of the IPR who have been named as Communists or espionage agents in sworn testimony before various Congressional committees:

INDIVIDUALS WHO WERE NAMED UNDER OATH AS COMMUNISTS AND WHO WORKED WITH JESSUP IN IPR

	NAMED BY	DATE	BEFORE THE
1. *Chen Han Seng* Writer and staff member under Jessup	Karl Wittfogel	Aug. 7, 1951	McCarran Committee
2. *T. A. Bisson* Writer and member with Jessup	Louis Budenz Louis Budenz	Aug. 22, 1951 Apr. 25, 1950	McCarran Committee Tydings Committee
3. *Chao Ting Chi* Served on board under Jessup and staff member under Jessup	Karl Wittfogel Elizabeth Bentley	Aug. 7, 1951 Aug. 14, 1951	McCarran Committee McCarran Committee
4. *Hilda Austern* Writer and staff member under Jessup	Louis Budenz	Aug. 23, 1951	McCarran Committee
5. *Harriet Lucy Moore* Writer and staff member under Jessup	Hede Massing Karl Wittfogel Elizabeth Bentley Louis Budenz Louis Budenz	Aug. 2, 1951 Aug. 7, 1951 Aug. 14, 1951 Aug. 22, 1951 Apr. 25, 1950	McCarran Committee McCarran Committee McCarran Committee McCarran Committee Tydings Committee
6. *Owen Lattimore* Writer, editor of *Amerasia* and Pacific Affairs. Served under Jessup.	Louis Budenz Alexander Barmine Louis Budenz	Aug. 22, 1951 July 31, 1951 Apr. 20, 1950	McCarran Committee McCarran Committee Tydings Committee
7. *Anthony Jenkinson* Writer and representative of news service with IPR while Jessup exercised control in IPR			
8. *Michael Greenberg* Writer and staff member under Jessup	Louis Budenz Elizabeth Bentley Karl Wittfogel	Aug. 22, 1951 Aug. 14, 1951 Aug. 7, 1951	McCarran Committee McCarran Committee McCarran Committee
9. *Maxwell S. Stewart* Writer of publications of IPR and served under Jessup's supervision.	Louis Budenz	Aug. 22, 23, 1951	McCarran Committee
10. *Lawrence K. Rosinger* Writer and staff member under Jessup's supervision	William Canning Karl Wittfogel Louis Budenz	Aug. 16, 1951 Aug. 7, 1951 Apr. 25, 1950	McCarran Committee McCarran Committee Tydings Committee

INDIVIDUALS WHO WERE NAMED UNDER OATH AS SOVIET AGENTS AND WHO WORKED WITH JESSUP IN IPR

	NAMED BY	DATE	BEFORE THE
1. *Frederick V. Field* Writer and Executive Secy. of IPR serving under Jessup	Louis Budenz Louis Budenz	Aug. 22, 1951 April 20, 1950	McCarran Committee Tydings Committee
2. *Owen Lattimore* Writer, editor of *Amerasia* and Pacific Affairs. Served under Jessup	Alexander Barmine	July 31, 1951	McCarran Committee
3. *Gunther Stein* Writer and paid employee of IPR when Jessup was Chairman	Louis Budenz Maj. Gen. Willoughby	Aug. 22, 1951 Aug. 9, 1951	McCarran Committee McCarran Committee
4. *Chao Ting Chi* Served on board under Jessup and staff member under Jessup	Karl Wittfogel Elizabeth Bentley	Aug. 7, 1951 Aug. 14, 1951	McCarran Committee McCarran Committee
5. *Michael Greenberg* Writer and staff member under Jessup	Louis Budenz Elizabeth Bentley Karl Wittfogel	Aug. 22, 1951 Aug. 14, 1951 Aug. 7, 1951	McCarran Committee McCarran Committee McCarran Committee

IDENTITY OF WITNESSES TESTIFYING TO COMMUNIST AFFILIATIONS OF JESSUP'S ASSOCIATES AND STAFF MEMBERS IN IPR

Dr. Karl Wittfogel—Professor at Columbia University; former member of Communist Party.

Elizabeth Bentley—Headed Communist Espionage Apparatus; has been used repeatedly as a Government witness in the trial and deportation proceedings of Communists.

Louis Budenz—Former member of national committee of Communist Party; served as editor of *Daily Worker*, official publication of the Communist Party; has testified in practically every case in which Communists were either convicted or deported over the past 3 years; one of key witnesses who testified against con-

victed 11 Communist leaders.

Gen. Alexander Barmine—Former General in Russian Military Intelligence who served as a Soviet Intelligence Officer for 14 years; fled the Soviet Union and is now under sentence of death by Soviet Military Court.

Major General Willoughby—Chief of General Douglas MacArthur's Intelligence Staff in the Far East for many years.

Hede Massing—Former Soviet Agent and wife of Gerhardt Eisler who fled behind the Iron Curtain and has since been active in Soviet-controlled East Germany; has testified in the trial of Alger Hiss and in other cases for the FBI and Department of Justice.

Prof. William Canning—Former member of the Communist Party who broke with the Party; former professor at City College, New York City and Xavier College.

CHAPTER VII

The Evidence on Owen Lattimore

Senator McCarthy, during the Tydings committee hearings you stated that you were willing to stand or fall on the Lattimore case. What evidence has been produced in his case?

Thirteen different witnesses have testified under oath to Lattimore's Communist membership or party line activities.* Some of the testimony and evidence follows.

Used by Russian Intelligence Agents

(1) Alexander Barmine, a former Russian General, was attached to Soviet Military Intelligence for 14 years. He renounced Communism and escaped to the United States. As result he is now under sentence of death by a Russian court. General Barmine testified under oath as follows:

—that Owen Lattimore was a member of Russian Military Intelligence.[194]
—that at one time General Berzin, the head of Russian Military Intelligence, had agreed to lend Lattimore to General Barmine for a secret Soviet project in China, which consisted of shipping to China Russian military equipment falsely labeled as truck parts for storage in Chinese warehouses for later use by the Chinese Communists.[195]
—that it was later decided that Lattimore could not be spared for the Chinese project but should be kept in his more important position in the Institute of Pacific Relations which was being used as a "cover shop for Soviet military intelligence work in the Pacific area."[196]

Considered Top Member by American Communist Party

(2) Louis Budenz, former editor of the *Daily Worker*, the official publication of the Communist Party, testified that Lattimore was considered by the Communist Politburo in this country as a top functionary of the Communist Party. Budenz testified that Jack Stachel told him to "consider Owen Lattimore as a Communist."[197] Budenz identified Stachel as follows: "Jack Stachel has been for years the most important Communist in the U. S. for all-around activity. He was one of the small commission of five which was in constant touch with Moscow."[198]

"Principal Agent of Stalinism"

(3) David N. Rowe, professor of Political Science at Yale University, a lieutenant colonel in military intelligence reserve, and consultant to Air Force intelligence, has testified under oath that "as of today among Far Eastern specialists in the United States, *Lattimore is probably the principal agent of Stalinism.*"[199]

American Communist Party Notified of Official Party Line Change Through Owen Lattimore

(4) Louis Budenz has further testified that the American Politburo learned of an important Communist Party

line change on China in 1943 through Frederick V. Field who stated he received those instructions from Lattimore. Budenz testified under oath that:

"Mr. Field just returned from a trip and I get the impression that he had talked to Mr. Lattimore personally, and Mr. Lattimore stated that information coming to him from the international Communist apparatus where he was located indicated that there was to be a change of line very sharply on Chiang Kai-shek, that is to say, that the negative opposition to Chiang Kai-shek was to change to a positive opposition and that more stress was to be put upon attacking Chiang Kai-shek."[200]

Budenz testified that the Communist Party in this country checked the accuracy of this important party line change and Moscow confirmed the instructions.[201]

Under Disciplinary Power of Communist Party

(5) Budenz further testified that he received orders from Communist Party leaders to treat Lattimore in the *Daily Worker* as a party member under Communist Party discipline.[202] After identifying Lattimore as "under Communist Party discipline," Budenz went on to say:

"Now in this respect there are Communist Party members, those who are smaller people, and out-and-out Communists under discipline.
"These Communists under discipline since 1939 or 1940, since the Hitler-Stalin Pact, are ordered not to have any vestige of membership about them, except in exceptional instances where the Politburo decides otherwise . . ."[203]

Secret Communist Orders Bore Lattimore's Symbol "XL"

(6) According to sworn testimony before the Tydings Committee, highly secret Communist Party documents, including reports to Moscow, often bore Lattimore's Communist Party identification symbols, which were "L" and "XL."

The testimony was that those reports were written on onion-skin paper with orders that they be destroyed after reading. People in key or delicate positions were desig-

---

*Louis Budenz, Freda Utley, General Alexander Barmine, Igor Bogolepov, Newton Steely, Professor Kenneth Colegrove, Dr. Karl Wittfogel, Ambassador William Bullitt, Governor Harold Stassen, Professor David Rowe, Professor William McGovern, Eugene Dooman, Frank Farrell, Harvey Matusow.

[194] McCarran Committee Hearings on IPR, Pt. 1, July 31, 1951, p. 201.
[195] McCarran Committee Hearings on IPR, Pt. 1, July 31, 1951, pp. 197-200.
[196] McCarran Committee Hearings on IPR, Pt. 1, July 31, 1951, pp. 201-202.
[197] McCarran Committee Hearings on IPR, Pt. 2, Aug. 22, 1951, pp. 552, 553; Tydings Committee Hearings, Pt. 1, April 20, 1950, p. 492.
[198] McCarran Committee Hearings on IPR, Pt. 2, Aug. 22, 1951, p. 555.
[199] McCarran Committee Hearings on IPR, March 27, 1952 (now being printed).
[200] Tydings Committee Hearings, Pt. 1, April 20, 1950, p. 492; McCarran Committee Hearings on IPR, Pt. 2, Aug. 22, 1951, p. 529.
[201] Tydings Committee Hearings, Pt. 1, April 20, 1950, p. 492; McCarran Committee Hearings on IPR, Pt. 2, Aug. 22, 1951, p. 529.
[202] McCarran Committee Hearings on IPR, Pt. 2, Aug. 22, 1951, pp. 552, 553.
[203] Tydings Committee Hearings, Pt. 1, April 20, 1950, p. 504.

nated in those reports by special initials or symbols. Lattimore's symbol was "XL" or "L."[204]

Member of Communist Cell in Institute of Pacific Relations

(7) According to testimony before both the McCarran and Tydings Committee, Lattimore was a member of a Communist cell in the Institute of Pacific Relations.[205]

Recruited Writers to Sell Communist Line on China

(8) Budenz testified under oath that Lattimore "was given an assignment by the Politburo" to recruit Communist writers to sell the American people the Communist Party line on China. For seven years, Lattimore was editor of *Pacific Affairs*, a publication of the Institute of Pacific Relations which constantly plugged the official Communist line on the Far East.

On this point, part of Budenz' testimony was as follows:

"At that time [1937] it was stressed by Earl Browder specifically as leader of the party, that Lattimore was performing a very great service for the party in *Pacific Affairs* by more and more bringing in Communist authors. Browder said: 'We appreciate that every writer for *Pacific Affairs* can't be a Communist,' that, however, the number must be increased and that Lattimore had shown a willingness and readiness to do so . . . so the emphasis on Lattimore was that he was getting more and more Communists."[206]

Used Soviet Diplomatic Pouch

(9) Lattimore admitted under oath that he used the Soviet diplomatic pouch to send material to Moscow.[207]

Communist Spy Under Sentence of Death Sends Secret Message

(10) W. Rudolf Foerster, who is now living in Switzerland, went to Moscow in 1928 where he was employed by the Soviet Heavy Industry Commissariat as an engineer. From there he went to Japan in 1932 where he became close friends with Max Klausen and Richard Sorge. Sorge headed the then-secret but now famous Sorge Communist Spy Ring. He was convicted by the Japanese as a Communist spy and was hanged. Klausen was also convicted and given a long prison sentence. The State Department ordered his release when our forces occupied Japan. Klausen immediately disappeared.

Foerster gave a sworn affidavit that his wife, who was returning to the United States from Japan, delivered a letter from Sorge to Owen Lattimore and that the reason for this method of delivery was that Sorge was afraid to send the letter through the mail. The affidavit states that when Foerster asked Sorge the purpose of the letter, Sorge got excited and begged him not to inform the Japanese police about the letter because it would "endanger my comrade."[208]

Edited "Amerasia"

(11) Lattimore was a member of the editorial board of the magazine, *Amerasia*, from 1937 to 1941.

FBI and OSS agents raided the *Amerasia* offices in 1945 and found 1,700 top secret and other classified government papers. Those documents had been stolen from the Department of State and other government agencies, including the Army, Navy, OSS, and OWI. Six people were arrested in connection with the notorious *Amerasia* case, including State Department officials John Stewart Service and Emmanuel Larsen. Larsen pleaded guilty and was allowed to resign from the State Department. Service was cleared but later ordered discharged by the Loyalty Review Board.

Declassified "Secret Documents"

(12) A few days before the arrest of John S. Service and Andrew Roth in the *Amerasia* spy case, which involved the theft of hundreds of secret State Department documents, both men were at Lattimore's home. According to affidavits made by other guests who were at the Lattimore home at the same time, they were working over papers which Lattimore first claimed had to do with a book that Roth was writing. The affidavits state that when Lattimore was later questioned about this after the arrest of Service and Roth, he then claimed that they had been "declassifying documents—a common Washington practice." Neither Lattimore, Roth, nor Service had any authority to declassify or pass out secret government documents.[209]

Louis Budenz has testified that the Communist Party was greatly concerned over the *Amerasia* arrests and called on Lattimore for assistance in the matter. According to Budenz:

". . . in the Amerasia case in 1945 there were many hurried meetings in the Politburo and in that connection Lattimore's name was mentioned several times; that is, that he should be appealed to for help, and, finally, Jack Stachel did report that Lattimore had been of considerable assistance in the Amerasia case."[210]

Wife Lectured at Communist Labor School

(13) Lattimore admitted under oath that his wife had lectured in the Tom Mooney Labor School in San Francisco.[211] The Tom Mooney Labor School has been cited as completely dominated by the Communist Party. It is recognized as the Communist Party school at which only Communist Party functionaries normally act as lecturers and instructors.[212]

Sold Property to Communist Without Down Payment

(14) The files of the Recorder of Deeds, Bethel, Vermont, show that in the summer of 1949 Lattimore bought an undivided half-interest in a home near Bethel, Vermont. Other property owners in that general area include

[204] Tydings Committee Hearings, Pt. 1, April 20, 1950, p. 495; McCarran Committee Hearings on IPR, Pt. 2, Aug. 22, 1951, p. 522.
[205] Tydings Committee Hearings, Pt. 1, April 20, 1950, p. 491.
[206] McCarran Committee Hearings on IPR, Pt. 2, Aug. 22, 1951, pp. 550, 551; Tydings Committee Hearings, Pt. 1, April 20, 1950, p. 491.
[207] Tydings Committee Hearings, Pt. 1, May 3, 1950, p. 883.
[208] Congressional Record (Unbound), August 1, 1950, p. 11620.
[209] Affidavits summarized in Congressional Record (Unbound), March 30, 1950, p. 4440.
[210] McCarran Committee Hearings on IPR, Pt. 2, Aug. 22, 1951, p. 555.
[211] Tydings Committee Hearings, Pt. 1, May 3, 1950, p. 882.
[212] California Committee on Un-American Activities, Report, 1947, pp. 63, 77-79.

John Abt, Nathan Witt, Lee Pressman, and Marian Bachrach—all of whom have been named under oath as Communists or as members of a Communist spy ring. Lattimore's co-owner was Vilhjalmur Stefansson, a man who has belonged to a vast number of organizations which have been listed by the Attorney General as fronts for and doing the work of the Communist Party.

Very recently Lattimore sold his half of the property to Ordway Southard, once a candidate on the Communist Party ticket for Governor of Alabama, and Mary Southard, who had run for the State Senate in Alabama on the Communist Party ticket and who also wrote for the *Daily Worker*.

Lattimore stated, however, that he never met the Southards who bought his half of the property from him. The town records show that the buyers made no down payment but gave a mortgage for the full amount. This creates the unusual situation of Lattimore's selling his half of the property to two people who had been well known as Communists whom he "had never met" and allowing them to take possession of the property without making even a $1.00 down payment.[213]

When questioned about this transaction by the McCarran committee, Lattimore stated:

"I did not sell the property. My wife and I empowered Mr. Stefansson to sell it on our behalf."[214]

Later, when confronted with a notary public's certification that Owen Lattimore and Eleanor Lattimore had signed the deed and swore to their signatures before the notary, Lattimore admitted that he personally had signed the deed. The testimony on this follows:

SENATOR FERGUSON: "Let me read it [the notary public's certification] to you . . .
" 'Personally appeared and acknowledged this instrument [the deed to Communist candidate Southard] by them sealed and subscribed to be their own free act and deed.'
"Did you or did you not do that?"
LATTIMORE: "Evidently I did."
SENATOR FERGUSON: "Do you want to put in the word 'evidently'?"
LATTIMORE: "All right, I did."[215]

Lectured Troops in Communist China

(15) Lattimore, in his testimony, admitted that he toured and lived at Communist headquarters at Yenan, Chinese Communist military stronghold, at a time when only "friendly" visitors were allowed through the lines. Traveling with Lattimore were Philip Jaffe and T. A. Bisson, both of whom have been identified in testimony before the McCarran committee as important Communist Party members. Lattimore testified before the McCarran Committee that he had personally made the arrangements with Communist headquarters for the visit to Yenan.[216]

In describing this visit to Yenan in the pages of the Communist Party's magazine, *New Masses*, Jaffe wrote: "Our visit to Yenan was climaxed by a huge mass meeting addressed by Chu Teh, Lattimore, and myself . . ." Chu Teh was and is Commander-in-Chief of the Chinese Communist armies.

In his testimony before the Tydings committee, Latti-

more grudgingly admitted he had addressed this Communist mass meeting, describing his speech by the phrase "partial address."[217]

At Yenan the party was joined by Agnes Smedley who was exposed by General MacArthur's Intelligence Headquarters as a Communist spy and who has been described as Russia's most valuable agent in China. Smedley recently died and left her estate to the Communist leader, Chu Teh.

After the Lattimore party left Yenan, Smedley wrote Lattimore as follows:

"I want to tell you that you left behind remarkable friends. I did not realize the effect of the meeting until 2 or 3 days had passed. Then it began to roll in . . . The meeting and your speech in particular has had a colossal effect upon all the people . . . There has never been anything like this here before."[217-A]

Incidentally, the Tydings committee found that Lattimore "never knowingly associated with Communists."[218]

Wanted to Retain an Important OWI Employee "Even if He is a Communist"

(16) When Lattimore was head of the Pacific Division of the Office of War Information, he wrote a letter on June 15, 1943, to Joseph Barnes, then head of the New York division of the Office of War Information and warned Barnes to keep the letter "strictly secret." Barnes has been named under oath as a Communist agent.[219]

In this letter, Lattimore advised Barnes to get rid of all Chinese in the Office of War Information except a Dr. Chi and a Mr. Chew Hong, and to recruit a new force of Chinese from the *New China Daily News*.

At the time I made this letter public, I pointed out that this meant Lattimore was directing Barnes to staff the Chinese Office of OWI with Chinese Communists or those sympathetic to the Communist cause.

After both the State Department and Lattimore denied this, I put into the *Congressional Record* the secret loyalty files on Chi and Chew Hong, which show that the Loyalty Board considered Hong to be a Communist and Chi to be at least a Communist fellow traveler, if not an actual Communist. The files showed that the Loyalty Board had rated Hong ineligible for government employment because of his membership in the Communist Party and that the ineligible rating was cancelled only because of Lattimore's strong insistence.

Those Loyalty files also showed that the *New China Daily News* was an *official* Communist paper and that any people recruited for the OWI from that paper would obviously be members of the Communist Party.

The files further show that Lattimore was advised of the fact that Hong was a Communist but that nevertheless Lattimore stated he wanted to keep him on "even if he were a Communist."[220]

Following are some excerpts from those Loyalty files:

213 Washington Times Herald, Aug. 3, 1950.
214 McCarran Committee Hearings on IPR, March 10, 1952 (now being printed).
215 McCarran Committee Hearings on IPR, March 10, 1952 (now being printed).
216 McCarran Committee Hearings on IPR, March 21, 1952, (now being printed).
217 Tydings Committee Hearings, Pt. 1, May 2, 1950, p. 870.
217A New Masses, Oct. 12, 1937, inserted in record of McCarran Committee Hearings on IPR, Pt. 2, Aug. 23, 1951, p. 658.
218 Tydings Committee Report, p. 73.
219 McCarran Committee Hearings on IPR, Pt. 1, July 31, 1951, p. 200.
220 Congressional Record (Unbound), June 2, 1950, pp. 8104-8108.

"*China Daily News*—The testimony is to the general effect that the China Daily News is a publication by and for Chinese Communists. It is described by some individuals as the Chinese equivalent of the *Daily Worker*.

". . . the OWI representatives were also informed of the unfavorable information secured regarding Dr. Chi and his son, which included testimony to the effect that the young Dr. Chi is or was, until recently, a Communist and that he at one time was a delegate to the Third Internationale in Moscow and to the effect that the elder Dr. Chi was removed from his position as Commissioner of Education in the Shansi Province because of Communist activities . . .

"On the one hand it can be argued that since we are reasonably convinced that Hong is pro-Communist, it is our responsibility to require his removal notwithstanding Mr. Lattimore's representations. On the other hand the Commission could, if it wished, take the position that since Mr. Lattimore has assumed responsibility, the Commission can afford to permit Hong's retention in the service. If the Commission takes the latter position it will be tantamount to saying that although we believe the individual is a Communist, we will be willing to rate him eligible provided the employing agency is willing to assume the responsibility. I doubt that the Commission can afford to avoid the issue in this manner. If we believe Hong is a Communist then we should rate him ineligible . . .

"It is concluded that the activities, affiliations, and associations of Hong, as shown by the Commission's investigation, are Communistic. A finding of ineligibility is considered necessary in this case . . .

"In view of the testimony obtained during the subsequent investigation of Mr. Hong in San Francisco and the evidence secured in the investigation of Dr. Chi regarding Communist activities on the part of him and his son, I can see no reason why the Commission should disturb its previous rating of ineligibility in Mr. Hong's case.

"During my interview with Mr. Marsh, Mr. Lattimore and Admiral McCullough, the evidence secured during investigation of Mr. Hong was discussed and they were advised fully regarding the substance of the derogatory information."

The Loyalty files quote Lattimore as having said:

"I know there is a law preventing the hiring of Communists. Personally and frankly I would not be too worried if an individual Communist were in Hong's position."[221]

The Loyalty files also quoted the following from a letter which Lattimore wrote to Joseph Barnes, former foreign editor of the New York *Herald Tribune,* who was then in the OWI and who has been named under oath by four witnesses as a member of the Communist Party. Lattimore was discussing the two Chinese named in the above Loyalty files. His letter, as quoted by the Loyalty Board, stated:

"I urge you not to be high-pressured into getting rid of either man."

In his letter to Barnes urging that a new force of Chinese be recruited for OWI from the *New China Daily News,* Lattimore described this newspaper as "unaffiliated." He has denied my statement that since the *New*

China Daily News was a Communist paper any people recruited from it, as he recommended, would necessarily be Communist. While the Loyalty files referred to above thoroughly established the fact that this newspaper was an *official* Communist paper, a recent development cast even more light on this subject.

On April 28, 1952, the president and the former managing editor of the *New China Daily News* were named by a Federal Grand Jury in a 53-count indictment as part of an "international racket entailing murder, extortion, torture and in general, commerce in human misery . . . a racket which is designed to further the aims of the Chinese Communist government." The Assistant United States Attorney stated that part of the scheme carried on by the *New China Daily News* was the printing of "editorials and news releases that urged American Chinese to send money in support of Mao Tse tung, head of the Red China government."[222]

Advised IPR to Back the Chinese Communists and Russia's International Policy

(17) For many years Lattimore was active in the Institute of Pacific Relations which has exerted a powerful influence on State Department policy, according to evidence uncovered by the Senate Internal Security Subcommittee. Several years ago the IPR was cited as a Communist front.[223]

Senator McCarran in *U. S. News* of November 16, 1951, had this to say about the IPR:

"The IPR originally was an organization with laudable motives. It was taken over by Communist design and made a vehicle for attempted control and conditioning of American thinking and American policy with regard to the Far East. It was also used for espionage purposes to collect and channel information of interest or value to the Russian Communists."

This year the McCarran committee began its investigation of the Institute of Pacific Relations and took possession of a vast number of Institute of Pacific Relations files which were hidden in a barn near Lee, Massachusetts. By carefully sifting those files and calling before them a large number of witnesses, the McCarran committee produced a mass of evidence about the Institute of Pacific Relations. That evidence was to the following effect:

1. That it was Communist-dominated. [224]

2. That it served as an "umbrella for Communist operations" and as "a covershop for [Russian] military intelligence."[225]

3. That the real leaders of IPR were Owen Lattimore, Philip Jessup, E. C. Carter,[226] and Frederick V. Field.

4. That it strongly influenced the United States Far Eastern policy.[227]

221 Congressional Record (Unbound), June 2, 1950, pp. 8104-8108.
222 New York Times, April 29, 1952.
223 California State Legislative Committee on Un-American Activities Report, 1948, p. 168.
224 McCarran Committee Hearings on IPR, Pt. 1, July 31, 1951, pp. 202, 203, 205, 208; Aug. 22, 1951, pp. 517, 518; Aug. 14, 1951, p. 412.
225 McCarran Committee Hearings on IPR, Pt. 1, July 31, 1951, pp. 202-204; Pt. 2, Aug. 23, 1951, p. 593.
226 McCarran Committee Hearings on IPR, Pt. 4, September 26, 1951, p. 1003 and March 27, 1952 (now being printed).
227 McCarran Committee Hearings on IPR, Pt. 2, Aug. 22, 1951, p. 517, Aug. 23, 1951, p. 593; Sept. 25, 1951, Pt. 3, pp. 920-924.

Following are excerpts from a letter which Lattimore wrote E. C. Carter, head of IPR, on July 10, 1938:

"... I think that you are pretty cagey in turning over so much of the China section of the enquiry to Asiaticus, Han-seng, and Chi.* They will bring out the absolutely essential radical aspects, but can be depended on to do it with the right touch ..."

"For the general purposes of this enquiry, it seems to me that the good scoring position, for the IPR, differs with different countries. For China, my hunch is that it will pay to keep behind the official Chinese Communist position—far enough not to be covered by the same label—but enough ahead of the active Chinese liberals to be noticeable ... For the USSR— back their international policy in general, but without using their slogans ..." (Emphasis mine.)[228]

While Lattimore swears that he was never a Communist, it would perhaps be impossible to find any member of the Communist Party, including Stalin, who would differ one iota from Lattimore's recommendations contained in the foregoing letter.

Conference with Russian Ambassador

(18) Documentary evidence presented to the McCarran committee showed that before leaving for China, Lattimore spent an "illuminating two hours" with Russian Ambassador Oumansky on June 18, 1941. At the time of this conversation, Russia was allied with Germany in a non-aggression pact, known at the Hitler-Stalin Pact.[229]

Disrupted Peace Talks with Japan 12 Days Before Pearl Harbor

(19) Before the Japanese attack on Pearl Harbor, Secretary of State Cordell Hull and the Japanese representatives were attempting to work out a *modus vivendi* which would stave off war. At that time, Lattimore was in China, having been sent there by President Roosevelt as advisor to Chiang Kai-shek.

On November 25, 1941, twelve days before Japanese bombs fell on Pearl Harbor, Lattimore sent an urgent cable to the White House advising against peace with Japan.[230]

The Pearl Harbor hearings and the testimony before the McCarran committee show that Lattimore, with the aid of Lauchlin Currie, an administrative assistant to the President, and Harry Dexter White, a top official in the Treasury Department (both of whom have been named under oath as having aided a Communist spy ring), worked frantically to prevent a peaceful settlement between the Japanese and the United States.[231]

Keep in mind that at this particular time, 1941, Communist Russia was extremely eager to have the United States come into the war and destroy Japan, which had long been a bulwark against Communism in Asia. The official Communist Party line at that time was to give all-out support to Chiang Kai-shek in his fight against Japan. It was obviously in the interest of Communist Russia for the war between anti-Communist China and anti-Communist Japan to continue. At the Comintern meetings it had been decided that first priority be given to the de-

struction of the highly industrialized Japanese empire which stood in the way of Communist conquest of China. The next step after the destruction of Japan would be to turn upon Chiang and communize China.

Advised Ambassador Jessup, in Line with Official Party Line, on Far Eastern Mission

(20) At the request of Dean Acheson, Lattimore submitted a secret memorandum in August, 1949, entitled "For the Guidance of Ambassador-at-Large Philip Jessup." This was prepared for Jessup prior to his departure on a special mission to the Far East to study its problems and work out a State Department policy for Asia and the Pacific.

Lattimore's recommendations in his memorandum for Ambassador Jessup's "guidance" are identical in all major aspects to the officially adopted program of the Communist Party insofar as Asia is concerned. For example, he recommends:

1. that the United States withdraw all support from Korea;
2. that we give no support whatsoever to the anti-Communist forces on Formosa;
3. that we refuse to support any league of Asiatic countries against Communism;
4. that the United States "accept a list of countries recommended for admission to the United Nations by Trygve Lie," (Trygve Lie had recommended that Communist China be admitted to the UN); and
5. that the United States withdraw its forces from Japan.[232]

When I first revealed the fact that Lattimore had been called upon for this secret memorandum, Acheson called a press conference and denied the existence of such a memorandum. I then notified the State Department that if they did not make the document public, I would. Within hours, Lattimore's advice to Ambassador Jessup was "found" by the State Department and made public.

Dominated State Department Conference

(21) Harold Stassen, former Governor of Minnesota, testified before the McCarran committee that he attended a State Department conference in October, 1949, which Lattimore also attended. General George C. Marshall and other members of the Board of the IPR were also there. The meeting was called for the purpose of determining a foreign policy for Asia and for advising Ambassador Jessup on a policy before he left for his tour of the Far East. Ambassador Jessup presided at the meeting.

Stassen testified under oath (1) that Owen Lattimore consistently argued for the adoption of a ten-point program on Asia which followed the official Communist line; (2) that the group led by Lattimore dominated the meeting; and (3) that Ambassador Jessup, for whose benefit

---

*These men have been repeatedly named under oath as Communists and are publicly recognized as members of the Communist Party.

228 McCarran Committee Hearings on IPR, Pt. 2, Aug. 22, 1951, p. 525.
229 McCarran Committee Hearings on IPR, Pt. 1, July 26, 1951, p. 150.
230 Pearl Harbor Hearings, Dec. 1945, p. 1160.
231 Washington Times-Herald, November 26, 1951, p. 1.
232 Tydings Committee Hearings, Pt. 1, April 6, 1950, pp. 459-462.

this meeting was called, told him he agreed with Lattimore's ideas because they "were the greater logic."[233]

Toasted by Communist Leader As "Responsible for Future of China"

(22) In 1944 Lattimore and John Carter Vincent (named by a government witness under oath as a Communist), upon the recommendation of Lauchlin Currie (named under oath as a member of a Communist spy ring), accompanied Vice President Henry Wallace on a tour of China. Upon his return Wallace wrote a book entitled, *Soviet Asia Mission.*

In the book, Wallace states that while he and Lattimore were travelling through China, Sergei Godlize, a high Soviet official—President of the Executive Committee of Siberian territory—and an intimate friend of Stalin, toasted Owen Lattimore and John Carter Vincent at a dinner as the men "on whom rests great responsibility for China's future."[234]

"Let Them Fall But Do Not Let It Look As Though We Pushed Them"

(23) On July 17, 1949, shortly before Lattimore prepared his secret advice (August, 1949) to Jessup, he wrote an article in the *Sunday Compass*, a left-wing New York publication, in which he stated, referring to the Marshall Mission:

"The problem was how to allow them [China] to fall without making it look as if the United States had pushed them."

In the same article, Lattimore suggests that what had been done in China should now be done in Korea also. This was before the Korean war. He stated:

"The thing to do, therefore, is to let South Korea fall—but not to let it look as though we pushed it. Hence the recommendation of a parting grant of $150 million." (Economic aid.)

In this connection, it should be noted that nearly a year before the Korean war started, Congress voted $10,300,000 military aid for South Korea. This was not done upon the recommendation of the State Department. The Congress was entitled to believe that this $10,300,000 was being spent rapidly for airplanes, tanks and guns for South Korea. However, whenever a member of Congress asked the State and Defense Departments how the $10,-300,000 was being spent, the answer was, "We cannot tell you for security reasons."

After the war in Korea began, Senator Knowland put into the *Congressional Record* the facts which showed that the State Department had succeeded in keeping the expenditures for the arming of South Korea down to $200, which was spent for loading some wire aboard a West Coast ship which never reached Korea.[235]

Thus did the State Department plan to "let South Korea fall" into the Communist hands without letting the Congress or the American people know that "we pushed it."

Writings Follow Communist Line

(24) Lattimore's writings, coupled with his acts, thoroughly identify him. The following excerpts from his writings give some idea of the extent to which he followed the Communist Party line. More complete documentation of his writings is contained in my speech reported in the *Congressional Record* of March 30, 1950.

The general line of Communistic propaganda put across by Lattimore in his writings is clearly shown by the following blurb in his book, *Solution in Asia.*

This is what the editor says about the book:

"He shows that all the Asiatic people are more interested in actual democratic practices such as the ones they can see in action across the Russian border, than they are in the fine theories of Anglo-Saxon democracies which come coupled with ruthless imperialism . . . He inclines to support American newspapermen who report that the only real democracy in China is found in Communist areas."

Lattimore's admiration for Russian "democracy" is characterized by the following passage in the same book:

"To all of these peoples the Russians and the Soviet Union have a great power of attraction. In their eyes —rather doubtfully in the eyes of the older generation, more and more clearly in the eyes of the younger generation—the Soviet Union stands for strategic security, economic prosperity, technological progress, miraculous medicine, free education, equality of opportunity, and democracy—a powerful combination."[236]

In another book, Lattimore writes:

"Throughout Asia today there prevails an atmosphere of hope, not of despair. There is not a single country in Asia in which people feel that we are entering on an age of chaos. What they see opening out before them is a limitless horizon of hope—the hope of peaceful constructive activity in free countries and peaceful cooperation among free peoples."[237]

The Communist *New Masses* on May 8, 1945, had this to say about one of Lattimore's books:

"*Solution in Asia* is a *must* book not only for our San Francisco delegates but for every one of us."

Lattimore Book "Required Reading" At Official Communist School

(25) According to sworn testimony given to the McCarran Committee by Harvey Matusow, an undercover FBI agent, Lattimore's book *Solution in Asia* was recommended by the New York State Educational Department of the Communist Party to all Communist Party members.

Matusow, a former member of the Communist Party, worked in three Communist Party bookstores. He testified that Lattimore's book and four others "were basically the books that the Party stated carried out Party line on China."

Matusow further testified that Lattimore's *Solution in Asia* was required reading for students at the Jefferson School of Social Science, a school run by the Communist

[233] McCarran Committee Hearings on IPR, Pt. 4, Oct. 1, 1951, pp. 1035-1074, Oct. 6, 1951, pp. 1111-1138, Pt. 5, Oct. 12, 1951, pp. 1251-1277.
[234] Henry Wallace, Soviet Asia Mission, p. 172.
[235] Congressional Record (Bound), Aug. 16, 1950, p. 12600.
[236] Owen Lattimore, Solution in Asia, (Little, Brown & Co., 1945), p. 139.
[237] Lattimore, The Situation in Asia, p. 238.

Party in New York City for the purpose of teaching Marxism and Leninism.[238]

It should perhaps be noted in passing that the Communist newspaper, *The People's Daily World,* which is the *Daily Worker* of the West Coast, ran an advertisement on June 8, 1945, urging their Communist readers to buy the books of Owen Lattimore, Communist Frederick Vanderbilt Field (who recently served a prison term in connection with the Communist trials in New York), and Communist William Z. Foster (convicted former head of the American Communist Party).

The books of these three individuals were being featured by the International Book Store in San Francisco which has been officially cited by the California Committee on Un-American Activities as "the Communist Party book center in the Bay area for the distribution of *its literature.*"[239]

Incidentally, when President Truman announced the surrender of Japan in 1945, according to newstories only two books appeared on the President's desk—one was Lattimore's *Solution in Asia.*

Lattimore's writing can perhaps be best summed up in the words of Freda Utley, well-known anti-Communist writer and lecturer who was formerly a member of the British Communist Party:

> "Soviet Russia, in all of Lattimore's writings, is always sinned against and is always represented by Lattimore as standing like a beacon of hope for the peoples of Asia, even when she is collaborating with the Nazis or aggressing on her own account. Russia is never in the wrong and if he is forced to take cognizance of a few slight misdemeanors on her part, he excuses them as only a reaction to American imperialism or some other country's misdeeds."[240]

Favorably Reviews Party Line Writings

(26) The Communist cause benefited greatly by Lattimore's book reviews for the New York *Times* and the New York *Herald Tribune,* in which he consistently endorsed and praised such books on China as those of Edgar Snow, Israel Epstein, Gunther Stein, and Laurence Rosinger.* Those books which received Lattimore's praise gave the Communist line on China, including the idea that the Chinese Communists represented the party of land reform, free and improved education, better sanitary conditions, and agrarian reform. In turn, of course, pro-Communists reviewed Lattimore's books in glowing terms.[242]

Part of Lattimore's New York *Times* review of Israel Epstein's book *The Unfinished Revolution in China,* follows:

> "In the last ten years, American writers have taken the lead over all others in raising the level of description and analysis in writing about China. From Edgar Snow's *Red Star Over China* to Theodore White and Annalee Jacoby's *Thunder Out of China,* the list of names is distinguished—and most of these writers won their distinction solely or primarily by what they had to say about China. Israel Epstein has without question established a place for himself in that distinguished company . . . It is noteworthy that the recent and current trend of good books about China, well-documented and well-written, has been well to the left of center . . ."[243]

Following is some recent sworn testimony on Lattimore given to the McCarran Committee.

Lattimore's Character Witness Refuses To Answer Whether He Was Member of Communist Party On Day He Defended Lattimore

Daniel Thorner, Assistant Professor of Economic History, University of Pennsylvania, testified on March 25, 1952, as follows:

> MR. MORRIS: "Mr. Thorner, did you hold a fellowship at the Walter Hines Page School at Johns Hopkins University?"
>
> MR. THORNER: "I did, Mr. Morris, in the year 1947-48."
>
> MR. MORRIS: "Who arranged for you to have that fellowship at Walter Hines Page School?"
>
> MR. THORNER: "Mr. Owen Lattimore invited me to accept an appointment as a Page School fellow . . ."
>
> MR. MORRIS: "Mr. Thorner, were you a contributor or a Co-Author with Owen Lattimore to *Pivot in Asia?*"
>
> MR. THORNER: "Yes . . ."
>
> SENATOR FERGUSON: "Who asked you to help on that volume?"
>
> MR. THORNER: "Mr. Lattimore asked me . . ."
>
> SENATOR FERGUSON: "At the time that you wrote that, I ask you the question as to whether or not you were a member of the Communist Party?"
>
> MR. THORNER: "I must respectfully decline, Senator, on the grounds of the First and Fifth Amendments and all other Constitutional rights and privileges [on the grounds of self-incrimination] . . ."
>
> MR. MORRIS: "Mr. Thorner, several years ago, Owen Lattimore appeared before the Senate Foreign Relations Committee."
>
> MR. THORNER: "Yes, sir."
>
> MR. MORRIS: "Do you know whether or not he sent in your name as a person who wrote in a letter on his behalf, expressing respect and admiration for his writings at that time?"
>
> MR. THORNER: ". . . I wrote Mr. Lattimore a letter at that time expressing my support of him . . ."
>
> MR. MORRIS: "At that time, were you a member of the Communist Party, Mr. Thorner?"
>
> MR. THORNER: "I must respectfully decline to answer that question [on the grounds of self-incrimination]."[244]

---

* All four named under oath by government witnesses as Communists.

[238] McCarran Committee Hearings on IPR, March 13, 1952 (now being printed).
[239] California Committee on Un-American Activities Report, 1947, p. 100.
[240] Tydings Committee Hearings, Pt. 1, May 1, 1950, p. 746.
[242] See Speech of Senator Owen Brewster, Congressional Record, June 5, 1951, p. 6301.
[243] New York Times, June 22, 1947.
[244] McCarran Committee Hearings on IPR, March 25, 1952 (now being printed).

IPR "Double-Way Track" to Russia

Igor Bogolepov, former Red Army officer, testified on April 7, 1952, before the McCarran Committee on Lattimore's record. Bogolepov, a graduate of Russia's University of Petrograd, has held a variety of positions in the Red Army and in the Russian government. He testified as follows about the Institute of Pacific Relations, which according to the evidence was dominated by Jessup, Field, Carter, and Lattimore:

MR. BOGOLEPOV: "I got the impression from talks with my comrades working in the Soviet Institute of Pacific Relations, in the foreign office, that they considered this institute as a very valuable organization from two points of view. As one of my former comrades expressed it, it is like a double-way track. On one line you got information from America through this Institute. On the other hand, you send information which you would like to implant in American brains through the same channel of the Institute."

THE CHAIRMAN: "What was the double-way track that you refer to?"

MR. BOGOLEPOV: "I mean two channels. One was the ingoing channel, the second outgoing channel."

THE CHAIRMAN: "What was that?"

MR. BOGOLEPOV: "The ingoing channel was military intelligence. We extracted military information."

MR. MORRIS: "When you talk about two-way track, do you mean that military intelligence was extracted from outside the Soviet Union through the medium of the Institute of Pacific Relations?"

MR. BOGOLEPOV: "That is right."

MR. MORRIS: "And on the other hand, by the outway track you mean information that you wanted to impart to the outside world was transmitted through that medium?"

MR. BOGOLEPOV: "Yes."

Lattimore Selected for Important Job By Litvinoff, Former Russian Ambassador

On page 7534 of the transcript of the Hearings, Bogolepov first discusses a conversation held between himself and Litvinoff, one-time Russian Ambassador to the United States, about the necessity of propagandizing the American people along certain lines. Bogolepov first explains that he and Litvinoff decided they had to pick a man who could "mobilize public sentiment in the West." His testimony thereafter follows:

SENATOR EASTLAND: "Who was that man who was decided upon?"

MR. BOGOLEPOV: "Litvinoff asked the officer of Mongolian Desk of the Foreign Office, who was present—"

MR. MORRIS: "What was his name?"

MR. BOGOLEPOV: "Parnoch, P-a-r-n-o-c-h—whom he would recommend, and before Parnoch could give his answer he asked 'Lattimore, perhaps?' "

SENATOR EASTLAND: "Litvinoff said 'Lattimore?' "

MR. BOGOLEPOV: " 'Lattimore, perhaps,' yes. And Parnoch answered, 'Yes, we will try to do that.' "

MR. MORRIS: "Was there a formal decision made by that body?"

MR. BOGOLEPOV: "There was a formal decision which was obliging for the corresponding bodies of the Soviet foreign group to take measures in order to fulfill the decision."

Bogolepov, the former Russian Red Army officer, testified as follows about Frederick Schuman, a university professor and part-time State Department lecturer whose case I gave to the Tydings Committee:

SENATOR FERGUSON: "Do you know of any other example of an American coming to Russia and getting materials and coming back and its being published?"

MR. BOGOLEPOV: ". . . Frederick Schuman [who wrote], 'Soviet Politics Abroad and at Home.' "

SENATOR FERGUSON: "What did he write on?"

MR. BOGOLEPOV: "He wrote a book which in my opinion is full of nonsense."

MR. FERGUSON: "Outside of its being nonsense, what was it on?"

MR. BOGOLEPOV: "It was very important nonsense because if you learned the wrong things about the Soviet Union, your thoughts are also wrong. That was the idea, to sell nonsense to the foreign newspapers."

SENATOR WATKINS: "Can you give us an example?"

MR. BOGOLEPOV: "Yes."

SENATOR FERGUSON: "Give us an example of what was in the book."

MR. BOGOLEPOV: "All right, for example, the book by Frederick Schuman stated that the unfriendly attitude of the Soviet Union toward the Western world was not caused by Communist doctrine or any other consideration on the part of the Soviet leaders themselves, but it was caused by Western intervention during the civil war [in Russia]. Mr. Schuman lets the American readers of his book believe that it is only because the American, Japanese, French and English people made their so-called intervention on the side of the Russian national against the Communist that the Communist Soviet Union is now reluctant to have good relations with the British. If you compare Schuman's book with the corresponding page of the official *History of the Communist Party of Soviet Union* you will very easily recognize that they say the same things. Frederick Schuman got his ideas from the Soviet propaganda."

SENATOR FERGUSON: "Do you know of any others?"

MR. BOGOLEPOV: "I recall Mr. Joseph Davies [Father-in-law and law partner of former Senator Tydings], the former American Ambassador to Moscow. Mr. Davies was in very good relations to Foreign Commissar Litvinoff, in such good relations—"

THE CHAIRMAN: "Joseph Davies?"

MR. BOGOLEPOV: "Davies!—in such good relations that some of the instructions which this American Ambassador received from the State Department—"

SENATOR FERGUSON: "You mean the American State Department?"

MR. BOGOLEPOV: "That is right—along confidential lines were simply read by the American Ambassador to Foreign Commissar Litvinoff. He received a cable from Washington. He came to the office of Litvinoff and he consulted Litvinoff on what to do with this cable."

On page 7528 of the hearings Bogolepov testified:

MR. BOGOLEPOV: "As I told you, besides my work for the foreign office, I was also a member of the Institute [IPR], a research worker, and I used to work two or three times a week in the library of this institute. In this library, by the way, worked also Mrs. Freda Utley, which name I remember having seen during your investigations. And when I was working in this library one of these mornings, a group of people entered the room, the library headed by Eugene Varga, who was director of the Institute."

THE CHAIRMAN: "How do you spell that?"

MR. BOGOLEPOV: "Varga, V-a-r-g-a. Eugene Varga. There were in this group of people some of them which were known to me and some which were unknown to me. Among the people known to me, I remember Mr. Abramson, Mr. Kantorovich, and Mr. Kara-Murza."

MR. MORRIS: "Let me ask you to pause there. Varga was a Comintern man?"

MR. BOGOLEPOV: "Varga was a member of the Executive Committee of the Comintern, the highest body."

MR. MORRIS: "What was Kara-Murza?"

MR. BOGOLEPOV: "Kara-Murza was intelligence officer in charge of Mongolian Relations."

MR. MORRIS: "Abramson?"

MR. BOGOLEPOV: "Abramson, as I told you, was a member of the Pacific group of this Institute, and at the same time also intelligence officer."

MR. MORRIS: "And then you say among them was Owen Lattimore? . . ."

MR. BOGOLEPOV: "Was two or more foreigners, and among them was Mr. Lattimore."

Bogolepov then goes on to describe how the three above named Russian Communists discussed with Lattimore the Communist aims in Mongolia, including the job they were doing of "purging the Mongolian population from the parasitic class of clergymen." According to Bogolepov they also pointed out on a map the road followed by the Russians through Mongolia to Manchuria. Bogolepov tells how, after Lattimore and the others left, he asked Kara-Murza, the above-mentioned Communist intelligence officer, to remain and suggested that he spoke too freely

before foreign visitors and was assured that it was "quite all right" to discuss such secret matters before them.[245]

In what official capacity has Lattimore represented the United States Government?

U. S. Aide to Chiang Kai-shek

(1) In 1941 Lattimore was appointed by the President as political adviser to Chiang Kai-shek in China.[246] As previously pointed out, the official Communist position at that time was to aid Chiang because, while Chiang was an enemy of Communism at that time, he was fighting Japan who was a more powerful enemy to world Communism than China.

Pacific Head of OWI

(2) From 1942 to 1945, Lattimore was first deputy director of Pacific Operations of the Office of War Information and then a consultant to the OWI.[247]

Member of Japanese Reparations Mission

(3) In October, 1945, Lattimore was appointed by the President as a member of the Pauley Reparations Mission to Japan. According to Lattimore's book, he was paid for his "services" by the State Department.[248]

Accompanied Vice President Wallace on China Mission

(4) In 1945 Lattimore, together with John Carter Vincent, accompanied Vice President Henry Wallace on his trip to China. As a result of this trip, Wallace prepared a report outlining a policy toward China for the United States. Wallace in the book he wrote on his return, *Soviet Asia Mission*, pays tribute to Lattimore for his invaluable assistance on this project of recommending a China policy to the State Department. He further states that President Roosevelt "urged me to take Owen Lattimore with me, who, he said, was *one of the world's great experts on the problems involving Chinese Russian relationships*."[249]

Lectured at State Department

(5) In 1946 Lattimore lectured and indoctrinated State Department foreign service officials during a State Department training course.[250]

Advised Truman Before Potsdam

(6) Two days before President Truman left for Potsdam where surrender terms with Japan were to be decided upon, Acheson, according to the following news-story, in a left-wing Washington newspaper, used Lattimore in an attempt to get President Truman to go along with the Communist plans for Japan:

"Finally, in order to convince Truman [to follow what was then the Communist line] Acheson asked him to discuss the matter with Owen Lattimore, one of the foremost American authorities on China and former adviser to Chiang Kai-shek.

245 McCarran Committee Hearings on IPR, April 7, 1952 (now being printed).
246 Lattimore, Ordeal By Slander, p. 67.
247 Lattimore, Ordeal By Slander, p. 67.
248 Lattimore, Ordeal By Slander, p. 66.
249 Wallace, Soviet Asia Mission, p. 17.
250 Washington Times-Herald, June 6, 1946.

"Lattimore talked to Truman for 30 minutes just two days before he departed for Potsdam. The President listened most carefully but made no comment."[251]

The fact that this meeting between Lattimore and Truman actually occurred was confirmed by former State Department official Eugene Dooman in his testimony before the McCarran Committee.[252]

Lattimore admitted, under cross-examination by the McCarran Committee, that he had a conference with the President and gave the President a written memorandum of his recommended postwar foreign policy for the United States.[253] One of the committee members pointed out that the memorandum served almost as a blueprint for America's postwar pro-Communist foreign policy in China.

What was the President's attitude toward Owen Lattimore after you presented the evidence on him?

I will let the President answer that.

The following is the New York *Times* account of the President's press conference at Key West on March 31, 1950:

> "The President paid a glowing tribute to Senator McCarthy's three major targets: Dean Acheson, Secretary of State; Philip C. Jessup, senior adviser to Mr. Acheson; and Owen Lattimore, one-time consultant to the State Department on Far Eastern Affairs . . .
>
> " 'You don't believe he is a spy?' asked a reporter, referring to Mr. Carthy's charge that Mr. Lattimore was Russia's leading agent in this country.
>
> "Of course, he did not believe that, Mr. Truman replied with asperity. It was silly on the face of it and people recognized it, he said."

Shades of Red Herring

This praise of Lattimore was given by Truman despite the fact that a sizable number of government witnesses gave the following testimony under oath about Lattimore: (1) that he was trusted and relied upon by the Russian Communists, (2) that he was assigned by the Communists the task of shaping our foreign policy to serve the Communist cause, (3) that he was trusted and relied upon by the American Communists, (4) that he was trusted, relied upon, and his advice followed by the State Department in determining foreign policy.

What about your statement that Lattimore had a desk in the State Department?

In 1950 Lattimore denied this under oath, and the State Department ridiculed it. However, some light is shed on Lattimore's truthfulness as a result of his cross-examination by the McCarran committee on this subject.

In his book, *Ordeal by Slander*, advertised on its jacket as "completely honest," Lattimore wrote:

> "I told the newspapermen that Senator McCarthy was crazy if he had got me mixed up with the State Department. I had never been in the State Department."[254]

In 1950, in his sworn testimony before the Tydings Committee, Lattimore said:

> "I do not have a desk in the State Department. I do not have a telephone there."[255]

In 1952, however, when Lattimore was testifying before the McCarran Committee, letters were produced, signed by Lattimore, which showed he had regular hours in the office of Lauchlin Currie [named under oath as a member of a Communist spy ring] in the State Department building.[256] Only then did Lattimore admit under cross-examination that he did have a desk in the State Department Building.

[251] Washington Post, Aug. 14, 1945.
[252] McCarran Committee Hearings on IPR, Pt. 3, Sept. 14, 1951, pp. 730, 731.
[253] McCarran Committee Hearings on IPR, March 10, 1952 (now being printed).
[254] Lattimore, Ordeal by Slander, p. 5.
[255] Tydings Committee Hearings, Pt. 1, April 6, 1950, p. 421.
[256] McCarran Committee Hearings on IPR, Feb. 29, 1952 (now being printed).

CHAPTER VIII

General George C. Marshall

Why did you spend so much time preparing the Marshall speech—especially in view of the fact that you knew it would be an unpopular speech?

A number of things contributed to my decision to write the history of General George Marshall.

Some of the reasons are set forth in the following passages of my book, "America's Retreat from Victory":

"My discussion of General Marshall's career arose naturally and inevitably out of a long and anxious study of the retreat from victory which this Administration has been beating since 1945. In company with so many of my fellow citizens I have become alarmed and dismayed over our moral and material enfeeblement.

"The fact that 152 million American people are officially asked by the party in power to adopt Marshall's global strategy during a period of time when the life of our civilization hangs in the balance would seem to make it imperative that his complete record be subjected to the searching light of public scrutiny.

"As a backdrop for the history of Marshall which I gave on June 14th, there is the raw, harsh fact that since World War II the free world has been losing 100 million people per year to international Communism. If I had named the men responsible for our tremendous loss, all of the Administration apologists and the camp-following elements of press and radio led by the *Daily Worker* would have screamed 'the Big Lie,' 'irresponsible,' 'smear,' 'Congressional immunity,' etc., etc., etc.

"However, it was the Truman branch of the Democrat Party meeting at Denver, Colorado, which named the men responsible for the disaster which they called a 'great victory'—Dean Gooderham Acheson and George Catlett Marshall. By what tortured reasoning they arrived at the conclusion that the loss of 100 million people a year to Communism was a 'great victory,' was unexplained.

"The general picture of our steady, constant retreat from victory, with the same men always found at the time and place where disaster strikes America and success comes to Soviet Russia, would inevitably have caused me, or someone else deeply concerned with the history of this time, to document the acts of those molding and shaping the history of the world over the past decade. However, an occurrence during the Mac-Arthur investigation was the immediate cause of my decision to give the Senate and the country the history of Marshall.

"A deeply disturbed Senator from the Russell Committee came to my office for information. 'McCarthy,' he said, 'I have always considered Marshall as one of our great heroes and I am sure that he would knowingly do no wrong. But, McCarthy,' he said, 'tell me who prejudiced the thinking of this great man? Why, for example, did he keep from Roosevelt the complete and correct intelligence reports at Yalta? Why did he, as Roosevelt's military adviser, approve that Yalta agreement which was drafted by Hiss, Gromyko and Jebb? Who persuaded him at Yalta to disregard the intelligence report of 50 of his own officers, all with the rank of colonel or above—an intelligence report which urged a course directly contra to what was done at Yalta and confirmed at Potsdam?'

"He handed a copy of that report to me and asked: 'Why did a man of Marshall's intelligence ignore such a report as this compiled by 50 of his own top intelligence officers?'

"The Senator went on. 'McCarthy,' he said, 'who of evil allegiance to the Kremlin sold him on the disastrous Marshall Mission to China, where Marshall described one of his own acts as follows: "As Chief-of-Staff I armed 39 anti-Communist divisions. Now with a stroke of a pen I disarm them."

" 'When that was done,' he asked, 'who then persuaded Marshall to open Kalgan Mountain Pass, with the result that the Chinese Communists could make contact with the Russians and receive the necessary arms and ammunition to overrun all of China?'

" 'McCarthy, who on earth could have persuaded Marshall to side with Acheson and against American interests on the question of Formosa and the use of the Chinese Nationalist troops?'

"Upon searching for the answers for the Senator, I found to my surprise that no one had ever written the history of Marshall—Marshall, who, by the alchemy of propaganda became the 'greatest living American' and the recently proclaimed 'master of global strategy' by and for the party in power. In view of the fact that the committee, the Congress, and the American people were being called upon either to endorse or reject Marshall's 'global strategy,' I felt it was urgent that such a study be made and submitted to the Congress and the people."

Marshall's First Attempt to Make General

Another thing which particularly interested me in Marshall's history was the unusual story of his promotions and rise to power. For example, General Pershing unsuccessfully attempted to have Marshall given a generalship 15 years after World War I. According to Walter Trohan's article, "The Tragedy of George Marshall," Marshall grew impatient over slow promotion and sought the intercession of General Pershing with General Douglas MacArthur who was Chief of Staff. As Trohan puts it:

"MacArthur was ready to oblige, but insisted that the promotion go through regular channels. Pershing agreed, confident Marshall could clear the hurdles. Friendly examination of the Marshall record showed what his superiors regarded as insufficient time with troops. MacArthur proposed to remedy this, giving him command of the Eighth Regiment at Fort Screven, Georgia, one of the finest regiments in the Army.

Army Inspector General Rejected Promotion for Marshall

"Marshall was moved up from Lieutenant Colonel, but his way to a General's stars appeared to be blocked forever when the Inspector General reported that under one year of Marshall's command the Eighth Regiment had dropped from one of the best regiments in the Army to one of the worst. MacArthur regretfully informed Pershing that the report made promotion impossible. To this day Marshall is uneasy in the presence of MacArthur."[257]

Six Years Later Became Top Army Man

This interested me particularly because only six years later Roosevelt put Marshall in command of the entire United States Army. I wondered what happened to change the unsuccessful regimental Commander into the first choice of the President for the highest Army post in the country.

During the depression years Marshall became interested in the Civilian Conservation Corps, known as the CCC, and it was because of this that he came to the attention of those persons in Washington interested in this commendable project—among them Mrs. Roosevelt and Harry Hopkins. It was at this point that Marshall, whose only troop command in the field was reported by the Inspector General as a complete failure, suddenly became a Brigadier General and then a General.

Great Memory Fails on December 7, 1941

Another contributing factor in my decision to conduct a searching scrutiny of Marshall's history was the unusual testimony of Marshall concerning Pearl Harbor morning. Here was a man with a great memory, reportedly the greatest memory of any man in Government, but on the morning of Pearl Harbor, for some reason or other, the Chief of Staff had no idea where he was.

Most people who read this will remember exactly what he or she was doing on December 7, 1941, when the news broke of Japan's attack on Pearl Harbor. But Marshall, charged with the safety of those who died at Pearl Harbor, first said he was riding horseback, then changed that story to say he was with his wife. However, Arthur Upham Pope, in his book containing a diary of Litvinoff (who in 1941 was Russian Ambassador) states that Marshall, on the morning of December 7, 1941, was at the airport meeting Litvinoff. While it may seem unimportant whether Marshall was with a horse, with Litvinoff, or with his wife, it does cause one to wonder why this man with the great memory, the Chief of Staff, charged with the lives of so many men, could not remember where he was when the bombs began to fall.

Sends Pearl Harbor Warning by Commercial Wire

In connection with Pearl Harbor, there was something else that caused me to wonder about Marshall. I wondered why it was that when he was finally found and given the decoded message that the Japanese were about to attack, that instead of picking up the phone on his desk, which was a direct, certain, and immediate way to contact his Commanders in Hawaii, he yawned and sent the message by regular commercial telegraph. Because the warning of the Japanese attack reached Hawaii too late, thousands of American boys were shot, burned, drowned, suffocated, and crushed above and below the Hawaiian waters.

I have not tried to tell why Marshall acted as he did. But I did become deeply disturbed about this man who was such a mysterious figure, whose story was never written and who with Acheson was again being offered to us by the Party in power as the global strategist—the man whose strategy was to chart our future.

Conflicting Reports on Who Wrote Instructions for Marshall Mission

Another reason why I began to wonder about Marshall was the mystery which surrounded the question of who wrote the instructions which Marshall followed on his mission to China—which mission, according to Admiral Cooke and others, played such an important part in the betrayal of China. The high points of the Marshall Mission to China have been previously covered in Chapter V.

Let us briefly review the conflicting reports about who wrote the instructions.

General Marshall before the Senate Armed Service Committee, September 19, 1950, said:

"... The policy of the United States was being drawn up in the State Department, and that was issued while I was on the ocean going over there [China]."[258]

Before the Russell Committee, May 10, 1951, he said some people were saying:

"... that I sat down in the State Department and drew up this policy. I did not."[259]

Here is what Acheson, under oath, had to say about this same subject before the Russell Committee, June 4, 1951:

"At the end of November, 1945, Secretary Byrnes and General Marshall met. This was after General Marshall had been asked to go to China.

"Secretary Byrnes read him a memorandum suggesting the outline of instructions for him. General Marshall did not approve of it. General Marshall said he would wish to try his own hand, assisted by some of his associates, in drafting the instructions. This he did, and a draft was prepared by him ..."[260]

And James Byrnes, who was Secretary of State at the time of the Marshall Mission, has stated in his book, *Speaking Frankly*:

"The President made no change in that policy except upon the recommendation of General Marshall or with his approval."[261]

Like others, I too wondered who was telling the truth—whether Marshall spoke the truth when he said that he was on the ocean at the time the instructions were drafted and had nothing to do with drafting the secret instructions, or whether Secretaries Byrnes and Acheson spoke the truth when they said that Marshall drafted his own instructions and no changes were made unless he recommended or approved them.

Public Scrutiny Essential

The thing that is so inconceivable about much of the criticism of the Marshall history that I gave, is the type of objections which are raised. If a man is—as Marshall's friends claim he is—a great man, he should not object to having his life scrutinized in great detail. If he made mis-

[257] Walter Trohan, "The Tragedy of George Marshall," *American Mercury*, April, 1951, pp. 267-275.
[258] Senate Armed Services Committee, Nomination of Gen. George O. Marshall to be Secretary of Defense, Sept. 19, 1950, p. 21.
[259] Russell Committee Hearings, Pt. 2, May 10, 1951, p. 467.
[260] Russell Committee Hearings, Pt. 3, June 4, 1951, p. 1848.
[261] James Byrnes, *Speaking Frankly* (Harper Brothers, 1947), p. 226.

takes, that is no disgrace. Only those who do nothing make no mistakes. To prove that Marshall made mistakes does not indict Marshall of being either incompetent or of following the Communist cause.

One of my vigorous critics, a defender of Marshall, wrote the following in defense of Marshall:

"'The History of George Catlett Marshall' is well documented and makes an impressive case that Marshall's decisions were, on the whole, disastrously bad from the standpoint of American interests and promoted the interests of the Soviet Union. With this thesis I am in complete agreement. But I do not think that because Marshall's policy decisions were disastrous, it raises a question as to his patriotism."[262]

If as Marshall's defender admits, "Marshall's decisions were, on the whole, disastrously bad from the standpoint of American interests and promoted the interests of the Soviet Union," then in the name of 152 million Americans whose futures are affected by the "global strategist" of the party in power, his record should be held up to the bright light and coldly and clearly scrutinized in the absence of any synthetic flag-waving and hero-worshipping.

This perhaps answers the question of why I felt it was my duty to spend unlimited time and energy to bring his story to the attention of the American people.

Good or bad, I did not make Marshall's history. He did. I merely wrote it.

That I would be misquoted, misunderstood, damned, and pilloried if I gave the uncolored facts became obvious as I began to delve into the history of Marshall. I knew the storm of opposition which awaited any man who dared to lay hands upon the laurels of a man who by the alchemy of propaganda became a great war hero—an unusual war hero, who during 50 years as a soldier spent less time within range of enemy bullets than any other war hero in recorded history.

Some of my well-meaning friends were horrified when they learned I planned to give a history of Marshall which was not completely complimentary of him. As one of my good friends in the Senate said, "McCarthy, criticize Abraham Lincoln or George Washington, but if you want to come back to the Senate, lay off George Marshall." Many of my other friends told me how unwise it would be from the political standpoint to intimate that Marshall actually was not the great hero into which he has been built. I gave my answer to them in a speech to the National Convention of Young Republicans at Boston in the following language:

"I recently prepared a documented history of Marshall—a documented history of his acts over the past ten years. Some of my good friends urged that I not do that—and they have urged that I not talk about Marshall tonight—because, they say, it is *politically* unwise.

"It reminds me of the advice I got 16 months ago when we started to bring out the facts on Dean Gooderham Acheson and some of the others who have been so bad for this country. Let me remind those well-meaning friends that the reason the world is in such a horrible condition today is that so many two-bit politicians do only those things they think are politically wise—only that which is safe for their own puny political futures.

"You young people here tonight will be running this country some day. I ask you in the name of Western civilization not to follow the disastrous footsteps of those who say, 'Don't do anything that is politically unwise.' If a task—unpleasant as it may be—must be done, do it. Otherwise, this nation, this civilization will pass from the face of the earth as surely as did those great empires of the past which were destroyed because of weak leadership which tolerated corruption, disloyalty, and dishonesty because that was the easier path to follow and perhaps to them the 'politically expedient' course.

"I have been through this nation much in the past year—from the Atlantic to the Pacific, from New Orleans to St. Paul. The American people are desperately searching, hoping and praying for leadership. They are not looking for men who only do the things that are politically wise or those who measure every act in terms of the votes gotten."[263]

Did you accuse Marshall of being a traitor?

No. I very carefully put together the history of General Marshall as it was found piecemeal in the writings of his friends and those who were neutral to him. I avoided quoting his enemies. I gave for the first time the complete, coldly-documented history of General George C. Marshall, as drawn by the pens of those who actively participated in World War II, or who were writing the story of the events as they happened. It was a tedious, disagreeable task. But it had to be done.

Right or wrong, brilliant or stupid, patriot or traitor, Marshall is one of the most important figures, if not the most important, in the last 10 years. If the history of that 10-year period is to be understood, Marshall's record must be understood.

Will you compare the Forrestal Plan, known as the Truman Plan for Greece and Turkey, with the Marshall Plan for Europe?

The Forrestal plan—which Truman fortunately adopted for Greece and Turkey—provided for all the necessary military aid to people who themselves were willing to fight Communism. While sufficient economic aid was given to make the military aid effective and workable, the emphasis at all times was to be on military aid. The Forrestal Plan proved very successful.

The Marshall Plan was directly opposite to the Forrestal Plan for Greece and Turkey. It consisted of giving the maximum economic aid with a minimum of military aid. The Marshall Plan fitted perfectly with Communist Russia's desire for a power vacuum in all of Western Europe.

The Forrestal Plan would have included Spain. The Marshall Plan excluded Spain, but originally included Russia. Russia, however, turned it down.

I voted for the Marshall Plan because it had some good aspects, for example, the feeding of the starving people of Europe. I strongly maintained then that the food and clothing which we were giving should be on the basis of need of the people themselves rather than

262 Tower Phelan, The Freeman, Feb. 11, 1952, p. 298.
263 Speech before National Convention of Young Republicans, June 29, 1951, Hotel Statler, Boston.

a gift to the governments involved, which sold it to the starving people on the basis of ability to pay. Another point which I maintained at that time was that the money for the rehabilitation of industry should have been loaned directly to the industry in question, taking back what security that industry had to offer instead of funneling the money through tottering, corrupt, and socialistic governments as the Marshall Plan proposed to do. Nevertheless, in the end I voted for it because it was a case of Marshall Plain aid for Europe or nothing.

What was the general newspaper reaction to your speech on Marshall?

Perhaps the best answer to this question is contained in the following columns and editorials:

George Sokolsky

"The immediate newspaper reports were based not upon the Senator's 60,000-word speech, but on a supposition of what he might have said.

"In current journalism, this is called 'high-lighting' and is generally inaccurate and distorted.

"So I waited until I could get a full copy of the speech; read the whole of 60,000 words and realized that the Senator had done a decent job of research and analysis.

". . . [His] bibliography is important because it shows not a single enemy—personal or political— of General Marshall, unless it be Winston Churchill, with whom Marshall did not see eye-to-eye during phases of the war.

"The point of this piece is to suggest that the speech ought to be read; ought to be taken seriously; and should be discussed.

"It is apparent throughout that Senator McCarthy, while not approving of General Marshall, devotes most of his long speech not to his own views but to quotations from others." (Column of July 1, 1951.)

Washington Times-Herald

"Senator Joe McCarthy made a 60,000 word speech about General Marshall on June 14. The kept columnists and newspaper errand boys of the Pendergast mobsters have been screeching the house down ever since.

"They have suggested the Senator is a skunk, traitor, mudslinger, faker of facts and all around candidate for horse-whipping. Are they right?

"We don't see how anybody possibly say unless and until after examining the evidence. And right here and now, we will place a small bet . . . that not one of those who have been calling Joe McCarthy names since June 14th has actually done the basic homework job of reading the speech itself. . . .

"The writer of this editorial has read McCarthy's speech and finds it is a challenge that will have to be met and dealt with, sooner or later." (Editorial of June 24, 1951.)

Polk County Ledger
Balsam Lake, Wis.

"We listened and read with growing alarm the comments of the daily press and radio. We heard Mc-

Carthy charged with crimes ranging from blasphemy to mere political dishonesty. Yet we were impressed, as we have been impressed on previous occasions, with the studied refusal of the McCarthy critics to discuss his basic charges. Nowhere did we read or hear direct references to McCarthy's text, or direct quotations from it. The critics simply told us that McCarthy had engaged in a wholesale slander of General Marshall. We began to suspect that there might be a vast difference between what McCarthy said, and what the critics who disagree with him would have us believe he said.

"So we did the logical thing—the thing the critics didn't do. We read the full text of McCarthy's speech on 'America's Retreat—The Story of George Catlett Marshall.' We read all 48 pages of it (not printed at government expense) direct from the Congressional Record."

Time Magazine perhaps best represents the attitude of those newspapers and magazines which sacrificed truth in reporting the Marshall speech. The reason for such complete distortion seems to lie in their continuous efforts to discredit McCarthy since the beginning of his exposure of Communist infiltration in government.

Here is how *Time* Magazine reported the Marshall speech:

". . . an attack on Secretary of Defense George Marshall by Wisconsin's poison-tipped Joe McCarthy . . . in familiar fashion, McCarthy twisted quotes, drew unwarranted conclusions from the facts he did get right . . ."[264]

Thereafter I suggested to Henry Luce, Editor of *Time, Life* and *Fortune,* that if *Time* knew of a single quotation that was twisted or a single statement that was untrue, they should point it out to me. To this date they have found no untruth or misquotation.

In order to understand the attitude of such publications as *Time* Magazine, it is important to review some of the adjectives used by *Time* during my anti-Communist fight.

"Loud-mouthed . . . irresponsible . . . wretched burlesque . . . completely without evidence . . . hashed-over charges . . . scarehead publicity . . . tired old loyalty cases . . . desperate gambler . . . conspiratorial secrecy . . . mad man . . weasel-worded statements . . . Senatorial immunity . . . noisily charging . . . vituperative smear . . . wild charges."

When one analyzes the camp-following, left-wing "news" coverage and comment on a carefully and thoroughly documented speech such as the Marshall speech, the question that arises is: Why the deliberate distortion and suppression? This question is discussed to some extent in the chapter entitled "The Smear."

The twisted reporting by a combination of Communist and left-wing, camp-following elements of press and radio, and the government-subsidized elements of the same, made it necessary for me to publish the history of Marshall in book form so that it would be available to the people of this nation.

264 Time Magazine, June 25, 1951, pp. 20, 21.

CHAPTER IX

The Tydings Committee

What was the Tydings Committee and why was it set up?

The Tydings Committee was set up as a result of information which I gave the Senate about the Communist connections of a sizable number of present and past State Department employees. I gave the Senate a brief review of the files of 81 individuals who were then or had been closely connected with the State Department. At that time I informed the Senate that I did not have the staff, the power of subpoena, or the facilities to produce all of the available evidence against those individuals, but that the evidence which I had clearly indicated that many of them were either Communists or doing the work of the Communist Party. Others were marginal cases who might be able to prove their loyalty.

The Senate thereupon voted unanimously that the Foreign Relations Committee should hold hearings. It ordered that committee to subpoena all of the files on those named by me. The Tydings Committee was given all the money, investigators, and power it needed to do the job.

The Tydings Committee was, of course, carefully selected to do the job which it finally did. At that time there was in existence a Special Senate Investigating Committee fully staffed with competent investigators which could have done the job. The Judiciary Committee, headed by a great American who is anti-Communist, Senator Pat McCarran, also could have done the job. But the Foreign Relations Committee was selected. The reason for choosing that committee can best be described in the words of ex-Senator Scott Lucas when he said on the Senate floor:

> "All we are trying to do is to give the Committee on Foreign Relations jurisdiction of the proposed investigation, rather than have the Committee on the Judiciary or the Committee on Expenditures in the Executive Departments, or some other committee immediately take jurisdiction . . ."[265]

Here we have notification from Democrat Leader Lucas that the reason for selecting the Tydings Committee was to make sure that no other committee would go into the matter. It seemed obvious in view of this that the committee was not formed to make a complete investigation but to prevent a real investigation. Why the Administration feared an investigation has, of course, since become obvious.

The Tydings Committee was ordered to obtain all of the files which might contain information on those you named. What files were they supposed to get?

State Department files, Civil Service Commission files, FBI files, Naval Intelligence files, Army Intelligence files, Secret Service files, and Central Intelligence Agency files.

Did the Tydings Committee obey the order of the Senate and subpoena all the files?

No.

What, if any, files were obtained by the Tydings Committee?

The loose leaf State Department files.

Why were not the files of the Central Intelligence Agency, Civil Service Commission, FBI, Naval Intelligence, Army Intelligence, and Secret Service subpoenaed by the Committee?

In this respect Tydings should not take the full blame because the President publicly announced that he would defy the Senate subpoena for the loyalty files, saying he would stand pat on his 1948 order instructing all government departments to refuse to let Congress look at loyalty records of Government employees. At the same time President Truman indicated that he would make available any files which would *disprove* Senator McCarthy's charges of Communist infiltration.[266]

In other words, if a file would prove that a man was guilty of treason or Communist activities, the Committee, according to Truman, could not see that file. If the file would prove that McCarthy was wrong then the file could be seen by the committee.

You have stated that the loose leaf State Department files which the Tydings Committee obtained had been stripped of all information about Communist activities before they were shown to the committee. Tydings claimed this was untrue. What evidence do you have to support your claim?

I gave to the Senate and to the Tydings Committee the written statements of four of the State Department employees—one of whom is now an FBI agent—who did the actual job of removing from the State Department files all evidence of Communist activities.[267] A reproduction of one of the four statements appears on the following page.

Tydings denied that the files had been tampered with —in spite of those signed statements. He refused to call Paul Sullivan or any of the four who stated they were willing to testify under oath that they themselves had removed material in State Department files. He announced he was calling on the Department of Justice to tell him whether the files had been stripped or tampered with.

On June 21, Tydings told newspaper reporters that "a special inquiry by the FBI has established as false McCarthy's accusations that the files had been raped, skeletonized, or tampered with in any way." On the

265 Congressional Record (Unbound), Feb. 21, 1950, pp. 2105, 2106.
266 Washington Times-Herald, Feb. 24, 1950, p. 1.
267 Congressional Record (Unbound) July 12, 1950, pp. 10137-10139;
Congressional Record (Unbound) July 25, 1950, pp. 11108-11109.

The following information is given by me freely and voluntarily without any promises whatsoever. I furnish this information because it is the truth and I feel it is my patriotic duty to furnish the facts as I experienced them.

I am living at 1902 North Fifteenth Street, Arlington, Virginia at the present time.

In August 1946 I was released from the U. S. Navy in California. I came to Washington, D. C. and while in Washington, D. C. I was looking for a job. I went into the Walker Johnson building of State Department at 18th & New York Ave., N.W. I talked to a fellow in the State Department by the name of Holcombe. I got a temporary clerical job in the files at the Walker Johnson Bldg. These files were the Departmental personnel files located in the Walker Johnson Bldg. I started work on these files on Sept. 1946. When I reported for duty I was told that I would be working on a project on these files. This project had been going on for some time before I started. There were at least 8 persons who were working on this project.

I was not formally and specifically instructed as to what the purpose of the project was, but from what I was instructed by the other clerks, I and the other clerks were to go through each personnel file and pull out all derogatory material from the file. In addition to the usual personnel forms, the files contained all kinds of letters, reports, memorandum concerning the individual person. As per instructions I received, all of the clerks on this project were to pull out of the files all matters considered derogatory either morally or politically.

The project was very confused but I and the other clerks pulled out of each personnel file any material which could be considered derogatory. This material was removed and some was thrown in wastebaskets by us and some was thrown in a cardboard box. I don't know what happened to the derogatory material we pulled out from the files but I do know of my own knowledge that a good lot of it was destroyed.

I do not recall details of each personnel file I examined, but the material I pulled out of the files pertained to either the morals of the person or in some way reflected on his or her loyalty. I recall one thick report on one State Department employee who was accused of being a photographer and a member of some subversive organization which published some sort of news report. This was removed from the file and disposed of.

I worked from September till the end of December 1946 working on this file project pulling out and disposing of the derogatory material as per my understanding given me.

I left on Dec. 31, 1946 and this project on the personnel files was still not finished, but my temporary appointment ran out and my employment with the State Dept. ended.

I can't recall who the official in charge of these files was. I met him only a very few times but I could easily recognize him if I saw him.

I have read this statement of three pages and the facts are true to the best of my knowledge and belief.

Signed

Paul E. Sullivan

July 6, 1950
1902 N. 15th Street
JAckson 4—0369

Witnessed:

Donald A. Surine
July 6, 1950

(Copy)

Tydings Asserts F. B. I. Cleared State Dept. Files

Says Check-Up Showed No Loyalty Data Tampering as Charged by McCarthy

By Raymond J. Blair

WASHINGTON, June 21.—A check by the F. B. I. has failed to substantiate Senator Joseph R. McCarthy's charge that eighty-one State Department loyalty files have been "raped" to eliminate damaging evidence, Senator Millard E. Tydings, Democrat, of Maryland, said today.

Senator Tydings is chairman of the Senate Foreign Relations subcommittee that has been intermittently investigating charges by Senator McCarthy, Republican, of Wisconsin, of communism in the State Department. The loyalty records were made available to the Tydings subcommittee May 4 by President Truman. Senator McCarthy recently charged they had been "raped, skeletonized or tampered with" so that they did not contain all of the relevant material.

Senator Tydings told reporters that upon hearing Senator McCarthy's charge, he asked the Justice Department to investigate. Today he received the department's report, he said, in a letter from Peyton Ford, assistant to Attorney General J. Howard McGrath.

The report said, Senator Tydings stated, that a study by F.B.I. agents had shown the files were "intact" and that all F. B. I. material on the eighty-one individuals involved, whom Senator McCarthy has accused of Communist leanings, was included.

Senator Tydings also said that study of the files would be completed by the subcommittee Sunday night. It was not clear, however, whether this program was acceptable to all subcommittee members.

McCARTHY IS HELD REFUTED ON FILES

Tydings Says F. B. I. Reports Dossiers Not Tampered With —Group to End Examination

By WILLIAM S. WHITE
Special to The New York Times.

WASHINGTON, June 21—Senate investigators will close on Sunday night their two-month examination of eighty-one confidential State Department loyalty files and will return them at once to the Administration.

This was disclosed today by Senator Millard E. Tydings, Democrat of Maryland, chairman of the Senate Foreign Relations subcommittee reading the dossiers in the White House in its investigation of Senator Joseph R. McCarthy's charges of communism in the State Department.

At the same time, Mr. Tydings asserted that a special inquiry by the Federal Bureau of Investigation had established as false Mr. McCarthy's accusations that the files had been "raped" before being turned over to the subcommittee.

A letter just received from Peyton Ford, First Assistant Attorney General, stated, that Senator Tydings added, that a special inquiry made by the Federal Bureau of Investigation produced the following results:

"That the files are intact, that they have not been raped, skeletonized or tampered with in any way and that the material turned over to the State Department by the F. B. I. is still in the files."

McCarthy charges are not substantiated by the facts." He declared himself unable to give out the text of Mr. Ford's letter because it would disclose the names of some of the persons whose files were under study.

OFFICE OF THE DIRECTOR

Federal Bureau of Investigation
United States Department of Justice
Washington 25, D. C.

July 10, 1950

Honorable Joseph R. McCarthy
United States Senate
Washington, D. C.

My dear Senator:

    I have received your letter dated June 27, 1950 inquiring whether this Bureau has examined the 81 loyalty files which the members of the Tydings Committee have been scrutinizing and whether such an examination by the FBI has disclosed that the files are complete and that nothing has been removed therefrom.

    The Federal Bureau of Investigation has made no such examination and therefore is not in a position to make any statement concerning the completeness or incompleteness of the State Department files.

    For your information, the Federal Bureau of Investigation furnished Mr. Ford, at his request, a record of all loyalty material furnished the State Department in the 81 cases referred to. For your further information, I am enclosing a copy of Mr. Ford's letter to Senator Tydings which I have secured from the Attorney General.

Sincerely yours,

J. Edgar Hoover

Enclosure

BY SPECIAL MESSENGER

The above reproductions of two newsstories demonstrate the typical deliberate misrepresentations engaged in by the Tydings Committee and the State Department during the entire course of the Tydings Investigation. It will be noted that the letter of J. Edgar Hoover, Director of the Federal **Bureau** of Investigation clearly brands the Tydings statement in the above newsstories as a lie.

previous page will be found reproductions of news stories on this Tydings' interview.

The matter would have ended there had not I decided to ask J. Edgar Hoover, the head of the FBI, about this. Mr. Hoover replied on July 10 that this was not true—that the FBI had not made an investigation of the files during the time the files were available to the committee.

"The Federal Bureau of Investigation has made no such examination," Mr. Hoover wrote, "and therefore is not in a position to make any statement concerning the completeness or incompleteness of the State Department files." His complete letter appears on the previous page.

Hoover's statement, the direct opposite of Tydings', was taken to the floor of the Senate and presented so all the country could see.

Had it not been for J. Edgar Hoover's frank and honest report the truth never would have been known.

Following Hoover's letter, Tydings tried again to cover-up this story through the following sequence of events:

(1) On June 16, 1950, Peyton Ford, the man who was at all times present and in charge of State Department files while the Tydings Committee "examined" them, obtained from the FBI copies of all FBI material previously sent to the State Department which should have been in the files. Proof of this is found in a letter from Ford to Tydings, dated July 17, which Tydings refused to show the press or put in the record. A copy of this letter was obtained by me and given to the press.

(2) Nearly a month later, July 20, after there was ample time to insert the above material in the files and *after the committee no longer had access to the files*, the Justice Department ordered the FBI to examine the files, to determine whether the material which it had sent to Ford on June 16 was now in the State Department files. Obviously the material was now in the files. Otherwise, why the request of the FBI to send its material to Peyton Ford who was in charge of the State Department files.

(3) Long after the Tydings "investigation" ended, J. Edgar Hoover was ordered by the Department of Justice to write a letter to Tydings describing the condition of the files. This he did, under date of September 8. That letter truthfully stated that the files, when examined by them—not during any of the time that the Committee was allegedly looking at the files but long thereafter—were then complete.

Rather involved, but a typical example of the committee's attempt to hide behind the excellent reputation of the FBI.

If the Tydings Committee was formed for the purpose of investigating your charges of Communists in Government, why was not all of your evidence given to that Committee?

Being a member of the Minority Party, I had no control whatsoever over the Tydings Committee. I had no power to order the Tydings Committee to hear evidence which it did not want to hear. We had available some thirty witnesses who were willing to testify under oath as to the Communistic activities, associations, and connections of those whom I had named. Senator Hickenlooper asked Tydings to call those witnesses.[268] This Tydings refused to do.

The evidence of Robert Morris, Minority Counsel, was repeatedly rejected by the chairman. For example, in one case, Morris said:

"There is a case of a man named Theodore Geiger. He has been an employee of the State Department. He is now one of Paul Hoffman's top assistants. He is doing work that is quasi-State Department in character. I have gone and gotten some witnesses together who will testify that he was a member of the same Communist Party unit as they were, and I think we would be delinquent if in the face of this evidence that is now on record . . ."

To this, Tydings replied:

"Turn it over to the FBI or do something else with it . . . We don't want to waste this afternoon."[269]

After Chairman Tydings refused to call the witnesses, the Democrat majority issued a report saying that I failed to prove my case. About the only analogy I can think of is that of a judge who refuses to hear any of the plaintiff's testimony and then renders a decision against him, saying he has failed to prove his case.

You were a judge. Why was not more "court room" proof presented on those you named?

A vast amount of legal proof was offered to the committee. Names of important witnesses were given to the committee with the request that they be called.

Failure to Call Witnesses

The following is an excellent illustration of the committee's failure to call witnesses.

Senator Hickenlooper challenged the committee on June 28, 1950, on its failure to call witnesses. He said he felt that the committee could not arrive at any final conclusion about my charges unless they called a list of witnesses which had been suggested to them. To this reasonable suggestion Senator Green replied sarcastically that the committee did not place "want ads" in the paper to find witnesses, adding,

"It seems to me that we have done all that we need to do in connection with the job that was imposed on us."[270]

Senator Hickenlooper then reminded Green that the committee had not called the list of 20 or 30 names of witnesses he wanted to testify before the committee.[271]

Incidentally, a number of the witnesses whom Tydings refused to call—such as General Alexander Barmine, who testified as to Lattimore's connection with Russian military intelligence—have since been called and testified under oath before the McCarran Committee.

A huge amount of documentary evidence—such as photostats of checks, letters, memoranda, signed affidavits

[268] Congressional Record (Unbound), July 25, 1950, p. 11110.
[269] Tydings Committee Hearings, Pt. 3, pp. 2521, 2522.
[270] Tydings Committee Hearings, Pt. 3, p. 2519.
[271] Tydings Hearings, Pt. 3, p. 2519.

and statements—was offered to the Tydings Committee.

Leads on other evidence were also given that committee. Those leads were never followed up even though the committee had a staff of investigators. Instead those investigators spent months investigating or trying to discredit McCarthy. An example of the failure on the part of the staff to investigate Communist infiltration of Government is illustrated in the following exchange between Robert Morris, Minority counsel for the committee, and the Chairman:

MR. MORRIS: "May I say, Senator, that the *first* basic request that I made in commencing this investigation was for the books and records of Frederick Vanderbilt Field, inasmuch as there was evidence that his money was the heart of the Communist cell in the Institute of Pacific Relations. I maintain that was necessary. It was *basically necessary* to start that kind of an investigation."

CHAIRMAN: ". . . We are pretty far away from loyalty in the State Department when we get out in the Instiute of Pacific Relations."[272]

(The McCarran Committee this year seized the missing IPR files, estimated at 200,000 documents. They were found hidden in a barn near Lee, Massachusetts. At the time this is being written, that committee has already demonstrated the extent to which Communists and pro-Communists in the IPR have shaped our disastrous foreign policy.)

Senator Lodge in a Tydings Committee meeting on June 25, 1950, pointed out 18 examples of leads the committee had failed to investigate—leads which I had provided the committee in the form of documentary evidence.

For instance, he brought up this question:

"Who in the State Department was responsible for obtaining the services of Frederick Schuman and Owen Lattimore as speakers for the Department's indoctrination course for Foreign Service employees?"[273]

Again, Lodge asked,

"Have we questioned those who have headed the China desk in the State Department to determine whether Lattimore gave advice on United States policy for China and whether this advice was acted upon?"[274]

It should be remembered I was not given any funds by the Senate to hire investigators. The Tydings Committee, on the other hand, was given $35,000 to conduct a thorough investigation into this matter.

By contrast with the Tydings Committee staff which did not look for or find a single witness who would testify to disloyalty in government except those whom I produced the McCarran Committee staff is doing an excellent job of exposing disloyalty and incompetence in government.

The McCarran Committee is investigating Communists while the Tydings Committee spent its time clearing, without investigation, those accused of Communist and pro-Communist activities.

Failure to Intelligently Cross-Examine Both Friendly and Hostile Witnesses

Despite the fact that I had been spending practically 18 hours a day for months on this subject, I was denied the right to examine or cross-examine even a single witness.

The Tydings Committee, on the other hand, had the full power to examine and cross-examine both friendly and hostile witnesses but completely failed to develop the evidence which is normally developed by careful examination of the witnesses.

As a member of the Minority Party, which controls no committees, you knew that you could not force the appearance of any witnesses unless the Democrat chairman was willing to subpoena them. Therefore, why didn't you wait until the Republicans were in control of the Senate so that you could produce all of the evidence instead of doing it in a piecemeal pattern which a member of the political party not in power must of necessity follow?

I suggest you put yourself in my position. If you were a Senator of the Minority Party who knew of individuals high in government who were betraying this nation, could you sleep on the evidence and refuse to give it to the public because you were not allowed to produce a complete "court room" case? Would you not feel you owed the duty to the people whom you represented to make public the evidence which might save our nation from further disaster? If you were in my position you could either follow the example of Nero and fiddle while Western civilization burned, or you could attempt to form a bucket brigade and wade in and try to put out the fire even though firebugs or arsonists were in charge of the Fire Department—even though you knew you might get badly burned—even though the odds were against success.

The report of the Tydings Committee signed by the three Democrats states that your evidence of Communists in the State Department was a "fraud and a hoax." Is not the average American justified in assuming that this report signed by three Democrat Senators is true?

Obviously, in the limited space of this book, it is impossible to give all of the vast amount of evidence against those named. For that reason, I shall take a typical case and let you decide whether the evidence is a "fraud and a hoax."

One of the cases given the Tydings Committee by me was that of William Remington. Remington at that time was on the Commerce Department payroll, but working closely with the State Department. The following excerpt from the Senate resolution shows that the Tydings committee was ordered by the Senate to examine cases such as Remington's:

[272] Tydings Committee Hearings, Pt. 3, p. 2519.
[273] Tydings Committee Hearings, Pt. 3, June 28, 1950, p. 2514.
[274] Tydings Committee Hearings, Pt. 3, p. 2515.

"... the committee is directed to procure by subpoena and examine the complete loyalty and employment files and records of all the Government employees in the Department of State, *and such other agencies against whom charges have been heard.*" (Emphasis mine.) [275]

After the Tydings Committee had cleared Remington and declared my evidence was a "fraud and a hoax," a grand jury indicted him on the grounds that he lied when he denied membership in the Communist Party. A jury of 12 men and women, by a vote of 12 to 0, decided that he had perjured himself when he stated that he had not been a member of the Communist Party. This perhaps better than any documents of mine should help the average American decide whether McCarthy was right when he gave evidence of Communists in government, or whether the Tydings Committee was right when it said that my evidence that men such as Remington were Communists was a "fraud and a hoax."

The Tydings Committee, of course, was not alone in refusing to recognize that there were Communists in government. It should be remembered that when the evidence on Alger Hiss was being made public, the President gave Hiss a clean bill of health by stating on a number of occasions that the Hiss case was merely a "red herring."

The Tydings Report has been called a "Whitewash Report." Can you give me one specific example of any "whitewashing" that committee did?

Yes. Take the case of Haldore Hanson.

Haldore Hanson was a State Department employee who was scheduled to be chief of the technical division of the Point IV Program which would spend millions of American dollars in underdeveloped areas of the world. A recent phone call to the State Department revealed that Hanson's current position is Acting Assistant Administrator of the Point IV Program.

The Tydings Report gave Hanson a complete clearance.

Louis Budenz, former editor of the *Daily Worker* and the government's top witness in the trial of the 11 Communist leaders, testified before the Tydings Committee on the Hanson case. Budenz' sworn testimony was that Haldore Hanson was a member of the Communist Party.[276]

Here is some of the evidence which I presented to the Tydings committee on Haldore Hanson.

Edited Communist Magazine in China

When the Japanese-Chinese war broke out in China, this young man in partnership with Nym Wales, wife of Edgar Snow—both of whom have been named under oath as Communists[277]—was running a Communist-line magazine in Peiping, China. He spent several years with the Communist Armies in China writing stories and taking pictures which the Chinese Communists helped him smuggle out of the country.

After his return from China, Hanson wrote a book—*Humane Endeavor*. On page 349 of his book Hanson condemns the anti-Communist groups in the Chinese Government for

"Fighting against the Democratic Revolution as proposed by Mao Tse-tung and the Communists."

Arrested by Anti-Communists in China

Hanson points out on the same page, 349, that anti-Communist officials within the Chinese government were making indirect attacks upon the Communists and that:

"leaders of the Communist Youth Corps were arrested by military officers at Hankow. I myself was the victim of one of these incidents and found that local officials were the instigators."

So, we find that this employee of the State Department has a record of arrest in China with leaders of the Communist Youth Corps.

On page 350 we find that Hanson's passport was seized by the police in Sian when they found that he was traveling from Communist guerrilla territory to the Communist headquarters. He states that:

"The man responsible for this illegal action was Governor Ching Ting-wen, one of the most rabid anti-Red officials in China. The governor's purpose was merely to suppress news about the Communists."

Communist Generals Smuggled Film and Newsstories for Hanson

Throughout the book Hanson shows that not only did he have complete confidence in the Communist leaders but also that they had complete confidence in him. On page 256 he tells how Communist generals Nie and Lu Chen-Tsao acted as his couriers smuggling packets of film and newsstories for him with the aid of Communist guerrillas into Peiping. In this connection, it is significant that Hanson admits that the Communists do not tolerate anyone who is not completely on their side.

Praises Communist Leaders

Hanson makes it very clear all through the book that he is not only on the side of the Chinese Communists but that he has the attitude of a hero worshipper for the Chinese Communist Generals.

His respect and liking for the Communist leaders permeates almost every chapter of his book. For example on page 284 and page 285, he tells about how some ragged waifs, whom he had gathered into his sleeping quarters, regarded as "gods" Mao Tse-tung, the leader of Communist China, and Chu Teh, heir of Soviet Agent Smedley's estate and the Commander-in-Chief of the Chinese Red Armies now fighting us in Korea. He follows the system used in Lattimore's books of praising the Communists, not in his own words but in the words of some nameless waif who, of course, is anonymous.

Describes Communist Generals as "Straight Shooting"

Hanson says on page 303 that Communist China's leaders "impressed me as a group of hard-headed, straight-shooting realists."

[275] Tydings Committee Hearings, Pt. 1, March 8, 1950, p. 1.
[276] Tydings Committee Hearings, Pt. 1, April 25, 1950, p. 591.
[277] Tydings Committee Hearings, Pt. 1, April 25, 1950, pp. 594, 595; McCarran Committee Hearings on IPR, Pt. 2, Aug. 23, 1951, p. 680.

After an interview with Mao Tse-tung, leader of Red China, he states:

"I left with the feeling that he [Mao Tse-tung] was the least pretentious man in Yenan and the most admired. He is a completely selfless man."

Following is Hanson's description of how the Communists took over China. I quote from page 102:

"Whenever a village was occupied for the first time, the Reds arrested the landlords and tax collectors and held a public tribunal, executed a few and intimidated the others, then redistributed the land as fairly as possible."

In connection with Hanson's position as acting assistant director of the Point IV Program, the following on pages 312 and 313 of his book would seem especially significant. He quites Mao Tse-tung, the Communist leader, as follows:

"China cannot reconstruct its industry and commerce without the aid of British and American capital."

Following are my concluding remarks about Haldore Hanson before the Tydings Committee:

"Can there be much doubt as to whether the Communist or the anti-Communist forces in Asia will receive aid under the Point-Four Program with Hanson in charge?

"Gentlemen, here is a man with a mission—a man whose energy and intelligence, coupled with a burning all-consuming mission, has raised him by his own bootstraps from a penniless operator of a Communist magazine in Peiping in the middle thirties, to one of the architects of our foreign policy in the State Department today—a man who, according to State Department announcement No. 41, will be largely in charge of the spending of hundreds of millions of dollars in such areas of the world and for such purposes as he himself decides.

"Gentlemen, if Secretary Acheson gets away with his plan to put this man, to a great extent, in charge of the proposed Point-Four Program, it will, in my opinion, lend tremendous impetus to the tempo at which Communism is engulfing the world.

"On page 32 of his book, Hanson apparently tries to justify 'the Chinese Communists chopping off the heads of landlords—all of which is true,' because of 'hungry farmers.' That the farmers are still hungry after the landlords' heads have been removed apparently never occurred to him.

"On page 31 he explained that it took him some time to appreciate the 'appalling problems which the Chinese Communists were attempting to solve.'

"Secretary Acheson is now putting Hanson in a position in which he can help the Communists solve the 'appalling problems' in other areas of the world with hundreds of millions of American dollars."[278]

[278] Tydings Committee Hearings, Pt. 1, March 13, 1950, p. 82.

WASHINGTON, D. C., April 6, 1950, (United Press-Photo)—Sen. Millard Tydings, left, chairman of Senate Foreign Relations Subcommittee investigating Sen. McCarthy's charges of Communist infiltration in the State Department, shakes hands with Owen Lattimore, right, who appeared today to answer charges made by McCarthy.

CHAPTER X

Guilt By Association

Is not a person presumed innocent until proven guilty?

Yes.

Why do you condemn people like Acheson, Jessup, Lattimore, Service, Vincent and others who have never been convicted of any crime?

The fact that these people have not been convicted of treason or of violating some of our espionage laws is no more a valid argument that they are fit to represent this country in its fight against Communism than the argument that a person who has a reputation of consorting with criminals, hoodlums, gamblers, and kidnappers is fit to act as your baby sitter, because he has never been convicted of a crime.

American People Entitled to Benefit of Doubt

A government job is a privilege, not a right. There is no reason why men who chum with Communists, who refuse to turn their backs upon traitors and who are consistently found at the time and place where disaster strikes America and success comes to international Communism, should be given positions of power in government.

What is your answer to the charge that you employ the theory of guilt by association?

This should properly be labeled *BAD SECURITY RISK BY ASSOCIATION* or *GUILT BY COLLABORATION* rather than *GUILT BY ASSOCIATION*.

The State Department, whose publicity agents complain the loudest about guilt by association, has adopted in their loyalty yardstick what they condemn as the theory of guilt by association.

For example, one of the categories of people they have declared unfit for service in the State Department is:

"A person who has habitual or close association with persons known or believed to be in categories A or B." (Defined as a Communist or one "serving the interests of another government in preference to the interests of the United States.") [279]

In this connection I might add that the State Department's loyalty and security yardstick is all right. The trouble is that they do not use that yardstick when the loyalty measurements are made.

In upholding the constitutionality of the Feinberg Law, the purpose of which was to weed Communists out of teaching jobs in New York, the United States Supreme Court said:

"One's associates, past and present, as well as one's conduct, may properly be considered in determining fitness and loyalty . . .

"From time immemorial, one's reputation has been determined in part by the company he keeps . . .

We know of no rule, constitutional or otherwise, that prevents the state when determining . . . fitness and loyalty of . . . persons, from considering the organizations and persons with whom they associate." [280]

In passing upon the constitutionality of that part of the Taft-Hartley Law which requires a non-Communist oath, the Supreme Court said:

"The conspiracy principle has traditionally been employed to protect society against all 'ganging-up' or concerted action in violation of its laws. No term passes that the Court does not sustain convictions based on that doctrine for violations of the anti-trust laws or other statutes. However, there has recently entered the dialectic of politics a cliche used to condemn application of the conspiracy principle to Communists.

" 'Guilt by Association' is an epithet frequently used and little explained, except that it is generally accompanied by another slogan, 'guilt is personal.' Of course it is; but personal guilt may be incurred by joining a conspiracy. That act of association makes one responsible for acts of others committed in pursuance of the association." [281]

I have not urged that those whom I have named be put in jail. Once they are exposed so the American people know what they are, they can do but little damage.

FBI Head States Exposure Cuts Down Danger

As J. Edgar Hoover said before the House Un-American Activities Committee:

"Victory will be assured once Communists are identified and exposed, because the public will take the first step of quarantining them so they can do no harm." [282]

Defense of "Innocence by Association"

Strangely enough, those who scream the loudest about what they call guilt by association are the first to endorse innocence by association.

For example, those who object most strongly to my showing Jessup's affinity for Communist causes, the Communist money used to support the publication over which he had control, and his close friendship and defense of a Communist spy, also argue Hiss' innocence-by-association. The argument is that Hiss was innocent because Justices Frankfurter and Reed testified they were friends of his, because Acheson chummed and walked with him each morning, because Hiss was the top planner at the United Nations conference and helped to draft the Yalta agreement.

We are not concerned with GUILT by association be-

[279] Hearings before Subcommittee of Senate Committee on Appropriations, Feb. 28, 1950, pp. 596-597.
[280] Justice Sherman Minton speaking for the majority in the decision on the Feinberg Law, March, 1952.
[281] Justice Robert H. Jackson in his concurring decision on Taft-Hartley oath, May, 1950.
[282] Hearings before House Committee on Un-American Activities, Pt. 3, March 26, 1947, p. 44.

cause here we are not concerned with convicting any individual of any crime. We are concerned with the question of whether the individual who associates with those who are trying to destroy this nation, should be admitted to the high councils of those planning the policies of this nation; whether they should be given access to top secret material to which even Senators and Congressmen are not given access.

The best analogy perhaps is the case of the applicant for a job as bank cashier who travels with safe-crackers, robbers, and gamblers. Naturally, such a man would not be hired as cashier and allowed access to depositors' money. The fact that the bank president does not give him a job as cashier does not mean the job applicant has been found guilty of any crime. It merely means that the bank president, using good common horse-sense, decides that his depositors are entitled to have this man kept away from their money while he has associates who are bank robbers and safe crackers. Certainly in dealing with the lives of countless sons of American mothers and the liberty of 150 million American people, we should be using the same good common horse-sense that the bank president uses.

CHAPTER XI

The Penalty For Loyalty In The State Department

Is not your claim of Communists in the State Department unfair to the loyal Americans in the State Department?

This perhaps can best be answered by asking you the question of whether it is unfair to the loyal, honest employees of a bank to expose and convict the cashier who is embezzling the bank's funds.

I am well aware of the fact that the vast majority of people working in the State Department are good, loyal, honest Americans. Some of them have unstintingly devoted their entire lives, and at meager salaries, in the interest of America. I know perhaps better than anyone how painfully aware those loyal people are of the minions of Stalin who have been betraying this nation. I have positive knowledge that they are heartily in favor of my fight to remove the traitors from their midst.

It is those who have insisted on protecting Communists in the State Department who are unfair to the vast number of honest, loyal employees in that Department. Perhaps I have no better supporters in my fight than the good Americans in the State Department.

Real Experts in State Department Ignored

In this connection, let me quote a statement I made before the Tydings Committee on March 14, 1950:

"The Department of State of the United States operates with thousands of employees and requires a tremendous budget which has aided materially in placing on the American people the greatest tax burden they have ever been called upon to bear.

"All but a small handful of those employees are honest and loyal Americans. The State Department is their life work. They have given to it years of service, unquestioned loyalty; and they have served it with great pride.

"In the far-flung places of the world, these loyal men and women have spent their lives and exercised all their ingenuity to give to their Department and their Government every possible bit of information and advice they thought useful.

"Career employees of the State Department, by virtue of their long residence in every foreign country on the globe and their close association and friendship with citizens and officials of those countries, have had access to, have reported on, every phase of economic and political affairs in the nations to which they are attached.

"These are the real 'experts' of the State Department.

"It is a tragedy when we find the advice and experiences of such outstandingly able employees stored in a multitude of steel filing cases and disregarded while the Department of State's closed corporation of 'untouchables' calls upon pro-Communist idealists, crackpots, and, to put it mildly, 'bad security risks' to advise them on American diplomatic policy."[283]

Where have you gotten your information on Communists in government?

From a vast number of sources.

One of the reasons why I have been able to get information is that every government employee who gives me information knows that he will be fully protected and that under no circumstances will his job be endangered because he, as a loyal American, has given a Senator information on traitors.

I have not and do not intend ever to break faith with those people. The Tydings committee tried to get their names, but failed. No other committee will get their names.

If a government employee has information on another employee, why should he not take that information to the security officer of his department rather than to you?

As far as I know, all information given me has been brought to the attention of the proper officials.

Unfortunately, experience has shown that a State Department employee who furnishes evidence of Communistic activities in the State Department merely endangers his job and the information is pigeon-holed.

State Department Security Officer Threatens Retaliation

Carlisle Humelsine, Under-Secretary of State in charge of security, publicly stated on a nationwide television network on August 19, 1951, that if the State Department could find out who is giving me information on the Communists in government, those individuals—not the Communists—would be discharged.

Can you give an example of what happens to a State Department employee who attempts to expose Communism?

On June 16, 1948, while General Marshall was Secretary of State, Robert C. Alexander, who was employed in the visa division of the State Department, testified under oath that Communists were allowed to enter the United States under the protection of the United Nations. Secretary of State Marshall immediately denied the truth of this statement and set up a committee which denounced Alexander's allegations as "irresponsible and untrue." On September 9, 1948, Alexander received a letter from the State Department which contained the following:

"The Department proposes to take appropriate disciplinary action against you . . . for misconduct in office and dereliction of duty.

"The intended action rose out of your testimony and inferences arising from your statements made before the staff of the subcommittee on Immigration and Naturalization, Committee on the Judiciary, United States Senate

---

[283] Tydings Committee Hearings, Pt. 1, March 14, 1950, pp. 141, 142.

"Specifically, the department charges that this testimony was irresponsibly made and at variance with the facts. In the opinion of the department, this testimony constituted an indiscriminate reflection on the United Nations and other international organizations and consequently embarrassed the department."[284]

"Irresponsible" Charges Proved True

On June 30, 1949, Senator McCarran wrote Admiral Hillenkoetter, who was then head of the Central Intelligence Agency, to inquire whether Communists spies actually were coming into the United States through the United Nations. He wrote as follows:

"Dear Admiral Hillenkoetter:
"There is attached to this letter a list of names of 100 persons.
"This is a partial list of those persons to whom visas have been issued for admission into the United States either as affiliates of international organizations or as officials or employees of foreign governments, and their families . . .
"How many of the persons whose names appear on the attached list have been engaged in subversive activity prior to their assumption of official duty in the United States as affiliates of international organizations or as officials or employees of foreign governments? The term 'subversive activity' as used in this question denotes active participation in foreign intelligence organizations or active Communist organizational work, rather than mere membership in the Communist Party."[285]

Many of the names given in this letter of Senator McCarran were names which had previously been referred to by Mr. Alexander.

Head of Central Intelligence Agency Confirms As Accurate Alexander's Charges Which Had Been Labeled "Irresponsible"

Following are two pertinent paragraphs from Admiral Hillenkoetter's answer:

"Thirty-two of the individuals named in your attached list have reported or allegedly been engaged in active work for the intelligence services of their respective countries.
"Twenty-nine of the individuals named in your attached list are high-ranking Communist Party officials."[286]

Shortly thereafter Admiral Hillenkoetter was removed as head of Central Intelligence Agency and assigned to a post of duty in the Western Pacific.

Robert Alexander's testimony, given under oath, was contradicted and publicly denounced by his State Department superiors including Secretary of State George C. Marshall. No apology was made to Alexander when his "irresponsible" charges were proved true in every respect.

Secret Trial of Alexander Ordered

The State Department proposed to hold a secret trial of this State Department official on charges of misconduct. Alexander, however, refused to attend the secret trial, demanding instead that he be given a public investigation.[287]

This case received such wide publicity—and the State

Department knew it was treading on such weak ground—that it was afraid to fire Alexander.

Robert Alexander is today still in the State Department. But Robert Alexander is not one of the so-called experts or one of the policy makers of the State Department today. Despite his intelligent action on a matter which has been of major concern to all loyal State Department employees, Robert Alexander—like Angus Ward and so many other loyal State Department employees—has been penalized for his service to America. Unlike John Carter Vincent, Ambassador Philip Jessup, and so many other State Department employees whose main qualification for the top positions they hold seems to be their softness toward Communism, Robert Alexander's advice is not being sought by the top policy planners, nor has he been given a position to help lead the fight against international Communism.

In what way have loyal people in the State Department been hampered in their work by fellow employees who are pro-Communists?

The case of General Patrick Hurley, Roosevelt's Ambassador to China, is one of many cases in point.

When Ambassador Hurley left China for a trip to the United States on February 28, 1945, George Atcheson, Jr., then Charge d'Affaires during Hurley's absence, sent a telegram to the State Department recommending not only that we cooperate with the Communists but also that we supply the Communists with arms. His message read in part as follows:

"We recommend that the President tell Chiang Kai-shek in no uncertain terms that we will cooperate and supply the Communists."[288]

This was completely against the policy of the United States at that time. Ambassador Hurley has said that the message:

". . . Recommended in my absence that the Chinese [Communist] armed party, a belligerent whose purpose was to destroy the government that I had to sustain, be furnished lend-lease arms and equipment . . . I opposed that as destructive of the government that I had been directed to uphold . . ."[289]

Hurley Exposes John Stewart Service and Urges His Recall

Hurley later named George Atcheson, Jr., and John Stewart Service as two of the State Department employees who persisted in their support of the Communist Party against the Government of the Republic of China.[290]

On November 26, 1945, when Ambassador Hurley resigned his position, he had this to say:

"We finished the war in the Far East, furnishing lend-lease supplies and using all our reputation to undermine democracy and bolster imperialism and Communism . . .

[284] Congressional Record (Unbound), June 14, 1951, p. 6720.
[285] Hearings before Senate Subcommittee on Immigration and Naturalization on S. 1832, Pt. 1, July 16, 1949, p. 357.
[286] Hearings before Senate Subcommittee on Immigration and Naturalization on S. 1832, Pt. 1, July 16, 1949, pp. 358, 359.
[287] New York Sun, July 28, 1948; Washington Post, Oct. 6, 1948.
[288] Russell Committee Hearings, Pt. 4, June 21, 1951, p. 2905.
[289] Senate Foreign Relations Committee Hearings on Investigation of Far Eastern Policy, Dec. 5, 1945, p. 38-A, (Transcript).
[290] New York Times, Nov. 29, 1945, p. 3.

"The professional Foreign Service men [in the U.S. State Department] sided with the Chinese Communist armed party and the imperialist bloc of nations whose policy it was to keep China divided against herself. *Our professional diplomats continuously advised the Communists that my efforts in preventing the collapse of the National (anti-Communist) government did not represent the policy of the United States.* These same professionals openly advised the Communist armed party to decline unification of the Chinese Communist army with the National army unless the Chinese Communists were given control . . .

"I requested the relief of the career men who were opposing the American policy in the Chinese theatre of war. *These professional diplomats were returned to Washington and placed in the Chinese and Far Eastern divisions of the State Department as my superiors.*

"Some of these same career men whom I relieved have been assigned as advisors to the Supreme Commander in Asia. In such positions, most of them have continued to side with the Communist armed party and at times with the imperialist bloc against American policy . . .

". . . At the same time a considerable section of our State Department is endeavoring to support Communism generally as well as specifically in China." (Emphasis mine.) [291]

Hurley left the State Department, but Acheson's crowd stayed on. It would appear that the only road to swift promotion in the State Department has been secretly to aid the cause of Communism while publicly voicing opposition to Communism.

What happened to the members of Hurley's staff who were relieved by him because of their aid to the Communist cause?

Hurley's answer to this appears on August 7, 1949, in the New York *Times*:

"Nearly all the officials relieved by me in China because they were pro-Communist are now in the State Department presumably writing alibi White Papers."

[291] White Paper on China, pp. 581-582.

"I have been warned by many that an outspoken course, even if it be solely of truth, will bring down upon my head ruthless retaliation—that efforts will be made to destroy public faith in the integrity of my views—not by force of just argument but by the application of the false methods of propaganda.

"I am told, in effect, I must follow blindly the leader—keep silent—or take the bitter consequences."

General Douglas MacArthur
Boston, Massachusetts
July 25, 1951

The Smear

What is the reason for the viciously intense smear attack which has been waged against you since you started to dig Communists out of government?

The official Communist Party line is to destroy the reputation of anyone who dares to expose any of their undercover Communists. Lenin long ago established this Communist rule when he said:

"We can and must write in a language which sows among the masses hate, revulsion, scorn and the like, toward those who disagree with us."[292]

The purpose of this Communist tactic is two-fold: (1) to smear and discredit the individual so that his evidence on traitors will not be believed and (2) to discourage others from entering the fight.

In this the Communists have been singularly successful. Time and again, men in the field of politics, writing, religion, and education who have spoken out against specific Communists have found themselves bitterly attacked, smeared out of office, and prevented from getting jobs.[293]

Louis Budenz, who for years was editor of the Communist *Daily Worker*, gave the Justice Department the names of 400 secret members of the Communist Party who are engaged in newspaper and radio work. He explained that one of the major aims of the Communist Party was to infiltrate as many newspapers and radio stations as possible so as to be able to twist and distort the news along the Communist Party line. It is very important to the Party that the Communists handling news in press and radio remain concealed, secret members of the Party because once their membership is known they can do but little damage.

In this connection, the following testimony of Igor Bogolepov, former Colonel in the Red Army who worked with Russian intelligence, is of interest:

"Once I read a memorandum written by Molotov in our secret files where the problem was discussed of our participation and utilization of the Western press. I have to explain that before 1931 it was a general rule that the Communists should not write in the foreign press. It was a shame. It was a disgrace. But Trotsky was expelled from the Soviet Union and he had written articles against Stalin in the *Daily Express*, and these articles became very popular because they were written in the British newspaper.

"This gave the idea to the Soviet authorities that it was wrong to seek only the Communist papers. In the memorandum of Molotov which evidently laid down the foundation for the new trend of Soviet policy, written in 1931, it was stated, Who Reads the Communist Papers? Only a few people who are already Communists. We don't need to propagandize them. What is our object? Who do we have to influence? We have to influence non-Communists if we want to make them Communists or if we want

to fool them. So we have to try to infiltrate in the big press, to influence millions of people, and not merely hundreds of thousands.

"After this argumentation the position was taken that we had to change drastically our policy, as I said before and do our best in order to *carry out the Communist ideas through non-Communist press.*" (Emphasis mine.)[294]

It has been claimed by some that instead of hurting the Communist cause you have aided it. How can the average American, who does not have access to all the records, decide whether you have helped or hurt the Communist cause?

To determine whether I have been hurting the Communists, we should perhaps refer to the Communist press. One of the principal functions of the *Daily Worker*, according to all the evidence, is to notify all loyal Communist writers, news commentators, etc., what the official Communist Party line is.

Louis Budenz, former editor of the *Daily Worker*, testified:

"The *Daily Worker* is not a daily paper in the normal sense of the word. *It is the telegraph agency* of the conspiracy giving directives to the conspirators.

". . . It parades under the guise of a daily paper in order to protect itself through the cry of freedom of the press, but it is not concerned primarily with how much circulation it has . . .

"Its concern is to get out every day to the Communists throughout the country, the active ones, the instructions upon which they are to act."[295]

"Every time the *Daily Worker* arrives in the district office of the Communist Party it is read immediately by the district leader. He calls together his staff, and he assigns to them their tasks as a result of the *Daily Worker* articles and editorials."[296]

How did the Communist Party order its membership in press and radio to handle the issue of Senator McCarthy vs. Communists in the State Department?

The national secretary of the Communist Party, Gus Hall, who has since been jailed for his Communist activities, advised all Communist Party members as follows in the *Daily Worker* of May 4, 1950:

"I urge all Communist Party members, and all anti-fascists, to yield second place to none in the fight to rid our country of the fascist poison of McCarthyism."

On April 5, 1950, the *Daily Worker* had this to say:

"Communists are keenly aware of the damage the McCarthy crowd is doing. They recognize that the McCarthy objective is destruction of the Bill of

292 Quoted by Max Eastman, Saturday Evening Post, November 5, 1949.
293 For more detailed information on this see Eugene Lyons' article in American Legion Magazine, September, 1951.
294 McCarran Committee Hearings on IPR, April 7, 1952 (now being printed.)
295 McCarran Committee Hearings on IPR, Pt. 2, Aug. 22, 1951, p. 515.
296 McCarran Committee Hearings on IPR, Pt. 2, Aug. 23, 1951, p. 601.

Rights with its precious safeguards of the freedom to think, to meet, and to express one's thoughts freely."

It will be recalled that almost identical language was used by Truman in his attack on McCarthy on August 14, 1951.

On March 22, 1950, the *Daily Worker* had this to say:

> "McCarthy today is regarded by many people, maybe by a majority, as a clumsy but dangerous clown. But it is possible that at some time in the future the ravings of McCarthy, together with the irresponsible charges of the Un-American Committee, will provide the 'evidence' upon which labor leaders, Negro leaders and progressive persons from all walks of life, will go to jail."

By "progressive persons" obviously was meant Communists. Some of those "progressive persons" have since gone to jail.

On October 9, 1951, the *Daily Worker* lavishly praised Henry Luce, publisher of *Time, Life,* and *Fortune,* for his intemperate attacks on McCarthy and ended with the following language:

> "A broad united front struggle against McCarthyism is necessary . . . The admissions made by Luce in his editorial on McCarthy offer some disinterested confirmation of our conviction that such a broad united front is definitely a tangible possibility at this time."

On December 27, 1950, the *Daily Worker* shed tears over the exposure of the activities of Drew Pearson. Pearson, it will be recalled, sprang to the defense of Owen Lattimore when I presented the evidence on Lattimore in 1950, and has been carrying on a smear against McCarthy ever since.

Opposite is a reproduction of a letter put out by the Communist Party of Maryland.

It will be noted that this letter was signed by Philip Frankfeld who has since been convicted.

Attached to this letter was a pamphlet also put out by the Communist Party of Maryland and widely distributed to Communists both in and outside of Maryland. The title page of that pamphlet is reproduced on the opposite page.

Following are a few excerpts from the body of the pamphlet:

> "Defeat McCarthyism or face the threat of political annihilation. . . .
> "At all times, remember the fact that the main enemy is McCarthyism . . . [we must] direct our main fight against it. . . .
> "Time is running out. The great need today is unity. Let us start fighting together—and victory is assured."

In September, 1951, an article entitled "Mass Tasks Facing the Party Today," appeared in *Political Affairs,* a magazine which has been cited by the House Committee on Un-American Activities as "an official Communist Party monthly theoretical organ." The article urged that "the major task" of the Communist Party was to "seize the initiative in the fight against McCarthyism." This Communist publication then urged the importance of getting labor groups to fight McCarthyism. It urged that the fight against McCarthy, to be successful, should be labeled "as a fight against monopoly, pro-fascist reaction, and for democratic liberties and the Bill of Rights."[297]

The above are a very, very small percentage of the Communist directives repeatedly carried by every Communist publication in the country. For over two years Communist officials and publications have constantly been proclaiming that their No. 1 task is to discredit and destroy McCarthy in the eyes of the people. Recently they have been equally intemperate in their attacks upon Senator Pat McCarran. Senator McCarran, with the power of subpoena, an excellent committee, and an excellent staff, is doing an outstanding job. He is doing great damage to the Communist conspiracy. The nearer he gets to nerve center of the Communist movement, the more vicious will become their attacks upon him.

What do you consider the principal purpose of the Communist Party line type of smear attack being waged against you?

The smear attacks on McCarthy are no longer being made with the hope that they can thereby force me to give up this fight to expose and get Communists out of government. They have learned by now that I am not much concerned and am in no way influenced by their smear attacks. The purpose now of the viciousness and intensity of the smear is to teach other men in public life that the same will happen to them if they dare to expose Communists.

Most of the attacks were thoroughly discredited and disproved charges which had been used against me in the campaign in Wisconsin in 1946. They were not used again until I publicly began my fight against Communists in government. Who dug up these old attacks in an attempt to stop my Communist fight? Where were they used? Why?

In Owen Lattimore's book, *Ordeal by Slander,* Mrs. Lattimore tells of spending days poring over the columns of left-wing writers to collect this material from the 1946 campaign.[298] The original source of practically every one of these attacks was the Madison *Capital Times,* whose city editor, Cedric Parker, has been publicly called by his own editor and boss, William Evjue, "the Communist leader in Madison."[299] These publicly disproved stories were picked up by Lattimore and used before the Tydings Committee to "prove" that Lattimore was not a Communist. Lattimore, incidentally, has since said that Joe Barnes, formerly foreign news editor of the New York *Herald Tribune,* helped him prepare his statement before the Tydings Committee.[300] Barnes has been named under oath as a Soviet agent. This smear, which was used in Lattimore's defense before the Tydings Committee, has been picked up with a few additional inventions and

[297] *Political Affairs,* September, 1951, pp. 26, 27.
[298] Lattimore, *Ordeal By Slander,* p. 40.
[299] Madison *Capital-Times,* March 14, 1941, p. 24.
[300] Lattimore, *Ordeal By Slander,* p. 56.

COMMUNIST PARTY

OF

MARYLAND AND THE DISTRICT OF COLUMBIA

November 27, 1950,
Baltimore, Maryland

Dear Sir or Madam:

The enclosed article, "UNITY CAN DEFEAT McCARTHYISM", is
being mailed out to thousands of Marylanders as a public service
by the Communist Party of Maryland and District of Columbia.

We have confidence that the onslaughts of McCarthyism
have not been that successful where men and women will refuse to
listen to the Communists of Maryland.

It is high time that we learn the lesson of Hitler
Germany. There a whole nation was betrayed under the slogan of
"Defeat Communism". Our country is following the same tragic path.

If the Communist Party of the USA is outlawed under the
McCarran, Smith or Ober Laws, then McCarthyism has won a signal
victory and the Constitution and Bill of Rights has been outlawed
for all Americans. Then our country has taken a great leap forward
towards a complete fascist state — and towards World War III.

The future of our country rests with YOU — individually
and collectively — and what YOU will do immediately together with
the many-millioned-majority who support Democracy against fascism.

The enclosed article is an "Appeal to Reason".

We urge you to read it.

Very sincerely yours,

Philip Frankfeld, Chairman
George A. Meyers, Labor Secretary
Roy Wood, Chairman, Washington, D.C.

UNITY
CAN
Defeat
McCarthyism!

by
Philip Frankfeld
"CHAIRMAN OF THE COMMUNIST PARTY OF MARYLAND"

Letter and pamphlet distributed by Communist Party

parroted over and over by the *Daily Worker,* Drew Pearson, the Milwaukee *Journal,* etc.

Most of the catch phrases, with which you are undoubtedly familiar, such as—"McCarthyism," "irresponsible charges," "mud slinging," "shotgun technique,"—were coined by the *Daily Worker* or Owen Lattimore.

Has the Administration aided the Communists in this smear?

From the day Truman announced on February 23, 1950, that he would do everything in his power to "disprove McCarthy's charges," the Administration has used all of its power—all of its publicity agents paid for by the taxpayers—to clear men like Lattimore, Davies, Vincent and Acheson, and to attempt to discredit and smear McCarthy.

Truman Begins Smear Campaign

As early as April, 1950, President Truman called to the White House for a conference William Evjue, editor of the Madison *Capital Times,* a man who, as previously stated, maintains on his staff as city editor, Cedric Parker, who Evjue himself in an editorial called "the Communist leader in Madison."

At the conclusion of the White House conference, Evjue announced to the press that the President assured him the Administration would continue to fight McCarthyism.

State Department "White Papers" on McCarthy

There is no secret about the fact that the State Department spent hundreds of thousands of dollars in a propaganda effort to discredit McCarthy. One phase of this effort was the series of six "White Papers," covering speeches which I had made during May and June 1950.

Those "White Papers" were sent to every newspaper throughout the country. Their purpose was to "prove" that McCarthy had lied. They were cleverly prepared, but with complete disregard for the truth—their hope apparently being that if they could get enough newspapers to repeat over and over the State Department's claim that McCarthy had lied, that some of it might stick in the minds of the people.

For example, when I exposed the fact that the Communist front publication, over which Jessup had editorial control, was supported by Communist money, a "White Paper" was issued, pointing out how unfair this was to Jessup and inferring that only $3,500 of Communist money had been taken.[301]

Since then the McCarran Committee has obtained the records of this Communist front and has found that over $60,000 of Communist money was used.[302] This obviously was known to Jessup and the State Department at the time the "White Paper" was written.

Another "White Paper" was issued after my Rochester, New York speech of May 25, 1950. In that speech I discussed Ambassador Jessup's connection with the Communist-front China Aid Council. The China Aid

Council has been repeatedly recognized and cited by legislative committees as a Communist front.[303] The sworn testimony of Elizabeth Bentley before the McCarran Committee is that Price, the Secretary of the China Aid Council, was a Communist agent and that the China Aid Council was completely controlled by the Communist Party.[304]

After I discussed Jessup's connection with this organization, the State Department sent a "White Paper" to newspaper editors throughout the country. In that "White Paper" they state:

"China Aid Council: Ambassador Jessup has never been affiliated with this organization."[305]

On December 8, 1949, Jessup testified during the trial of Alger Hiss, and in answer to questions on the China Aid Council, he testified as follows:

QUESTION: "Did you know whether *your wife in 1947 was a member of* the directors of the China Aid Council?"
JESSUP: "I believe she was."

———

QUESTION: "Are you a member or have you been associated with the China Aid Council?"
JESSUP: "I have never been a member of it. *I had some association with it."*
QUESTION: "Did you tell us in what manner you were associated with—your description now is—"
JESSUP: "I don't remember specific contacts. I remember that *we had questions of common interest about arranging meetings, publications, things of that kind."* (Emphasis mine.) [306]

In my speech to the American Society of Newspaper Editors on April 20, 1950, I exhibited a letter written by Lattimore, while he was Deputy Director of Pacific Operations, Office of War Information, to Joe Barnes, then head of the New York office of the Office of War Information. That letter labeled "secret" told Barnes to fire all Chinese in OWI except two (Chew Hong and Chi) and to recruit a new Chinese force from the *New China Daily News.*[307] I pointed out in my speech that the *New China Daily News* was a Communist controlled paper. Therefore, this was in effect an order to Barnes that in hiring Chinese, only Chinese Communists or those sympathetic to Communism should be hired. The State Department "White Paper" on this ridiculed my statement and claimed that the Lattimore letter actually was an admonition to Barnes to be careful not to hire Communists.[308]

This sounded plausible enough to many editors who were not aware of the identity of Chew Hong and Chi or of the fact that the *New China Daily News* was Com-

[301] Department of State Bulletin, Vol. XXII, No. 571, June 12, 1950, p. 964.
[302] McCarran Committee Hearings on IPR, Pt. 1, July 25, 1951, p. 7.
[303] Cited as "subsidiary" of the American League for Peace and Democracy. (Special Congressional Committee on Un-American Activities, House of Representatives, Report, June 25, 1942, p. 16); Cited as a "Communist front and a subsidiary organization of the American League for Peace and Democracy." (California Committee on Un-American Activities, Report, 1948, pp. 151, 319, 336).
[304] McCarran Committee Hearings on IPR, Pt. 2, Aug. 9, 1951, pp. 406-407.
[305] Department of State Bulletin, Vol. XXII, No. 572, June 19, 1950, p. 1014.
[306] U.S. of America v. Alger Hiss, C-128-402, Hon. Henry W. Goddard, District Judge, testimony of Philip Jessup, Dec. 8, 1949, pp. 1510, 1512.
[307] Congressional Record (Unbound), June 2, 1950, pp. 8104-8106.
[308] Department of State Bulletin, Vol. XXII, No. 571, June 12, 1950, p. 966.

munist controlled and directed. Some of those editors, in fact, editorialized about another "wild McCarthy charge."

The facts are, however, that Chew Hong and Chi had been labeled by the Civil Service Commission as Communist and pro-Communist respectively. Civil Service files label the *New China Daily News* as Communist controlled. Those files have been made part of the McCarran Committee record.[309] In addition, the President and the former managing editor of the *New China Daily News* were recently indicted "as part of an international racket involving murder, extortion and torture in which American-Chinese have been mulcted of millions of dollars for Red China." The U. S. attorney described the *New China Daily News* as "a racket which is designed to further the aims of the Chinese Communist government."[310]

Maryland Campaign Investigating Committee Part of Smear

There are many other indications of the Administration's taxpayer-supported propaganda machine being used against anyone who attempts to remove Communists from government. The Maryland Campaign Investigating Committee went all-out as a part of the smear. My documented report on that committee's activities appears in the *Congressional Record* of August 20, 1951, page 10526 (unbound edition).

Benton Resolution Supported by Communist Party

The Benton resolution to expel McCarthy from the Senate and the Gillette-Monroney Committee which has been "investigating" Benton's charges for almost a year are also a part of the Administration's smear machine which is used against a fight such as mine.

The Communist Party has fully supported all of these efforts of the Administration. In an article entitled "How to Fight McCarthyism," which appeared in the October, 1951, issue of *Political Affairs*, the Communist publication which presents the current tasks and problems of the Communist Party, Communist Party members are ordered to "support the Benton resolution to oust McCarthy from the Senate."[311]

It is impossible to estimate how many hundreds of thousands of dollars have been spent by the State Department and the above mentioned Democratic-controlled Committees in an attempt to discredit this fight against Communism.

Some idea of the extent to which the State Department has used taxpayers' money for this purpose was revealed by Congressman Hill of Colorado and Willard Edwards, long-time Washington newspaperman. After weeks of work these men uncovered a large number of secret contracts made by the State Department, which showed that the department used a $27 million slush fund in 1950 to subsidize a number of radio commentators, cartoonists, writers and publishers. For example, the State Department paid over $2,000 for a book of Herbert Block's cartoons entitled *Herblock Looks at Communism*. Herbert Block is the political cartoonist for the Washing-

ton *Post*. He has cartooned violently against every attempt to dig out unexposed Communists, including my anti-Communist fight.

Time Magazine which has consistently distorted the news on my anti-Communist fight and which referred to misquotations in the Marshall speech—misquotations no one has yet been able to find in the speech—also received a heavy subsidy from the State Department this year, and in addition, according to a speech of Senator Harry Cain of Washington (April 10, 1950), was subsidized, as of December 31, 1949, in the amount of $343,800 by the government.

Why has President Truman repeatedly asked for an all-out fight against McCarthyism?

Perhaps for the same reason that he felt the exposure of Alger Hiss was a personal attack upon himself and labeled it as a "red herring."

Do you claim that all the newspapers that condemn you for exposing underground Communists are Communist controlled?

Certainly not. In that connection, we quote General Douglas MacArthur:

"This campaign to subvert the truth and shape or confuse the public mind with its consequent weakening of moral courage is not chargeable entirely to Communists engaged in a centrally controlled worldwide conspiracy to destroy all freedom. For they have many allies, here as elsewhere who, blind to reality, ardently support the general Communist aims while reacting violently to the mere suggestion that they do so."[312]

It should also be borne in mind that newspapers oppose one for different reasons.

There are, for example, the completely honest newspaper editors who are sincerely opposed to what I am doing. They honestly believe that there is some better way of digging out the under-cover Communists. Then there are papers—like the Sheboygan *Press* which is a Democrat paper in my state—which oppose anyone who threatens the security of the Democrat administration. Then there is a third group into which category fall papers like the Milwaukee *Journal* and the Madison *Capital-Times* in my state. The city editor of the *Capital-Times*, who also writes for the Milwaukee *Journal*, is Cedric Parker. As previously stated, he has been editorially described in his own paper, the *Capital-Times*, as "The Communist leader in Madison." Papers in this group are found consistently paralleling the editorial line of the Communist *Daily Worker*. They, of course, criticize Communism generally to obtain a false reputation of being anti-Communist. They then go all-out to assassinate the character and destroy the reputation of anyone who tries to dig out the really dangerous under-cover Communists. To this group, the real villains are men like General MacArthur,

309 Congressional Record (Unbound), June 2, 1950, pp. 8104-8108.
310 New York Times, April 29, 1952, p. 1.
311 "How to Fight McCarthyism," Political Affairs, October, 1951, p. 29.
312 General Douglas MacArthur, Revitalizing a Nation (The Heritage Foundation, Inc., 1952), p. 58.

James Forrestal, Chiang Kai-shek, Martin Dies and Senator Pat McCarran.

There are a sizable number of papers outside of my state that fall into the category of the Milwaukee *Journal* —papers such as the New York *Post*, Washington *Post*, St. Louis *Post-Dispatch*, and the Portland *Oregonian*. Some who read those papers may at first blush violently differ with me. However, you need not take my word. Make your own decision. First check the editorial policy which the *Daily Worker* consistently follows. Then determine for yourself the extent to which the above papers follow that editorial policy. Do not be deceived, however, by any general condemnation or tossing of pebbles at Communism generally. That is a perfectly safe sport which was indulged in even by Alger Hiss. The test is not whether they are willing to condemn Communism generally and the well-known, previously exposed Communists. The test is whether they follow a pattern of supporting or condemning the exposure of the sacred-cows—the dangerous, under-cover Communists who have been promoted to positions of untouchability by the Communist and left-wing press.

Incidentally, the Washington heads of the three major wire services are honest, capable men apparently dedicated to the task of supplying the papers throughout the country with the straight, uncolored news as it happens in Washington. They, of course, cannot personally check every one of the thousands of stories that daily emanate from Washington. Their attempt to do a good job is made extremely difficult by the sort of thing that happened on June 26, 1950. On that day the President of the Newspaper Guild, Harry Martin, attacked McCarthy and made it clear to the membership that any favorable coverage of my fight against Communists was taboo. At the time he made this speech, he was also on the State Department payroll working as Director of Labor Information for the ECA. The membership of the Guild consists of newsmen with practically every important newspaper in the country and on the desks of all the wire services. Fortunately, the majority of the members of the Newspaper Guild do not take dictation from their president, Harry Martin.

Those who have denounced you in connection with the dismissal of men like Service, because he was not convicted of a crime, have not objected to the dismissal of men suspected, but not convicted of graft and corruption in government. How can this attitude be explained?

The exposure of graft, corruption, and dishonesty of every kind in government is vigorously supported by two widely separated elements of American life—as far apart as the North and South Pole. The good, honest, decent people want dishonesty in government exposed so that there may be a housecleaning. The Communists are eager to have dishonesty flourish in a republic and exposed to the view of the people, with the hope that it will cause the people to lose confidence in their government and hasten the day when the Communists can impose Communism upon us.

In this connection I quote an editorial from the Washington *Times-Herald* of December 5, 1951 on this subject:

"Some 50 men and women, concerned in one way or another with federal tax collections, have been fired or have resigned under pressure. They were accused of accepting bribes and of various other irregularities and improprieties. Their separation from government service can be credited largely to the activities of Senator Williams of Delaware and the King Committee of the House. A few of the suspects have been indicted but none has yet been tried.

"So far as we know, there has not been a whisper of protest against the summary dismissals, and this is remarkable only because an enormous hullabaloo has been raised by the Administration and in its press against dismissals from the federal service on well-founded suspicion of disloyalty.

"The parallel is close. The evidence of disloyalty as of bribery was developed largely through Congressional committees. If there is any difference in the quality of the evidence, it is not in favor of those suspected of disloyalty, for the investigation of subversive activities has been going on for years and the facts have been documented and redocumented.

"Surely those who shout McCarthyism when the demand is made for the summary dismissal of men in government whose usefulness to the Communist cause has been well established, ought to shout Williamism or Kingism when an internal revenue hand is fired, without trial, on suspicion of cheating. We call this disparity to the attention of the editors of the New York *Herald-Tribune*, the Washington *Post*, the St. Louis *Post-Dispatch*, the Milwaukee *Journal*, the Louisville *Courier-Journal*, and the *New Yorker*, Mr. Henry Luce, and others who have been horrified by what they call McCarthyism. We think they ought to explain what the difference is.

"They have all told us that the loyalty investigations were discouraging good men from entering the public service. For our part, we expect that crooks today are a little more reluctant to take Internal Revenue or Justice Department jobs than they were a few weeks ago. Maybe if something like summary dismissal had been accorded those reasonably suspected of disloyalty, the other government bureaus, and notably the State Department would be in better shape today than they are.

"Surely it cannot be said that the tax fixing scoundrels are a greater menace to the American people than the State Department's disloyalists.

"Nobody knows as yet how much money the Treasury did not collect as a result of dishonesty within its ranks and in the Attorney General's department, but the loss was only in money and the evidence now available suggests that the sum can be measured in millions.

"By the way of contrast, look at the record of the disloyalists. In money they have cost us billions. The dollar outlay for the Korean war alone must now approximate 10 billions, and this war never would have been started except for the Communist sympathizers in the Administration who helped bring about the Communist victory in China. They also made it easy for Stalin to gain possession of his satellite countries in Europe. Except for that circumstance, there would be no Communist threat in Europe today to warrant the 6 billions we are spending there this year and the immensely greater sums that will be demanded tomorrow.

"The disloyalists were largely responsible for prolonging the Japanese war for months after the enemy had indicated a willingness to surrender on the terms finally accepted. They are largely responsible for conscription, which is costing each young man in this country two years of his life. They are largely responsible for the 100,000 American casualties in Korea, including more than 16,000 dead. They are largely responsible for the crushing taxes we are forced to pay and, it can even be argued, they are largely responsible for the corruption in the Treasury and the Attorney General's office, for if the taxes were not as heavy as they are, there would be less temptation to use illicit means of avoiding them than there now is.

"In the light of these circumstances, the tenderness toward those suspected of disloyalty and the approval of summary dismissal of those under suspicion of fixing taxes need to be explained. Can anyone suppose that disloyalty which has cost tens of thousands of lives and billions of money is a less grievous offense than tax fixing, grave as that offense is?"

Do you believe in freedom of press? If so, how do you explain your attacks on _Time_ Magazine?

I, of course, believe in freedom of the press. It might be well, however, to define freedom of the press. I understand freedom of the press to mean freedom to print all of the truth regardless of how pleasant or unpleasant it may be, and regardless of who may be helped or hurt thereby. I understand freedom of the press also to mean freedom to editorialize as the editor sees fit so long as he does not misstate facts. Freedom of the press does not mean freedom to lie and twist and distort the facts, as some would have the American people believe.

I did not "attack" _Time_ Magazine; I "exposed" _Time_ Magazine for gross, deliberate lying. I disagree with those who apparently feel that it is proper to expose a liar unless he owns a newspaper or a magazine. I feel that it is much more important to expose a liar, a crook, or a traitor who is able to poison the streams of information flowing into a vast number of American homes than to expose an equally vicious crook, liar, or traitor who has no magazine or newspaper outlet for his poison.

I have no personal fight with Henry Luce, owner of _Time_, _Life_, and _Fortune_. In fact, as far as I know, I have never met him. There is nothing personal about my exposing the depth to which this magazine will sink in using deliberate falsehoods to destroy anyone who is hurting the Communist cause—nothing any more personal than there was about a very unpleasant task which I had as a boy on the farm. That task consisted of digging out of their holes and destroying the skunks which were killing Mother's chickens. That was not a pleasant job. I had no personal feeling toward those skunks. But someone had to do that unpleasant job also.

You have given _Time_ Magazine as an example of dishonest reporting. Where can I get the complete story and all the facts in the _Time_ case?

Nora de Toledano, wife of Ralph de Toledano who was the co-author of _Seeds of Treason_ and who wrote _Spies, Dupes and Diplomats_, did an excellent job of documenting the extent to which _Time_ Magazine deliberately twisted and distorted the facts. Her story under the heading of "Time Marches on McCarthy" was published in the February issue of _Mercury_ Magazine and is available in booklet form at 10 cents a copy from _The American Mercury_, 11 East 36th Street, New York 16, New York.

On February 19, 1952, Congressman Shafer inserted the entire article in the _Congressional Record_. At that time he said:

"Mr. Speaker, the _American Mercury_ Magazine, in its February issue, has done a great service to America in exposing and refuting the deliberate smear attack by _Time_ Magazine on Senator Joseph R. McCarthy, of Wisconsin.

'Senator McCarthy is doing a great job, a necessary job, and one which no one else has dared undertake. The article by Nora de Toledano in the _American Mercury_ is convincing evidence that every right-thinking American should stand behind Senator McCarthy in his fearless exposures of these enemies in our midst.

"Let _Time_ Magazine try to answer this.

Following are two brief excerpts from the de Toledano article:

"But for the most part, _Time's_ editors, so boastful of the labor of verification that goes into their cover stories, repeated the whole rag-tag of slanders out of which the liberals, aided by the Communists, have manufactured the scarecrow called McCarthyism . . .

"In the past, when _Time_ was caught editorially in flagrante, it explained away the error by blaming the writers, proofreaders, or the pressure of an approaching deadline. But in the case of the Senator McCarthy cover story, _Time_ compounded the deliberate error of its writer by even more deliberately reaffirming and defending it. The editors reason that the public's memory is short—and that old sins are forgotten sins. But if the cancellations are any indication, it will be a long day before _Time_ will be able to forget its shoddy effort to write off Senator Joe McCarthy."

Is it not extremely unwise politically to fight powerful combinations of magazines and newspapers which can carry their story to millions of Americans every day? Won't they ultimately succeed in discrediting you?

Certainly it is politically unwise. I agree that only a miracle will keep them from discrediting me and perhaps ultimately causing my political defeat. In the meantime, however, I shall have done the type of job which I think my people in Wisconsin who elected me expected I would do. I like my job in the Senate, but not so well that I will bow and scrape to dishonest radio commentators and newspapers in order to keep that job. Besides, I have seen politicians who loved office for the sake of office so much that almost their every act was guided largely by the effect it would have upon their votes. I have watched those men morally shrink in their own eyes week after week, month after month, until they were of no benefit to either themselves or the people whom they allegedly represented.

Certain Senators have claimed you were endangering freedom of the press by bringing the facts in

the *Time* Magazine case to the attention of their advertisers. What is your answer?

To begin with it should be remembered that there is no question about the fact that *Time* Magazine lied and that the lying was deliberate. Their own files which I made public prove this. Even Henry Luce, owner of the *Time-Life-Fortune* chain, has failed to deny that and has failed to accept an invitation which I sent to him on November 14, 1951, to see the documentation and proof that *Time* was deliberately lying. There can be no question either about the fact that the lying was done for the purpose of discrediting my fight against Communists in the Administration.

It is equally true that *Time's* advertisers make it possible for the Luce chain to send the above proved, deliberate lies into the homes of millions of American families. Many of those advertisers are militantly anti-Communist and intensely American. When I know that they are not aware of the facts and because of that are unknowingly helping to pollute and poison the waterholes of information, I have a duty to bring that to their attention.

I feel strongly about labeling products for what they are. Poison should be labeled as poison; treason should be labeled as treason; truth should be labeled as truth; lies should be labeled as lies. Luce should not object to that. I have not asked a single advertiser to shift his advertising from *Time* to magazines like *U. S. News and World Report*, *Newsweek*, *The Freeman*, or any other specific magazine. But I feel that I have the duty to let those advertisers know that *Time* Magazine publishes falsehoods for a purpose. Those advertisers, who are extremely busy in their work, are entitled to have it called to their attention if unknowingly they are flooding American homes with Communist Party line material. Those advertisers sell not only their own product but also the magazine in which they advertise. If they continue to advertise in *Time* Magazine after they know what *Time* is doing, in my opinion no one who is for America and against Communism should buy their product.

At this point I want to make it very clear that I have never contacted the advertisers of any newspaper or magazine because they have differed with me or editorially criticized me. That is their right. That is their duty if they differ with me. Many good, honest American publications have vigorously differed with me without finding it necessary to twist and distort facts and dishonestly give to their readers untruths labeled as truths. Naturally I would prefer to have those papers on my side, but I cannot help but respect the vigor of their opposition as long as they honestly and truthfully report the facts.

Those who rail against McCarthy for letting an advertiser know that he is distributing lies instead of the truth would be the first to ask for criminal prosecution of the butcher who sold to their wives spoiled meat which made their children physically ill. Food for the mind, however, is far more important than food for the stomach.

I shall continue to expose every type of dishonesty or treason which I consider a threat to this nation. The fact that a man may have inherited or accumulated money with which he has bought control of newspapers, magazines, or radio chains will not make him immune from exposure.

What about the specific smear attacks made on you since you began your fight to expose and remove from government Communists and pro-Communists?

The pattern followed by the Communist-inspired smear brigade differs but very little from case to case. Never do they meet the facts head on and try to demolish them. Never do they answer the documented evidence. Always they avoid the issue by trying to discredit and destroy the character of whoever is a threat to the Communist conspiracy. Innuendo, half-truths, and untruths about the person exposing under-cover Communists are their answer.

Keep in mind the Communist directive issued by Lenin:

"We can and must write in a language which sows among the masses hate, revulsion, scorn and the like, toward those who disagree with us."

An excellent example of a case in point is that of James Forrestal. He was Secretary of Navy and later Secretary of Defense. Forrestal was one of the few truly intelligent anti-Communists in both the Roosevelt and Truman administrations. As early as 1942, Jim Forrestal in clear, unmistakable terms predicted exactly what would happen if we continued to bow and scrape to Communism abroad and promote Communists at home in high policy making positions. Forrestal not only spoke out for America, he acted for America and against Communism. He knew that as a result they would try to destroy him.

A good description of how the Communists, their sympathizers, and the left-wing "liberals" destroyed Forrestal is contained in an article in the *American* Magazine written by William Huie, editor of the *American Mercury*.

Following is an excerpt from that article:

"The country has never witnessed a more dishonest smear campaign. Forrestal was accused of having defrauded the Government in a tax case. He was a fascist, a warmonger, a racist, a bedfellow of I. G. Farbenindustrie, a dealer in near eastern oil. As a climax, Drew Pearson screamed that Forrestal was a personal coward, that he had once run out of his house and abandoned his wife to burglars."[313]

Drew Pearson while under cross-examination in the $5 million lawsuit which he brought against me for having referred to him as the mouthpiece of international Communism, admitted that it was untrue that Forrestal ever ran out of any house in which his wife was being robbed. He admitted, for example, that Forrestal's wife was robbed while she was out with some friends, that Forrestal was home in bed at the time and knew nothing

---

[313] William Bradford Huie, "Some Uncensored Footnotes to The Forrestal Diaries," Cosmopolitan Magazine, September 1951, pp. 38-41, 112.

about the robbery. He knew this on January 16, 1949, when he broadcast to millions of people:

"and I would go further and state that a man who runs out the back door of his house into the alley, leaving his wife to cope with a jewel robber alone, would not appear to have the courage or chivalry to be the best secretary of National Defense."

The same pattern of completely dishonest, degenerate character-assassination has been followed in the case of the other people who have seriously threatened the Communist conspiracy—men like Chiang Kai-shek and Douglas MacArthur, whom the Communists recognized as major threats to the creation of a Communistic world.

In the case of Forrestal they succeeded. The Communists killed him just as surely as though they had physically thrown him out of that 16th story window at Bethesda Naval Hospital from which he hurdled to a death that was such a victory for Communism.

In the case of Chiang-Kai-shek their victory for a while appeared complete though that victory may yet turn to defeat.

In the case of MacArthur, it temporarily appeared that the Communists had scored a victory on that dark day in history when he was removed from his Pacific command. Their apparent victory over MacArthur, however, may well be the most Pyrrhic victory the Communists have ever scored. History may record that the apparent breaking of MacArthur marked the end of the forward roll of Communism and a reversal of the trend.

The Communist Party line attack follows the same pattern in the case of Senator Pat McCarran, another great American who is making them bleed profusely.

The Communist smear brigade has followed the same tactic in my case—namely, the tactic of avoiding ever meeting facts, but rather using such a barrage of mud and dirt that people forget the facts.

In the case of Jim Forrestal they dishonestly screamed that he had avoided paying taxes, which after Forrestal's death was admitted to be untrue. The "tax smear" in my case was not as vicious as in Forrestal's case but the identical pattern was followed.

For example, in 1944 I wrote to the tax collector from the Pacific, where I was serving in the Marine Air Corps, setting forth the facts and asking for an opinion from the tax collector's legal department as to whether certain income would be considered taxable. Under Wisconsin law all such correspondence with the tax department is public property, as are all income tax returns. Nevertheless, this letter which was public property from the time it was received by the tax collector, was "exposed" by the Madison *Capital Times*, a paper which, as previously stated, has bragged that its city editor, Cedric Parker, was "the Communist leader in Madison." By constant repetition on the part of the Communist and left-wing press, that request for a decision from the tax department's legal staff has become "cheating on taxes." Not until *two years later* after I began my campaign for the Senate was my 1944 letter to the Tax department answered. Their legal office then advised it was their interpretation of the law that the income I outlined was tax-

able. Having neither the time nor inclination to contest this interpretation, I thereupon filed that income. According to the rules of the Communist smear brigade, this became "failure to file taxes."

Another example of the Communist type smear follows:

When the housing shortage was greatest, I suggested to the Joint housing committee that not only was it important to pass laws which would make it possible for the young veterans to buy or build a house but also that it was equally important to write a simple explanation of how they could take advantage of those laws—an explanation which would be easily understood by the typical home-seeking veteran unacquainted with legal jargon. The committee, while agreeing with me on the importance of such a task, did not make this a committee project. I, therefore, personally undertook the task of writing such an explanation of the housing laws in simple understandable language—an explanation which would clearly show the average young home-seeker how to take advantage of the vast conglomeration of involved, confused housing legislation.

At that time the Henry Luce chain of *Time, Life* and *Fortune* had much to say about the terrible housing conditions. I offered them the book on housing free if they would run it. *Time, Life* or *Fortune* Magazine could thereby have performed a great service to the millions of young men who wanted to build or buy homes but who did not know how to take advantage of the existing housing legislation. Henry Luce's publications refused, however, on the ground that this would not be a money-making venture.

After the public phase of my Communist fight began, *Time* suddenly "discovered" how unethical it was for me as a last resort to give the rights of such a book to the pre-fabricated company which would promise the greatest circulation for the book. To Luce's chain of *Time, Life,* and *Fortune* it suddenly became improper for me to keep the book up to date (at a fee of 10 cents for each copy sold)—as to changes (1) in housing legislation, (2) in presidential restrictions on housing credit, (3) in the Federal Reserve Banking system restrictions on housing credits, etc.

At that time it was general knowledge in Washington that I was writing such a book and that copies were presented for criticism and suggestions to every government department having anything to do with housing. The idea of writing such a book for the home-seeker was applauded by both Democrats and Republicans.

When I could persuade no national magazine to publish those simple instructions to the young home-seeker I contacted practically every publisher in the country to see if they would be willing to put the book out at a low price which would insure wide circulation. The publishers' replies boiled down to the statement that they could not afford to publish such a specialized book at a low cost. The letters of refusal are contained in the *Congressional Record* of June 19, 1950, starting at page A-4764.

I then offered the book to manufacturers of good prefabricated homes, such as Harnischfeger in Milwaukee and Lustron of Columbus. Lustron offered an arrangement which appeared to guarantee the widest dissemination of this important simplified information on housing.

At the time the book was sold to Lustron I held a press conference explaining that I was receiving a royalty on the book and that I had a contract to keep it up to date until my present term in the Senate ended. That was about a year and a half before the public phase of my fight against Communists commenced. Strangely, no one considered this "improper" or "unethical" until I started to expose Communists in government.

Strangely, an Administration Senator who has received sizable amounts of money for magazine articles and for a book, "discovered" that it was "unethical" for McCarthy to charge 10 cents a copy under a four-year contract to write and keep a housing book up to date.

Shortly before Christmas in 1950, the Democrat Administration sunk to a new low in attempting to aid the Communist-inspired smear brigade. A week before Christmas Drew Pearson announced that he was going to really "expose" McCarthy in a broadcast on Christmas Eve. The Administration's notoriously corrupt Internal Revenue Bureau was ordered to put as many men as necessary on McCarthy's federal tax returns and find something for Pearson's Christmas Eve broadcast. Reports are that George Schoeneman, who was Commissioner of Internal Revenue at that time, had nothing to do with this. The Internal Revenue Bureau was unable to produce anything for the Pearson broadcast. A year and a half was then spent carefully examining every item of McCarthy's tax returns, with the hope that some income could be found which I had failed to report. But not one penny could be found that I had not reported. Under Administration orders, however, something had to be done to embarrass McCarthy.

After a year and a half, someone came up with the bright suggestion, which was accepted, that even though their audit showed that McCarthy had painstakingly reported every penny of income, they could take income upon which tax had been paid in 1946 and decide that tax should have been paid upon that income in 1949 instead of 1946. Five years having elapsed since the 1946 tax had been paid, McCarthy, of course, would not be entitled to a rebate on what he paid in 1946 but could be forced to repay the same amount for 1949. In this way he would have to pay more taxes. When I pointed out to the collector that it was completely dishonest to make a man pay the same tax twice, his rejoinder was that if he wanted to protect his job, he had to "hook" McCarthy. A record was kept of this conversation.

My tax returns, of course, showed that I was heavily in debt and was paying large amounts of interest, and that in some years I had to make arrangements with my creditors to defer the interest payments. The interest was logically taken as a tax deduction the year that it was paid, not the year it became due. The following additional method of "hooking" McCarthy was devised: It was ruled that the interest should have been deducted the year it was due rather than the year it was paid.

Another clever method of "hooking" McCarthy was to shift income from a low bracket year to a high bracket year and to shift deductions from a high bracket year to a low bracket year—cleverly dishonest, of course, but done on the theory that while McCarthy would have to pay lawyers to fight this dishonesty, the Internal Revenue Bureau's lawyers would be paid by the taxpayers. This was done with the full realization that McCarthy had to pay this Administration blackmail or legally fight it, thereby distracting attention from McCarthy's fight against the Communist conspiracy.

This use of the Internal Revenue Bureau by the Communist-ridden Truman Administration as a political weapon against anyone hurting the Administration is not new. In this case it cost me a very sizable amount of money which I could ill afford, but I wrote it off as part of the high cost of exposing treason. I do not regret paying this or any of the price which I have paid and will in the future pay as a result of this fight. The price has not been too high!

Gillette-Monroney-Hennings Committee Sets a New Record of Political Dishonesty in Promoting the Smear

Gus Hall, the national secretary of the Communist Party, issued and published in the Communist *Daily Worker*, on May 4, 1950, the following official order to all Communist Party members:

"Yield second place to none in the fight to rid our country of the fascist poison of McCarthyism."

Shortly thereafter former Assistant Secretary of State (now Senator) Benton commenced a campaign of yapping at my heels and screaming imprecations at me. Since the Communist Party Secretary issued the above order to all Communists, 10 of those whose cases I gave the Tydings Committee have either been convicted, or removed from government jobs under the loyalty program.*

Each time one of the "innocent people" who were cleared by the Tydings Committee (some of whom worked under Benton in the State Department) were forced out of government as a result of my evidence, Benton launched a new shrill and squealing attack upon McCarthy's "awful" methods. Thus for months did Benton try to make himself the champion of what was also the No. 1 Communist cause—namely, discredit and smear McCarthy at all costs and throw so much mud in his direction that the more cautious and timid politicians will steer clear of the Communist fight.

I ignored Benton because of the type of attacker and the nature of the attack and because I was sure no decent respectable Senator would join hands with Benton. I was amazed to find Senators Gillette, Monroney and Hennings crawling into Benton's bed. For nearly a year they spent large amounts of taxpayers' money hiring investigators, paying for their travel expenses, etc., in an attempt to dig up witnesses who would be willing to make charges against McCarthy. Finally, the ideal witness was found. He was Robert Byers, Sr., of Columbus, Ohio, apparently a fine individual at one time with a very fine family, but who became mentally affected after a streak

* See page 13.

of bad luck. At least the Gillette-Monroney-Hennings staff reported to them that he was mentally unsound and that his mental condition caused him to develop a hatred for McCarthy. The staff reported that this man's testimony would be completely unreliable but that he would "make an excellent witness against McCarthy."

It was therefore decided to call him as the witness to supply the first day's headlines. It looked like a clever and perfectly safe procedure. After all, the public did not know that the staff had reported to Gillette, Monroney, and Hennings that the man was unreliable and mentally unsound. He, of course, would testify to anything suggested to him. If McCarthy tried to explain that Byers was a mental case, it would be heralded by the committee members as an "irresponsible charge"—the "smearing of another innocent person." So a member of the committee staff was sent to Columbus, Ohio with a subpoena for Bob Byers. But, as Robert Burns once wrote, "The best-laid schemes o' mice an' men gang aft agley." A few days previously a judge had committed this star witness to an institution for the insane at Lima, Ohio for observation.

When I first gave the press the story of this witness, according to the AP, the committee staff indignantly denied that they ever intended to call him before the committee. However, too many of the staff members knew the subpoena had been issued, so it was later reluctantly admitted by the committee counsel that a subpoena had been issued for him.

Incidentally, the Democrat Organizing Committee has published and distributed throughout Wisconsin hundreds of thousands of pieces of campaign literature quoting this man's statements about McCarthy.

This is undoubtedly the only time in the history of this nation that a Senate Committee deliberately attempted to use a mentally unsound witness to smear and discredit a fellow Senator. Thus did this committee establish an all time record of political dishonesty.

Another example of complete dishonesty in the committee's frantic attempt to make the smear stick occurred the day Stanley Fisher, one of the committee staff, testified. He had been sent by the committee to my home town of Appleton, Wisconsin, at considerable expense, to make a thorough investigation and to subpoena every letter, etc., having to do with my financial condition since long before I became a Senator. Before the public hearing was called, Fisher had reported to the committee that everything about my finances was completely in order—that while I had been heavily in debt, no creditor of mine had ever lost one penny of either principal or interest.

But this did not stop the committee. With a great fanfare there was announced that McCarthy's "finances" were to be publicly investigated—that the committee's investigator, Fisher, would be put on the stand where he could publicly "expose" what he had "discovered." This gave left-wing Democrat papers in my state, like the Milwaukee *Journal* and the Madison *Capital Times* the opportunity to headline for days the fact that "McCarthy's Finances Are Being Investigated," with the implication that a sinister picture was about to develop.

The dishonesty did not stop here, however. According to the testimony of one of the committee's witnesses,

Clark Wideman, he was present in the committee room while the press and public were absent, and heard staff member Fisher being criticized and browbeaten for having volunteered the testimony that his auditing showed that McCarthy had paid all of his debts and all of his interest. Thus did Fisher let the committee down by failing to leave a false impression of McCarthy's finances.

It was almost humorous to watch the committee attempt to escape criticism for this dishonesty after they became aware that the obvious smear attempt was sickening even some of their good friends in the press. After hours of smilingly watching their Chief Counsel Moore concoct the headline smears and after every drop of slime and mud had been squeezed from their own carefully coached witness, Monroney, Gillette, and Hennings suddenly with a great show of virtue discovered the dishonesty of what was being done, and vigorously and publicly criticized their Chief Counsel Moore who was operating under their direct control.

Here we see "honest," "upright," "virtuous" Democrat "statesmen" "protecting" America and "fearlessly," and "bravely" "fighting" Communism.

If the committee is trying to prove that I am guilty of the crime of not being wealthy, I must plead guilty. The money I have spent hiring investigators and paying their traveling expenses to dig out the evidence on Communists has, of course, not improved my financial condition. Then also there are the very heavy legal and investigators' fees which I have had to pay in connection with the lawsuits which have resulted from this Communist fight. According to Louis Budenz, former member of the Communist Party's National Committee, and editor of the *Daily Worker*, the strategy of the Communist Party is to force into lawsuits anyone who dares expose Communists, and thus through the payment of attorney's fees bleed them financially white. If I were on the other side of the fight, protecting Communists, unlimited legal services would have been offered to me and there would be no objection by Benton and no investigation by the Gillette-Monroney-Hennings Committee.

Do you claim that Senators Monroney, Hennings and Gillette are knowingly aiding the Communist cause?

No, but stupidity and eagerness to keep a corrupt party at the public trough can destroy a nation as effectively and as quickly as treason—especially when traitors can use men of little minds who put party above country.

There is no secret about the fact that 10 of those whom I named before the Tydings Committee have either been convicted or removed from the State Department under the loyalty program. Neither is there any secret about the fact that my exposure of the Truman Administration's whitewash and cover-up of Communist traitors in government has awakened and sickened the American people to the extent that a change in administration—either to a decent Democrat or Republican—is inevitable unless McCarthy can be personally discredited and smeared to the extent that his clearly documented proof of treason will be ignored.

95

Your Marine Corps record has been attacked. What are the facts?

The editor of the New York *Post,* who admits membership at one time in the Young Communist League, and Drew Pearson launched an attack upon my combat record as part of the smear campaign. This attack was suddenly called off when the Marine Corps allowed Senator Cain to inspect and make photostats of my complete Marine Corps file.

After examining and photostating my Marine Corps file, Senator Cain made a complete report on it to the United States Senate on July 13, 1951. Following are some excerpts from that report which appeared in the *Congressional Record* on pages 8328 to 8331:

"Until the Pearson broadcast of July 8, I had only known that Joe McCarthy had seen service as a Marine in World War II. It never occurred to me that Joe McCarthy had been anything other that a first-rate fighting Marine. One has a good habit of taking for granted that every Marine is a top-flight American.

"Following the Pearson broadcast of July 8, I sought to determine what Pearson was talking about. I secured copies of the three Pearson broadcasts and I secured Joe McCarthy's official record as a Marine . . .

"Mr. President, now that we know what Drew Pearson said about Joe McCarthy's record as a Marine, I can legitimately and properly offer Joe McCarthy's official record, which will speak for itself, and which every American can judge for himself.

"In Drew Pearson's second broadcast he indicated that he had seen Joe McCarthy's Marine Corps file. I do not know whether he saw it or whether he did not see it. If he saw it, I would wonder why he was permitted to see it. If he saw it, I believe I can establish it to be a fact that he did not see what he told his audience he did see.

"The Senator from Washington has seen that file and I have photostatic copies of the pertinent parts of it right here in front of me. These photostats indicate that Mr. Pearson has been providing his large audience with misinformation. There is nothing strange or new about this Pearson habit . . .

"Drew Pearson has sought to attack and destroy Joe McCarthy's war record . . .

"The first charge begins when Pearson states that there is nothing in McCarthy's Marine file to indicate that McCarthy was ever on any combat missions.

"As an answer to that interesting observation of nonsense or criminal maliciousness, I believe that Admiral C. W. Nimitz, of the United States Navy, ought to be called as a witness. Permit me to call him at this point."

Senator Cain then presented the Senate the following citation:

" 'UNITED STATES PACIFIC FLEET
Flagship of the Commander-in-Chief
The Commander in Chief, United States Pacific Fleet, takes pleasure in commending
CAPTAIN JOSEPH R. McCARTHY,
UNITED STATES MARINE CORP RESERVE
for service as set forth in the following
CITATION:
"For meritorious and efficient performance of duty as an observer and rear gunner of a dive bomber attached to a Marine scout bombing squadron operating in the Solomon Islands area from September 1, to December 31, 1943. He participated in a large number of combat missions, and in addition to his regular duties, acted as aerial photographer. He obtained excellent photographs of enemy gun positions, despite intense anti-aircraft fire, thereby gaining valuable information which contributed materially to the success of subsequent strikes in the area. Although suffering from a severe leg injury, he refused to be hospitalized and continued to carry out his duties as Intelligence Officer in a highly efficient manner. His courageous devotion to duty was in keeping with the highest traditions of the naval service."
C. W. NIMITZ,
Admiral, U. S. Navy.
Commendation Ribbon Authorized' "

"Another qualified witness who wishes to testify this afternoon is Maj. Gen. Field Harris, major general, United States Marine Corps. I read from a letter dated May 14, 1945:
" 'Dear Judge McCarthy: I note with gratification your unusual accomplishments during 30 months of active duty, particularly in the combat area, and that you received a citation from Admiral Nimitz for meritorious performance of duty. Without exception, the commanding officers under whom you served spoke of the performane of your duties in the highest terms.
" 'The Marine Corps will not forget the fine contribution you have made. It is largely through the devoted efforts and sacrifice of patriotic Americans like yourself that the corps is able to maintain its unbroken tradition of defeating the enemy, wherever, whenever, and however encountered.
" 'You have my warm appreciation of your services, and my wishes for your continued success and good luck in the years ahead.
" 'Sincerely yours,
FIELD HARRIS
Major General, United
States Marine Corps,
Assistant Commandant (Air).' "

"During the war, Joe McCarthy was a captain in the Marine Corps. At one period in 1944, his immediate superior officer was Maj. E. E. Munn. This Marine officer had something to say about our friend McCarthy, who was under Major Munn's command. This is what he said:
" '1. It is recommended that this officer be given a letter of commendation for his outstanding devotion to duty and achievement during the training period of the squadron and in actual combat as described hereunder . . .' "

"In 1944, Maj. Gen. H. R. Harmon of the United States Army commanded all Army, Navy, Marine, and New Zealand aircraft in the Solomon Islands area. Joe McCarthy was attached for a period of time to General Harmon's command where he served as a combat intelligence officer. It is good to note in passing that the Air Force and the Marine Corps were working hand in hand. Before Joe McCarthy was returned to his basic assignment with the Marine Corps, General Harmon reported on Joe McCarthy's efficiency and devotion to duty. It delights me to read what General Harmon said about the man McCarthy:
" 'This officer has shown marked qualities of leadership, cooperative spirit, and loyalty. His initiative, good judgment, determination, and diligence have made him an unusually useful member of the section in which he is assigned and his unfailing

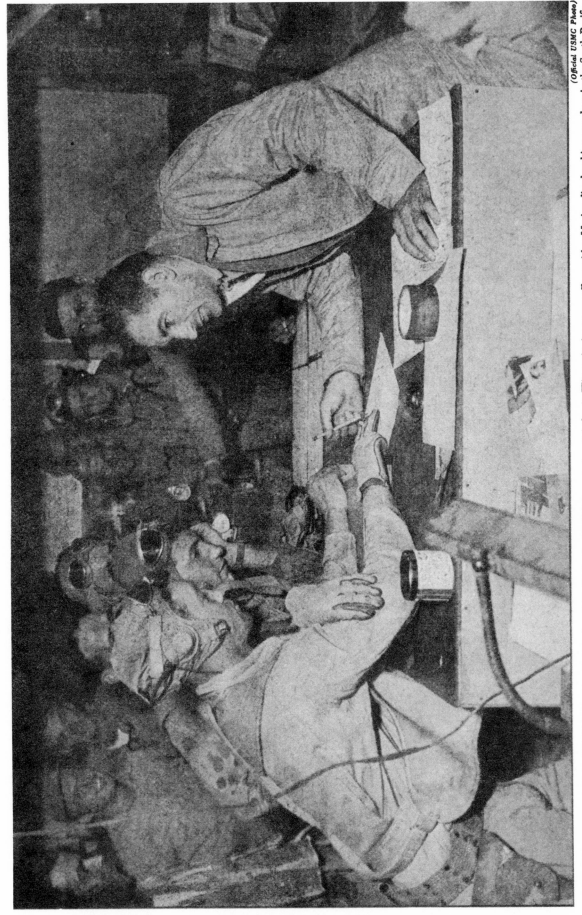

GUADALCANAL, Oct. 6, 1943 (USMC Release).—Captain Joseph R. McCarthy, USMC, former circuit judge in Wisconsin, is now an officer with a Marine dive bombing squadron in the South Pacific combat zone. Here he is seen interviewing pilots who have just returned from raids on Japanese installations in the Solomons.

97

good nature and ready wit has made him well liked and respected by his associates.

" 'This officer deserves to be classified as excellent. It has been a pleasure to have had him in this command.

" 'H. R. HARMON, Major General, United States Army, Commanding.' "

"Mr. President, I believe that what I have read from Joe McCarthy's Marine Corps record has completely destroyed every single one of the silly, unprincipled, and untrue allegations made by Mr. Pearson . . ."

To what extent has the Communist Party line smear against you hampered your work or been personally disturbing to you?

It disturbs me not at all. In fact, the louder the screams of the left-wing elements of press and radio become, the more damage I know I am doing to the Communist Party.

It has hampered the task to some extent, because it scares off the more timid of our friends who are afraid of the effect of the smear upon their political futures. To those people I commend the following quotation of Abraham Lincoln, which hangs over my desk:

"If I were to read, much less answer, all the attacks made on me, this shop might as well be closed for any other business.

"I do the very best I know how—the very best I can, and I mean to keep doing so until the end.

"If the end brings me out all right, what is said against me won't amount to anything. If the end brings me out wrong, then ten angels swearing I was right would make no difference."

CHAPTER XIII

The Evil Genius

You claim that Communism is evil. Why do hundreds of millions of people submit to Communist rule?

To answer this question I call upon Stanislaw Mikolajczyk, prime minister of Poland before its fall to Communist Russia, who personally witnessed the dark evil cloud of Communism blot out the sunlight over his nation.

In the Preface of his book, *The Rape of Poland*, Mr. Mikolajczyk earnestly asks Americans to learn the lesson that Poland learned too late.

"A raging question in Poland has become, 'How long will it take them to communize us completely?'

"To my mind, however, the question is badly framed. I am convinced that human beings cannot be converted to Communism if that conversion is attempted while the country concerned is under Communist rule. Under Communist dictatorship the majority become slaves—but men born in freedom, though they may be coerced, can never be convinced. Communism is an evil which is embraced only by fools and idealists not under the actual heel of such rule.

"The question should be phrased: How long can a nation under Communist rule survive the erosion of its soul?

"Never before in history has there been such an organized attempt to demoralize men and whole nations as has been made in Communist-dominated countries. People there are forced to lie in order to go on living; to hate instead of love; to denounce their own patriots and natural leaders and their own ideas. The outside world is deceived by Communist misuse of the organs of true democracy, true patriotism—even, when necessary, true Christianity.

"Who rules Poland today, and by what means? The answer is as complex as the nature of Communism itself.

"The pattern of Communist rule in Poland goes back to 1939, when Molotov and Ribbentrop agreed to partition my country. After stabbing Poland in the back while Hitler was engaging the Polish Army in the west, the Communists established their iron rule in the east of Poland. This *de facto* rule was tacitly recognized in the conference rooms of Teheran and Yalta.

"Therefore it is important to recognize the real aims of the Communist, his methods, the pattern of Soviet aggression.

"By October, 1947, the month in which I began my flight to freedom, the Communists ruled Poland through secret groups, open groups, Security Police—including special Communist units called the Ormo, the military, the Army, Special Commissions, and Soviet-patterned National Councils. A million well-armed men were being used to subjugate 23,-000,000. Control of all top commands was—and remains—completely in the hands of Russians. Their orders, even some of the more savage ones, were and are now being carried out by Poles. These Poles are either Communists or men of essen-

tially good heart whose spirit has at long last snapped. They are mainly chosen from among the 1,500,000 Poles transferred by Stalin to Russia in 1939. Stalin has 'prepared' them thoroughly for their work.

"The American reader who scans these words while sitting comfortably in a strong, free country may wonder at many aspects of Poland's debasement. He may wonder why the nation did not revolt against the Communistic minority which has enslaved it. On the other hand, he may wonder why Russia needed two and a half years to impose its rule. Or why Russia went to the trouble of camouflaging its aggression during much of that period.

"But the Communist minority has gained absolute control simply because it alone possessed modern arms. History reveals instances where a mob of a hundred thousand, armed with little more than rocks and fists, has overcome despotic rule by one assault on a key city or sector. Today is another day. If the despot owns several armored cars, or even a modest number of machine guns, he can rule. The technology of terror has risen far beyond the simple vehemence of a naked crowd.

"We in Poland fell—for this reason and for many others. We fell even before the war had ended because we were sacrificed by our allies, the United States and Great Britain. We fell because we became isolated from the Western world, for the Russian zone of Germany lay to our west, and Russia leaned heavily on the door to the east. In the morbid suspicions of the Kremlin, the plains of Poland had become a smooth highway over which the armor of the west might someday roll. Thus, much of our nation must be incorporated into the USSR, and the rest must be made to produce cannon fodder to resist such an advance. We fell because the Russians had permitted—indeed, they encouraged—the Germans to destroy Warsaw. In the average European country the capital remains heart, soul, and source of the nation's spirit. Our capital was murderously crushed; its wreckage became not alone the wreckage of a city but the debris of a nation.

"We fell because while so many of our best youths were dying while fighting with the Allies, so many of the people who knew the dream of independence were slaughtered and so many who constituted the backbone of our economy were herded like cattle into Germany or Russia. We fell because Russia stripped us of our industrial and agricultural wealth, calling it 'war booty.'

"We lasted two and a half years because we were the largest nation being ground down to fragments behind the Iron Curtain. We held out because we are a romantic people who can endure much if the prospect of liberty remains on the horizon. We lasted because the deeply ingrained religion of the country brought solace and hope. We existed because, through centuries of hardship, we have learned to fend, to recognize the tactics of terror and propaganda. We held out because the Poles have loathed the concept of Communism since it first showed its head, and because the strong-armed bands of Communism—strong as they were—were still not huge enough to blanket all the scattered farm lands which make up so much of Poland. The sparks of freedom flicker and sparkle through the length and breadth of agricultural Poland, fanned by priests and members of the intelligentsia who hide with the simple peasants when the horrors of life in the cities become too great to bear.

"Russia carefully camouflaged its actions in Poland for much of two and a half years, because it wished to make certain that the Americans and British would again disarm and drop back to their traditional torpor of peace. The Reds took into consideration Poland's status as an ally, not in any humane way, but with an eye to the possibility that if they raped us too abruptly, the West might remain armed and thus complicate the job of grabbing another country.

"The Western mind may find it hard to comprehend rule by a fanatic handful. Yet such rule is a fact, both in Poland and elsewhere in eastern Europe. After the fixed elections of January, 1947, the Communist Party was itself a party subjected to purge. Its size in Warsaw, for example, was cut from 40,000 to 24,000. This murderous group no longer had to wear the cloak of democracy, shielding itself as the 'Polish Workers Party'; 'window dressing' became superfluous, as well as the people who filled the windows.

"The Western mind may find difficulty, too, in reconciling the facts about Poland's rule with the apparparent enthusiasm of the vast mobs one sees at Communist rallies, grouped around the speaking platforms of tirading, frenzied leaders. It must be remembered, however, that these mobs have been commanded to gather. A worker who does not obey the command of the NKVD's 'adviser' in each plant—to appear at a given place and time—is dismissed, and his dismissal means personal catastrophe. For he and his family cannot find work, cannot have a food-ration card, and cannot have housing for himself and his loved ones, if he does not yield. The newsreel cameras, whose film reaches the free countries, never show the empty side streets, can never film—at close range—the gaunt faces in the marching mobs. 'I have never seen so many thoroughly unhappy people marching,' Cavendish Bentinck whispered to me the day the Warsaw people were commanded to file past the reviewing stand in honor of Tito's visit.

"Will Communist control eventually spread itself thin and snap, as did the military rule of Adolf Hitler? I wondered about this, too, in the dark hours of my struggle before I left Poland. The answer appears to be an emphatic no. Hitler attempted both to rule and to administer with Germans; Stalin rules with key Russians in control positions and administers with traitorous, corrupt, or weak nationals of the country to be ruled. In Russia today men and women of every nation are now being trained and schooled for the day when they will return to their native lands, which they know so intimately, to rule under direct command from Moscow. Stalin trains Frenchmen to rule France, Italians to rule Italy, Englishmen to rule England, Latins to rule the Latin countries, Japanese to rule Japan, Chinese to rule China, Indians to rule India, blacks to rule blacks, and Americans to rule America. . . . For Stalin, an evil genius, is more grimly efficient than any other tyrant in history. And he intends to conquer the world."[314]

314 Stanislaw Mikolajczyk, Preface to The Rape of Poland.

CHAPTER XIV

A Question For Americans

Senator McCarthy, what can I—an average American, holding no public office, and owning no newspapers or radio stations—do to fight Communism?

You can do a tremendous job if you will. You can help alert America to a danger much greater than Communists in the State Department or any other branch of the government—a danger much greater than any threat from Communist Russia.

Hitler once said, "Give me control of the minds of the youth of a country—give me control of the educational system for five years—and I shall control that country indefinitely."

The Communists thoroughly recognize the truth of that statement. One of their major efforts, therefore, is to infiltrate the educational system of this country and control school and college publications.

The May, 1937, issue of *The Communist* Magazine, sets forth the following directive to all Communist teachers:

"Communist teachers are . . . faced with a tremendous social responsibility . . . They must take advantage of their positions, without exposing themselves . . .

"Only when teachers have really mastered Marxism-Leninism will they be able skillfully to inject it into their teaching at the least risk of exposure."

In a speech at Brown University on April 22, 1952, Dr. J. B. Matthews, former research director of the House Committee on Un-American Activities, gave some general statistical facts on the support given by college and university professors to Communist and Communist-front organizations. Dr. Matthews stated:

"Approximately 28 percent of all the top collaborators with the deceitful Communist-front movement in recent years have been college and university professors.

"Exhaustive research into the personnel of Communist-front organizations reveals that some 3,000 professors from approximately 600 institutions of higher learning have been affiliated more than 26,000 times with these instruments of the Communist Party. This is not 'guilt by association' but guilt by collaboration."

Every man and woman in America can appoint himself or herself to undo the damage which is being done by Communist infiltration of our schools and colleges through Communist-minded teachers and Communist-line textbooks.

Countless times I have heard parents throughout the country complain that their sons and daughters were sent to college as good Americans and returned four years later as wild-eyed radicals. The educational system of this country cannot be cleansed of Communist influence by legislation. It can only be scrubbed and flushed and swept clean if the mothers and fathers, and the sons and daughters, of this nation individually decide to do this job. This can be your greatest contribution to America. This is a job which you can do. This is a job which you must do if America and Western Civilization are to live.

I warn you, however, that the task will not be a pleasant one. When you detect and start to expose a teacher with a Communist mind, you will be damned and smeared. You will be accused of endangering academic freedom. Remember, to those Communist-minded teachers academic freedom means *their* right to force *you* to hire *them* to teach *your* children a philosophy in which *you* do not believe. To Communist-minded teachers academic freedom means *their* right to deny you the freedom to hire loyal Americans to teach your children. As a practical matter we should remember that good generous salaries are necessary to attract to the teaching profession the kind of people whom you want molding the mind of young America.

We cannot win the fight against Communism if Communist-minded professors are teaching your children. We cannot lose the fight against Communism if loyal Americans are teaching your children.

INDEX

Anti-Movements in America

An Arno Press Collection

Proceedings of the Asiatic Exclusion League, 1907-1913.
1907-1913

Beecher, Edward. **The Papal Conspiracy Exposed.** 1855

Beecher, Lyman. **A Plea For the West.** 1835

Budenz, Louis F. **The Techniques of Communism.** 1954

Burr, Clinton Stoddard. **America's Race Heritage.** 1922

Calhoun, William P[atrick]. **The Caucasian and the Negro in the United States.** 1902

Ministers of the Established Church in Glasgow. **A Course of Lectures On the Jews.** 1840

Dies, Martin. **The Trojan Horse in America.** 1940

Dilling, Elizabeth. **The Red Network.** 1935

East, Edward M. **Mankind At the Crossroads.** 1926

Evans, H[iram] W. **The Rising Storm:** An Analysis of the Growing Conflict Over the Political Dilemma of Roman Catholics in America. 1930

Fairchild, Henry Pratt. **The Melting-Pot Mistake.** 1926

Fulton, Justin D. **The Fight With Rome.** 1889

The Fund for the Republic, Inc. **Digest of the Public Record of Communism in the United States.** 1955

Ghent, W[illiam] J. **The Reds Bring Reaction.** 1923

Grant, Madison. **The Conquest of a Continent.** 1933

Hendrick, Burton J. **The Jews in America.** 1923

Huntington, Ellsworth. **The Character of Races.** 1925

James, Henry Ammon. **Communism in America.** 1879

King, James M. **Facing the Twentieth Century.** 1899

Kirwan (pseudonym of Nicholas Murray). **Letters to the Right Rev. John Hughes, Roman Catholic Bishop of New York.** 1855

Ku-Klux Klan. **Papers Read at the Meeting of Grand Dragons Knights at Their First Annual Meeting.** [1923]

McCarthy, Joseph. **McCarthyism:** The Fight for America. 1952

McDougall, William. **Is America Safe for Democracy?** 1921

Monk, Maria. **Awful Disclosures.** 1836

[Morse, Samuel Finley Breese]. **Foreign Conspiracy Against the Liberties of the United States.** 1835

National Americanism Commission of the American Legion, Compiler. **ISMS:** A Review of Alien Isms, Revolutionary Communism and Their Active Sympathizers in the United States. 1937

Nevins, William. **Thoughts on Popery.** 1836

Pope, Or President? Startling Disclosures of Romanism as Revealed by Its Own Writers. 1859

[Priest, Josiah]. **Slavery.** 1843

Reed, Rebecca Theresa. **Six Months in a Convent** and **Supplement.** 1835

Roberts, Kenneth L. **Why Europe Leaves Home.** 1922

Ross, Edward Alsworth. **Standing Room Only?** 1927

Schaack, Michael J. **Anarchy and Anarchists.** 1889

Schultz, Alfred P. **Race or Mongrel.** 1908

Stripling, Robert E. **The Red Plot Against America.** 1949

Tenney, Jack B. **Red Fascism.** 1947

[Timayenis, Telemachus T.] **The Original Mr. Jacobs:** A Startling Exposé. 1888

Wiggam, Albert Edward. **The Fruit of the Family Tree.** 1924

Anti-Catholicism in America, 1841-1851: Three Sermons. 1977

Anti-Semitism in America, 1878-1939. 1977